Our Least Important Asset

Our Least Important Asset

Why the Relentless Focus on Finance and Accounting is Bad for Business and Employees

PETER CAPPELLI

OXFORD
UNIVERSITY PRESS

OXFORD

UNIVERSITY PRESS

Oxford University Press is a department of the University of Oxford. It furthers
the University's objective of excellence in research, scholarship, and education
by publishing worldwide. Oxford is a registered trade mark of Oxford University
Press in the UK and certain other countries.

Published in the United States of America by Oxford University Press
198 Madison Avenue, New York, NY 10016, United States of America.

CIP data is on file at the Library of Congress
ISBN 978–0–19–762980–2

DOI: 10.1093/oso/9780197629802.001.0001

Printed by Sheridan Books, Inc., United States of America

To friends who were most important to my work and career:
Tom Kochan, Bob McKersie, Nevzer Stacey, and Bob Zemsky

Contents

Preface: The Background to This Manuscript

This book reflects the path that the practices of employee management have taken since the recession of 1981, which is now recognized as a crucial turning point in the economy, the labor market, and in business. Since then, we have seen a steady erosion in traditional practices for hiring and managing employees, first for production workers with the decline of unions and then for white-collar and office workers. In their place we now mainly have stripped-down versions of the older model that are cheaper but on many other dimensions obviously worse for the employers, let alone the employees.

The advantages of taking employee management seriously—from quality circles to Japanese management approaches and lean production to more basic ideas about engaging and involving employees to agile project management systems—are as clear as anything is in the world of management. But over time, interest in each of them faded.

This has happened often enough that it is hard to believe that management cannot hold onto a good idea. When these ideas fade, we head back to that same stripped-down mode. There is something powerful that pushes managers back in the same direction each time.

This book is not another account about why it is important or even why it pays off to take care of employees and manage them carefully, although I certainly believe that. It is about why evidence of better practices never seems to be persuasive and the factors that keep pushing back in the other direction.

Every academic book about contemporary management is almost required to refer to Southwest Airlines and its unique approach to managing employees at least once, and so here is mine. The idea of trying to get employees to care about the company and to use their discretion to help the business that is at the heart of Southwest's approach is not quirky or new. Management stumbled on it, but the principles have been well known in management since the 1930s. It stands out in an industry where virtually every other competitor is very much rule-based, top-down, and focused on optimization. It also stands out by being the most profitable and financially successful airline in the history of the industry. This is despite being unionized, paying about the highest wages in the industry, and facing cost disadvantages that virtually all its US competitors achieved through repeated bankruptcy proceedings. Its Christmas 2022 operational debacle was traced to underinvesting in systems and a lack of backup resources that were unrelated to its employee management practices. Outside of classes on management, however, Southwest remains as an outsider. It gets little attention for its incredible and continued business success.

By contrast, compare it to GE in the 2000s when the business community was obsessed with learning its secrets, where endless conferences and programs focused on learning "the GE Way," where almost every story about the state of business featured it and the financial control system on which it was based. Even today with its reputation vastly diminished, a Google search for GE gets three times as many mentions as does Southwest. When Southwest is discussed, it is treated as a quirky example that can't be replicated.

At least part of the reason for the relative lack of attention for Southwest is that its model plays down the role of financial controls, planning, and top-down decisions and therefore runs contrary to the accepted norms in business. Those norms developed in part because of the business leaders themselves and their background. They are likely to have been schooled thirty years ago in neoclassical microeconomics with its focus on rationality and incentives and in engineering and business school tools aimed at optimization. Management development programs and rotational assignments where new managers would have learned about management practices that work with employees started disappearing before this generation arrived.

The most persistent reason, however, is because of the underlying limitations of financial accounting, which in the age where shareholder value is preeminent has become the roadmap business leaders and their companies follow to be judged as successes. Maximizing shareholder value is a mantra used to explain all kinds of things about modern business, but in fact that goal gives no guidance as to how to do it. Financial accounting is what provides the roadmap for businesses to follow. It is far too aggregated to reveal much of anything about operating efficiency, and it treats employment in very odd and adverse ways. Under the modern practice of accounting, a dollar spent on employees is arguably the worst expenditure a company can make, especially as compared to any physical asset. Simply moving dollars from employment to other categories—including nonemployee labor—immediately makes companies more valuable.

The reason why ideas about managing employees better fade despite evidence they are more efficient is that they do not fit with financial accounting and the now prevailing orthodoxy of business leaders. That orthodoxy is more consistent with the ideas of Frederick Taylor and scientific management from a hundred years ago than they are with ideas from the past generation or two. It is not surprising these practices don't turn out well for employees. More surprising is that they do not seem to turn out well for the business, either. While they may make the financial accounts look better, that is only because of the limitations of those accounts.

This book also follows something of my own journey through these topics, starting with *The New Deal at Work* published in 1999 that documented the breakdown of internal careers and the rising use of outside hiring. The question was, how were companies managing employees without lifetime employment and internal labor markets? In the early 2000s all the attention was on GE as the model, which was surprising since GE was doing what most other large corporations had always done, using the traditional internal labor market with long employment, if not lifetime. Companies without the scale and systems that GE had could not copy the GE approach, and frankly few actually tried. What companies were actually doing was what they had always done—workforce planning, succession models based on the assumption of long or lifetime employment—but just not doing it well, because their budgets and staff had been slashed.

I wrote a follow-up book in 2009 called *Talent on Demand* that documented why the old models for managing talent had to be adjusted to deal with the uncertainty of contemporary business and how that might be done. The preferred approach in practice was to continue using the existing tools even though they were not working.

What I did not anticipate is the extent to which businesses and other large organizations were able to get by with no systematic planning or practices for managing talent. Every vacancy was a treated as a surprise—as illustrated by the periodic discovery in the business press that employees are retiring with no successors to replace them. Employers could simply wait until there was a vacancy, then look for candidates who had done the same job someplace else and grab them to fill it. Why not, one might wonder, as it cut out all that planning and practices. The answer, described in detail here, is because it costs a lot more to hire outside, and skills and knowledge that employers needed for many jobs simply do not exist outside their own company. As an economy, we cannot operate simply by hiring from other people. This is why we keep hearing persistent complaints about skill shortages: it's because we stopped training.

After the Great Recession in 2009, complaints from employers on precisely this problem became common: in spite of the high levels of unemployed people who had held jobs just before, employers complained there was simply no one to hire to replace the people laid off a few years before. The truth was that very few people could step right into those jobs without needing any training. I wrote *Why Good People Can't Get Jobs* to explain that this situation was the result of giving up on training and the emerging practice of hiring on the outside job market—badly—to provide talent.

Employers expected colleges to provide the skills they were no longer provided through training and job experience. In 2016 I wrote *Will College Pay Off?* out of frustration with the common view that college education was the answer for anyone seeking a good job, highlighting the fact that employers actually cared more about the work experience of students in school than about their academics.

Since then, I have written a number of descriptive articles for the *Wall Street Journal* and the *Harvard Business Review* describing how poorly employment practices such as performance appraisals and hiring actually work. The theme of looking at what is actually happening—as opposed to theories or wishful thinking—animates this book, which both extends the prior work and pulls it together.

There are three questions raised and I hope answered in this book. First, how are employees actually managed? This sounds like an obvious question that must have been answered already, but it has not. Textbooks about workplace management are largely still organized around the model of corporate management from the 1950s and the tools developed then in personnel psychology. Few employers actually use them today. The reality is that contemporary practices are simpler, cheaper, and unlikely to achieve their stated purpose.

Second, are there any common themes to the current practices, and if so, what explains those themes? As shareholder value became more important, financial accounting that determines what is success in shareholder value became more important as well. It determines what is "profit," and the complicated answer is what keeps the field of accounting in business.

Financial accounting is an extremely limited and quirky set of standards when it comes to employees and the workplace. Compared to other kinds of spending, money spent on employees is seen as substantially worse for affecting the value of a company. That leads to the practical goal of minimizing everything that involves employment costs, because financial accounting punishes those costs.

This is not about becoming efficient, reducing operating costs, or even cutting labor costs more broadly defined. The easiest ways to cut employment costs—and to cut them the most—are to simply shift them to other categories of expenses. The most important example may be leasing workers employed by vendors rather than employing them directly, making the company instantly more valuable under financial accounting.

The goal of cutting the category of employment costs helped drive a second, related development: the use of optimization models designed by engineers, which are best at minimizing a single outcome, in this case those costs. But the optimization push has other sources as well, such as the increased number of contemporary business leaders who have engineering and quantitative backgrounds and now the new data science tools that have optimization at their heart. It does look like the return of scientific management.

Together, these practices create what researchers would call "suboptimization," pushing for optimal outcomes in one area at the expense of other areas, and what others call "pennywise and pound foolish," the British term for being so cheap as to cause bigger problems elsewhere or later on. A good example is the quip sometimes attributed to Harry Truman that he almost had his mule weaned off food until it up and died.

The third question is, to what extent are financial accounting and the resurgence of scientific management responsible for the continued decline in the quality of jobs in the United States? Prior research on job quality, especially in economics, has focused on causes in the marketplace, such as competition from China. Those explanations do not account for much of the decline, however. They also shift attention away from businesses themselves and the decisions that business leaders make. Management decisions have rarely been considered before as an explanation of the decline. Such decisions have gotten little play in policy discussions in part because they do not fit neatly into the economics paradigm and in part because they are hard to measure and analyze in traditional deductive-normative models. We can see evidence of management efforts to squeeze employment costs at the expense of costs and efficiencies elsewhere in many places, the connections to job outcomes and quality are straightforward, and it simply has not received sustained attention before now.

The good news is that others have recognized the limitations of financial accounting, although it is virtually always investors. Intangible assets, which do not appear in financial accounting like tangible assets, also matter for the value of companies. The most important of those assets has to do with people, not surprisingly. Prominent investors have pushed for more data that will help them measure those intangible human assets.

The concern here is not with helping investors make more informed investment decisions, although certainly that is a reasonable goal. It is with the fact that the current financial accounting practices distort management decisions such that we get worse decisions, worse outcomes for employees, and worse outcomes for organizations. Addressing investor concern about the lack of information on intangible assets does not necessarily solve the problems of employment decisions, but opening the door to think differently about financial accounting with respect to people issues could very well improve both outcomes.

Many people helped me put this story together, and I am indebted to them. Recovering accountant Dan Schliesmann, CFO Greg Warshaw, and professor Christina Zhu helped me understand the accounting issues. Seminars at McGill and Cornell Universities gave helpful feedback. Tom Kochan at MIT read important parts of the first draft. Lisa Warshaw, Wharton's emeritus head of the communications program, offered her usual insightful thoughts on messaging. Among the many executives who offered their experiences were a group of chief human resource officers: Benito Cachinero, Diane Gherson, Raghu Krishnamoorthy, and Susan Peters. My editor at *Harvard Business Review*, Steve Prokesch, polished many of these ideas. James Cook, my editor here at Oxford, saw promise in the original idea and nurtured it through the publication process.

Introduction

The New Model and How We Got Here

For average workers, and especially those at the bottom, jobs have gotten worse even as the economy has grown and the stock market boomed. Real wages adjusted for inflation have been stagnant for the average employee since the 1970s and declined for those without a college degree, and job insecurity has increased, especially for employees in positions that had been seen as lifetime or at least long term in larger companies. Retirement income is less secure as we have moved from pensions, where payments are guaranteed, to defined contribution plans, where returns are uncertain. Hours of work for white-collar employees who are exempt from wage and hour laws increased steadily, and evidence of the negative effects of workplace stress and insecurity on employee health continues to accumulate.

There is no real agreement about why this has happened. Economists, who are the most interested in the topic, look to events outside the organization in the overall job market for explanations, such as competition from China or IT investments substituting for labor, but those factors explain little of the change. There is agreement in the research literature that the decline of unions played a big role, but there is less interest in that story perhaps because it is not clear what to do about it. It is revealing that the most popular explanation is one that we cannot measure—skill-biased technological change—an assumption that somehow developing economies inexorably demand higher skills.

But at the same time, what goes on inside the firm has changed enormously, specifically the practices for managing employees such as who does what work, how are people hired, and whether they are trained. Opportunities for advancement have declined while expectations for performance have risen. There are several linking themes among the new practices. First and most important, they are simpler and cheaper. Second, they ignore what research and experience demonstrated about employee behavior and performance in earlier periods. Third, they are much less likely than in the past to be handled by human resource experts, whose ranks continue to thin, and are more likely to be carried out by vendors who operate at arm's length from the original employer. Or they are added to the list of tasks that line managers are supposed to handle.

There is little doubt that pushing work out of the organization and onto other providers—outsourcing, defined broadly—has been a major factor in shifting work from good jobs to worse, lower-paying jobs, as David Weil's important work identifying "the fissured workplace" has demonstrated.[1] This kind of outsourcing that drives work down to low-wage, individual contractors exists even in the hi-tech world of Silicon Valley.[2] It is only one manifestation of a broader development, however.

I doubt most observers ever believed the company slogan that "people are our most important asset." A more accurate description today would be that "employment costs are our biggest liability." The problem is specific to employment per se and does not apply to nonemployee labor, which seems perverse from an efficiency perspective. The shift in the last few decades has been to see employees and employment largely as a cost to be minimized, much worse than other costs, even when doing so raises costs elsewhere, such as having to pay more for the labor of nonemployees.

An explanation that we have heard for some time about what is wrong with jobs—indeed what is wrong with business—is the rise of the shareholder value movement, which gave primacy to the interests of shareholders as opposed to other stakeholders (such as employees). The problem with that explanation is that shareholder value might tell us how to distribute what's left over from revenue after we pay our costs, but it does not tell us how to maximize the amount paid to shareholders or how to run the companies.

It is tempting to assume that the problem lies with leadership. The eminent organizational psychologist Ben Schneider echoes the views of many observers in arguing that companies manage employees so poorly because their leaders think of them as liabilities rather than assets.[3] In other words, this is a failure of imagination by business leaders. The question, though, is why do they think of them that way?

The answer is that financial accounting and its underlying assumptions tell them to do it that way. These rules did not come down in stone tablets. They were created by accountants and then turned into stone tablets by regulators like the Financial Accounting Standards Board, which enshrined them as standard and accepted accounting practices. Financial accounting is not the same as internal accounting, with its detailed categories of all costs and sources of revenue. For the purposes of our discussion here, what is important is the odd way they treat employment costs as compared to other costs. Perhaps the best-known example is that investments in equipment are treated as assets that can be paid for and depreciated over time as we get value from them, but investments in employees are treated as current expenses that must be paid in full in the year in which they are accrued even though we get value from them over time as well. Wages and salaries are seen as worse than other current expenses because they are seen as fixed costs that somehow cannot be cut in downturns, even though layoffs are commonplace. Then we tax the cost of employing people with payroll taxes, adding to the burden of employment. I remember the CEO of a Fortune 50 company telling me that his job was to employ as few people as possible. At the time, I assumed that view was just a shorthand for the goal of increasing productivity where fewer workers would be needed, but now it seems clear that having fewer employees is a goal *in itself* even if doing so does not lead to greater effectiveness or even profitability. Indeed, even if it raises costs elsewhere.

It is important to remember that investors, who drive the shareholder value agenda, are not interested in accounting for settling up who was most profitable at the end of the year. They are trying to predict who will be more profitable next year, and they rely on financial accounting to tell them largely because that is the only financial data companies give them. Cutting employees immediately improves the perception of value because many performance measures are reported on a per employee basis, not a per worker basis. Moving from defined benefit plans to defined contribution plans and from earned vacation time to "unlimited vacation" plans immediately make a company appear more valuable because liabilities of future obligations go away.

The move to minimize accounting measures of employment and employment costs in particular has been pushed along by the rise of a now huge industry that helps companies shift employee costs onto other categories of spending by moving them onto the payrolls of specialized businesses. By some estimates, US corporations now spend 30 percent of their entire budgets for labor on nonemployees, mainly on "leased" employees who work for them at least a year but are actually the employees of someone else.

It has also been pushed along by the expanded application of optimization in management tools. Optimization models focus on one goal only, and a goal that matters a lot and is easy to measure is costs. We minimize employment costs by minimizing the number of employees and what is spent on them, even if we expand the use of nonemployee labor by the same amount.

The optimization approach has also been pushed forward by a new generation of leaders whose backgrounds are much more sympathetic to optimization thinking. Executives are far more likely now than in previous generations to come from engineering and finance backgrounds where optimization is assumed to be the priority. They are also far less likely to have had any management development training or experience in other functional areas to suggest that how employees are managed plays a huge role in what we get from them.

Optimization can be extremely useful, of course, and it is an important concept in improving productivity. A reasonable observer might ask, isn't that what business is supposed to do, to employ as few people as possible and pay them as little as we can? The answer, of course, is no. What we want to optimize is value per unit of cost. When we optimize by minimizing costs, especially if it is on only one aspect of cost, we are likely raising costs elsewhere and being very inefficient.

To illustrate, as described further in Chapter 3, the number-one criterion used by employers in the United States to assess their hiring practices is costs per hire. What almost none of them track is quality of hire. It would seem absurd in any other context to focus only on the cost of something and not what it was delivering. I was at a meeting of heads of corporate human resources where one participant noted that a particular vendor had saved them millions in hiring costs. When questioned, though, they had no idea whether the vendor's practices led to better or worse hires, what it did to employee turnover, or any other consequence of its hiring practices. Until that moment, he did not appear to have realized that simply because something is initially cheaper does not mean that it is better or even that it will lower overall costs.

In practice after practice, we see employers squeezing down the current accounting costs of employees and in the process shifting costs elsewhere: getting rid of their recruiters by pushing hiring responsibilities onto line managers; paying fees to vendors to use the vendor's employees under contract who are paid roughly the same amount as the client's regular employees, simply to reduce costs in the "employment" accounting category; hiring more expensive temps to fill labor shortages rather than raising pay levels for current employees; moving from pension plans to defined contribution programs that provide less security for retirees for the same cost in order to reduce financial liabilities in accounting.

One of the most common justifications for some of the changes such as using the employees of vendors rather than one's own is the idea that they increase flexibility. But there is nothing that makes the legal contracts that govern those arrangements more flexible than employment, remembering that most US employees are "at-will" where they are few restrictions on cutting them. The same cannot be said for abrogating contracts. As we will also see, the rules that companies put in place to restrict hiring actually make it less flexible for operating managers to use employees than to use vendor labor.

One of the best examples of the suboptimization approach of squeezing visible costs comes from a careful study of productivity and profits in the retail industry done by colleagues at Wharton. They found that stores on average were running staffing so lean that it hurt sales, especially because it meant that there were not enough workers who were keeping track of inventory at "the last mile," getting stock from the back rooms onto the shelves. If items are not on shelves they cannot be bought, and customers are likely to go elsewhere not only to find that missing item but also whatever else is on their shopping list.

The authors calculated that the stores with higher staffing levels and higher pay were substantially more profitable and that the advantage was more than enough to cover those additional labor costs.[4] When pointing out to the companies that they could raise their profitability substantially by making those changes, they got a very cold shoulder from their leaders.

In fairness to business leaders, they are rarely experts on employment and workplace issues. That is clearly the case for CFOs, who call many of the shots on spending. They try, sensibly, to cut costs wherever they can, and most every department has an argument as to why their budget should not be cut. Consider the common experience of cutting recruiter jobs, which may pay $75,000 per year, and pushing the task of hiring onto the desk of operating executives, who may be paid $200,000 per year. It may not seem sensible, but if those executives and managers are willing to take it on, it saves the company money reducing headcount. The problem, however, is that the easiest way for those people to take on the hiring task in addition to their other work is to do it poorly and quickly. Given that few of them know anything about hiring and no one is checking to see how well it is done, why would they do otherwise?

The pushback should come from pointing out that making poor hiring decisions is extremely costly. It leads to hiring workers who either quit or have to be fired, repeating all the costs of the first process. If that does not happen, it means having poor performers whose lack of contributions holds business down. If business leaders heard that argument, their response would likely be, "OK, show me." To do that requires first having data on the costs of bad hires, and the contemporary problem caused by outsourcing so many tasks is that the data needed to answer questions like these are siloed in different parts of the organization or, more likely, with different vendors. Conducting analyses was not part of the goal of cutting costs when the systems were created. The data that was collected could not answer these cost-related questions because human resources was rarely pushed to demonstrate the value of its practices. "Did people like our training program?" is quite a different question than demonstrating whether it generated more value than it cost to undertake.

Because HR departments could not answer questions like these, they were typically pushed aside. It became common, for example, not to consult the HR departments even about fundamental HR decisions such as layoffs— until they were told to execute them—because they did not have much to add to the question as to whether it would improve performance. As described in more detail below, HR officials were also extremely nervous about suggesting to operating managers that they were simply not good at executing the HR tasks like hiring that were pushed onto them.

Even if we could show that skimping on something like hiring led to costs such as turnover, doing something about it probably requires increasing the budget for human resources. Then the company would look worse in terms of its financial accounting by adding headcount, even though internal accounting might show a savings.

It is important to note there are no clear villains in this story. As we will see, the rise of shareholder value as a priority was the result of a long-standing academic argument. But that development alone would not have caused the management problems described here without limitations of financial accounting in dealing with human capital. Even then, it required that CFOs champion employment cost cutting, that CEOs support it, and HR leaders not present an effective counter. As with most widespread and important developments, this one had a thousand fathers.

The Goals of This Book

A central aim of this project is to describe how employees are actually managed. The chapters outline how employees are hired now, how work is allocated between vendors and employees, how performance is managed and work is organized, how careers are managed (or not), how employees are paid, and other aspects of employee management.

As a simple illustration, textbook accounts of hiring discuss crafting job ads, waiting for candidates to apply, sorting them out to determine who to test and interview, and especially how to do the latter. Census data suggest, however, that more than half the people who changed employers last year were not even looking for a job, and they did not apply in the usual sense: a recruiter came and found them, usually based on their LinkedIn profile. When we look at the practices that are used by employers, they typically ignore and undercut what research has shown works. In the hiring context, systematic testing has given way to unstructured interviews by inexperienced and untrained managers, one of the least valid ways to select candidates.

The second and more important goal of the book is to identify a common theme and explanation for these practices. That is the operating principle of squeezing anything that looks like employment costs, guided by financial accounting, even when the result simply shifts those costs elsewhere and makes workplace processes more difficult and expensive.

The goal of squeezing down one element contributed substantially to the return of optimization thinking in the management of employees. Artificial intelligence—in practice, data science—became popular in part because it is driven by that same goal of optimizing on a single element. In pursuit of practices that use as little labor as possible, it has taken back decision-making from employees and even supervisors and transferred it to systems. This process undercuts decades of evidence about the importance that empowering employees has for improving quality, productivity, and now creativity.[5] Instead of allowing employees to make decisions on things like schedules and organizing work, we turn to data science–driven algorithms and math formulas that calculate optimal assignments and job design, even if employees hate them. Practices like agile project management, which were all the rage at the end of the 2010s, have now been redefined so that they no longer mean the empowerment of teams, which had been its central attribute.

Engaging employees, making use of their insights, and managing organizational culture so that they feel willing to contribute is a lot of work. It is also not the kind of work that draws accolades from the business and investor community the way fancy financial deals with immediate outcomes do. If these optimizing approaches save me time and energy to devote to those rewarding activities, and they also make me look better to the financial community by cutting my employment costs, which look especially bad in financial accounting, what is not to like? The response, based on decades of empirical studies, is that it simply does not work well in the long run to treat employees like widgets.

A related concern is that to make optimization work and to build tools like algorithms, we need data. New information technologies make it easier to collect data of all kinds about employees. As it has become easier and perhaps necessary to measure what employees are doing, it has also become easier to monitor them.

The great working from home experiment driven by the COVID-19 pandemic in 2020 began with high levels of trust that employees would somehow get their work done. Despite the fact that this seemed to be going well, in part because employers had little choice other than to give employees more control over their work, employers began investing in more and more tattleware that monitored what employees were doing at home. As described in Chapter 6, monitoring extends past working hours with wellness programs that track employee behavior and fitness outside of work down to their blood sugar and serum cholesterol levels. It looks more and more like scientific management is back.

The third goal of the book, which follows from the one above, is to help explain why jobs appear to have gotten so much worse over the last two generations, even as the economy and especially the stock market have roared ahead. We see employers using every angle to hold down wages, such as mandating that employees sign restrictive covenants that have covered a staggering 38 percent of US employees, lowering turnover and wages in the process. Employment law violations have gone up, especially at the low end, as well as widespread anti-trust issues where employers conspire to keep wages down. They also do it by shifting work away from their employees not so much to contractors and gig workers but to leased employees who are the employees of vendors; by moving employee benefits like vacations from a guaranteed, accrued basis where they count as liabilities on the balance sheets to voluntary or unlimited arrangements where they are not; by dismantling training, development, and career advancement for current employees.

These developments have been bad for employees. They haven't always been great for business, either. An important and widespread illustration of how this squeeze on employment costs at the expense of business success came when the COVID-19 restrictions began to lift in 2021, allowing more businesses to open. At the beginning of the pandemic, employers placed a huge number of their employees on furlough, a category that means involuntary, unpaid time off. Those workers typically remain on the books as employees but are unpaid. Because the expectation was that restrictions would lift quickly (in March 2020, the guess was that it would be a matter of a few weeks), it made perfect sense for employers to keep these workers on the books because they were expected to be back at work soon. The evidence is clear that recalling those laid off turns out much better for both the employer and the employee than trying to find new workers.[6] Those furloughed workers could take jobs in the meantime, and they could also collect unemployment insurance in this period, so their interest in trying to find a new, permanent job was low.

Jobs continued to come back, but by August of 2020, the percentage of the unemployed who were furloughed no longer accounted for the majority of the unemployed.[7] From that period on, employers began complaining about the difficulty in finding workers to replace those that they had cut loose permanently. The number of permanent unemployed rose in absolute terms and as a percentage of all unemployed from then on. A reasonable conclusion is that employers cut too many workers on a permanent basis rather than use furloughs. Then they could not find enough workers.

Once vaccinations began in December 2020, the lifting of government restrictions on reopening was telegraphed well in advance and was widely anticipated. The economy responded and grew at the blistering pace of 6.4 percent in the first quarter of 2021, but hiring during that quarter barely kept pace with separations until March. After that point, employers scrambled to fill the positions they had laid off earlier, and at the same time everyone else was trying to hire the same people. The consequence in many cases was leaving positions open and having to turn away business. As described in more detail later, the fact that so many companies also got rid of their recruiters is one of the not-so-well-known reasons why they struggled to fill those jobs.

The airline industry exemplifies these trends. Despite receiving special and substantial government subsidies to keep employees on the job during the pandemic, it lost significant business due to staffing issues. Yet in 2021 the airlines told industry analysts that they were intentionally bringing back fewer staff than before the pandemic in an effort to run even leaner, which contributed to the rash of flight cancellations during the holiday season when demand for travel predictably surged.[8]

The Outline of the Text

Chapter 1 describes these accounting issues and the related factors that have pushed management to squeeze employee costs typically at the expense of increasing other costs, including nonemployee labor. Then we turn to the related rise of optimization thinking as and why it occurred.

Chapter 2 outlines the role of management thinking and ideas in these new developments. In part they are a function of the different experiences of a new generation of business leaders. That experience includes coming of age during the shareholder value period as well as experiencing the optimization ideas of contemporary business education.

Chapter 3 describes in stark terms what happens in arguably the most important people management task—hiring—and how it plays out in the suboptimization problem of cutting HR staff at the expense of making poor hiring decisions.

Chapter 4 picks up the related and extremely consequential move of shifting work from employees to the liquid workforce dominated by leased workers who are employed by a vendor to work at a client's location in place of regular employees. The remarkable web of contracting and legal agreements required in this approach challenges the argument that it is efficient or even flexible.

Chapter 5 takes on how work is now organized and the role that optimization thinking plays in it. The approach undermines employee involvement by taking decisions away from employees, and undermines supervisors for the same reason. One might argue that the rise of employee involvement had been the most important development in management since the 1960s until its current reversal.

Chapter 6 addresses how this is all playing out for employees and the changes associated in job security, pay, and benefits. The connection between the decline of the quality of jobs and the roadmap provided by financial accounting as to how to manage human capital is straightforward.

1

Employment Practices Are Choices

Despite the talk of gig work, all but about 6 percent of people in the work-force are employees, a number that has barely budged in recent decades.[1] Employment is still what matters. The policies and practices that employers use to manage their employees are therefore fundamental to our experiences at work and also to our well-being outside of work: whether we have the sta-bility and security to handle other life demands, whether we bring home stress or self-respect, and of course whether we have enough money to live a decent life.

These practices are choices. The market does not dictate how to interview employees or what type of performance appraisal system to use or how to set wages. Saying that the goal is to maximize profit or to be efficient tells us very little about how to do that. The choice of practices has huge impacts on employees and on their organizations. What gets chosen and why are the questions we address here.

We think about these practices collectively as "management" broadly de-fined and also as "human resources," a contemporary derivative from the original "personnel" created to signal a greater focus on business goals in the management of people.

In historical terms, employee management is a relatively new develop-ment. While individuals and small businesses have hired workers at least since the construction of the pyramids,[2] the notion of employment as a con-tinuing relationship where the worker is paid for their time, rather than for explicit outcomes, and can be directed by the employer, dates only from its common-law creation in the 1700s. Systematic practices for managing employees came much later, with the rise of large organizations and the crea-tion of corporations in the early twentieth century.

Since the 1920s, arrangements for organizing work and then for managing employees in corporations have been heavily influenced by engineering principles, especially by scientific management. Those principles were laid out by industrial engineers, a subset of the engineering field that basically applied math principles to workplace issues, especially in manufacturing and most noticeably in assembly lines. The underlying goal of those principles is optimization: How do we get the most out of our operations and out of our employees?

The details of employment practices and most of the rules for white-collar jobs after World War II were filled in by the specialized branch of psychology—industrial-organizational psychology and the even more applied personnel psychology—that supported the engineering decisions. These helped shape the basic organization structures created by the engineers and the specific rules for running them. To illustrate, corporations had operating requirements to meet their planned goals many years out; those plans required workers, so plans had to make sure there were enough workers available. If someone was out on a given day, production could then go ahead, and if a key employee left, successors were always prepared to step into vacancies.

The practices for hiring employees, picking successors, and other aspects of talent management were determined by those psychologists. The practices they created are familiar to anyone who has ever worked in a large organization, at least in older organizations. Filling out job applications, taking tests to get hired, looking at the organizational chart to see our prospects for our career advancement, figuring out the possibilities for pay increases within the compensation system, and enduring performance appraisals and training programs were all practices created to fit in and support the industrial model.

Critics of business noted then and now how these practices helped bend employees to the interests of the business, but it is also true that in the process, they buffered employees from the harshest consequences of market forces—layoffs in particular—and changes in business strategies. The internal labor markets, where employees advanced inside the organization, were reinforced by no-layoff practices for white-collar workers in most large corporations, built around the recognition that employees with a lifetime tie to the business would be much more committed to it than otherwise. The archetype of that model was probably IBM, which mandated forty hours of management training each year and a lifetime career. It argued that the lifetime commitment to look after its employees allowed it to restructure and change quickly. In a typical year before 1981, it moved 7,000 of its 50,000 or so managers to new locations—hence the joke that IBM stood for "I've Been Moved."[3]

That model began eroding in the 1980s, again most notably at IBM, which led the way with layoffs of white-collar employees for the first time, and has picked up speed since with a new generation of companies and leaders coming to power. The end of lifetime employment and the fact that it is incumbent upon the individual to find a new job remains the most profound aspect of that change, one that continues to resonate.[4] The usual justification for the churning of employees is—ironically—exactly the same as the justification that IBM gave for not churning them: the belief that it made restructuring easier.

We can see it in literature about work, especially office work. Before the 1980s, one could argue that the dominant theme was the crushing conformity required of corporate jobs, epitomized by Sloan Wilson's *The Man in the Gray Flannel Suit*. Boring tasks and a lack of control over them was the price of any job that paid a white-collar salary. After the 1980s, the themes were less about the psychological costs of boring jobs and much more about basic needs: dealing with the enormous economic and personal consequences of losing jobs and struggling to find new ones. Both Walter Kim's *Up in the Air* and Mike Freedman's *King of the Mississippi* revolve around the new corporate role of downsizing consultants, the work they do, and the callousness that such work demands. Ed Park's *Personal Days* and Joshua Ferris's *Then We Came to the End* follow employees in companies that are shrinking down, waiting for their inevitable layoffs. Donald Westlake's *The Ax* takes job hunting to an extreme, where a middle-aged and unemployed manager kills off the other candidates to get a new job.[5]

Involuntary job loss and the restructuring that drives it leads to another profound change, and that is the movement of employees across employers. The fact that the average fifty-year-old employee in the United States has already worked for twelve different employers suggests how careers are now driven by movement across organizations. Typical hires now are not new graduates or leavers, as had been the case a generation ago. Instead, as described in Chapter 2, they were already employed, and they were approached by another employer or more likely recruiters working on their behalf who persuaded them to move. Despite the rise of layoffs and targeted recruiting, which drives turnover, we somehow point to employees as the ones responsible for job hopping, as if they were responsible for pushing people out of their jobs and looking outside for their replacements. In particular, the idea that there is something different about the job-hopping tendencies of millennials has been debunked.[6]

Almost as big a change, described in more detail in Chapter 4, is that some 30 percent of the individuals at work for a typical corporation are not its employees but members of an alternative, liquid workforce, mainly agency workers provided under contract, and also employees of vendors who work at the client's location. This does not count the outsourcing of tasks now done outside the organization under contract. Many human resource tasks—from hiring to administering benefits to laying off employees—are now outsourced to vendors. There are still many large firms where the older practices, such as internal career advancement, are recognizable, although none are as central as they had been.

We often assume that the evolution of business and management is always toward more sophisticated and rigorous approaches that work better, and that good practices drive out bad ones. There is no evidence this is the case in management and plenty of evidence that it's simply not effective, even for business success. On issues from hiring to (not) developing talent to the declining interest in employee involvement, employers have backed away from practices that evidence showed worked, not only for the business but also for employees. Practices that are good for employees and good for business are sometimes referred to as "high road" practices. They get a lot of interest, but then fade, and we move back to stripped-down, low-cost models. It is never because of evidence showing that these high-road ideas do not work. Why this happens is a puzzle, and is what this book is about. Something continues to push us back in the other direction.

It's Not Shareholder Value

We often hear "finance" as the explanation for many of the changes in contemporary business. The term "financialization" is used to describe both the growing importance of the financial industry in the economy and also the increased financial motivation behind how companies are run. It can easily make a claim to being the most important development in business in the last fifty years. What is so surprising about it, especially to hard-nosed businesspeople, is that it is almost completely an academic idea about values and ethics that has no clear answer. What are the obligations of business? Researchers have examined this topic and financialization at length.[7]

The consensus answer before the early 1990s had been that for-profit business had multiple objectives corresponding to different stakeholders: employees, shareholders, customers, and the broader community, what was known as the stakeholder view. It is true that Milton Friedman had long advocated that business had no obligations to any group but shareholders, but that position was on the fringe of practical discussions, in part because it suggested the clear need to regulate such a powerful group that explicitly had no interest in the broader good of society.

Despite its profound consequences and academic roots, the change to the shareholder value view was not the result of a deep or even interesting debate. The role that public companies should play in society is the topic of corporate governance, which is in practice a legal question. Courts and legislation have addressed it over time, and there was no big shift in any relevant laws to suggest that companies only had obligations to shareholders. Shareholder value, by contrast, is a normative argument about what should be. It was long advanced as an assumption in economics because it allowed for complex optimization models and insights that were not possible if we assumed that firms had multiple objectives. It isn't possible to optimize across many different outcomes at the same time.

As a close observer of how the shareholder value view took hold in business schools, I can say that the shift involved no debate. Few business schools had courses on corporate governance, and even fewer had lawyers on the faculty who knew the reality of what corporate governance actually entailed. Economics and finance faculty taught shareholder value as an assumption because it made formal modeling easier. Finance professor Michael Jensen became the fiercest advocate for this view, arguing that shareholders were the residual claimants of the proceeds of public companies so that companies should be run solely for their benefit.[8] A simple way to state the claim is that the system as it exists assumes that maximizing shareholder value is the goal. As the finance world and finance curricula grew in size and importance, the shareholder value view grew because more students heard it more often, and in most cases students heard no alternative because there were few, if any, courses where the topic was covered.

By 1997 the Business Roundtable, arguably the most important US business group, issued a statement about the purpose of the corporation that stepped away from the stakeholder model and fell sharply in line behind the shareholder view: "The Business Roundtable wishes to emphasize that the principal objective of a business enterprise is to generate economic returns to its owners."[9] It was a coup with no opposition.

The most important developments following this coup were on the investor side: activist investors who buy stakes in public companies and then push hard to raise share prices, sometimes forcing out CEOs and board chairs who resist;[10] huge institutional investors who own so many shares of individual companies that simply selling them if they feel a company is performing poorly is untenable. They also lean on the company's leaders to improve share price more than individual shareholders.[11] There is also an extensive literature suggesting that different kinds of shareholders may push companies toward different kinds of practices, such as short-termism.[12] There is little doubt that thinking about companies as having one real stakeholder—the shareholders—did matter to how they operated. Although the Business Roundtable repudiated the extreme shareholder value notion in 2019,[13] it has been difficult to see any change yet.

Short of not wasting resources or giving money away, the shareholder value goal gives no indication as to what actions businesses should take to pursue that goal. Does it maximize profits to treat employees so that they perform better or to pay them as little as possible and squeeze them, or something else? Shareholder value offers no guidance.

It's Financial Accounting

The guidance comes from financial accounting, the tool that investors and the industry analysts who guide them use to determine how profitable companies are and will be. Financial accounting differs substantially from other kinds of accounting. Cost accounting or internal accounting describes the detailed books that a business would keep about its operations: how much it spent by type of expense in producing each product or service, how much it took in for each of those, and so forth. Managerial accounting takes that information and uses it to create an overall picture of how a company is doing from a financial perspective to guide the decisions of executives. Those two types of accounting stay inside the company, and investors rarely if ever see them. Financial accounting presents the accounting results to an outside audience according to highly standardized and regulated rules. The separate categories within internal accounting are aggregated together into summary categories in financial accounting.

The rules of financial accounting are ultimately enforced by the US Securities and Exchange Commission, but it delegates the setting of those rules to the Financial Accounting Standards Board (FASB). The FASB is a private organization that is run by and essentially responds to the concerns of the finance and accounting industries. The data from internal accounting are molded into the reports according to these accounting rules known as GAAP—the generally accepted accounting principles. That information and reports that the SEC requires are all the investors and shareholders see be-cause it is all that public companies are required to report. The companies do not want them to see internal accounting data at least in part because without detailed knowledge of the context, it would raise more questions than it answers, and once they start reporting it, investors will assume that if they stop it is because something bad has happened.[14] What analysts and investors know about a company's financial situation comes almost com-pletely from financial accounting. The accounting rules, therefore, define what is success and provide the map that tells executives how to run their businesses in order to get ahead. While private companies do not have the same reporting requirements as public companies, FASB standards apply to what they report as well and what investors expect to see.

Fans of traditional economics models, possibly apoplectic by this point, would say that it is obvious what to do: just make as much profit as pos-sible. But something has to determine what is profit. If we consider a sports analogy, the reason the game of basketball is not as simple as just putting the ball in the basket more often than the other team is because many separate and complicated rules determine what counts as a basket: several actions can prevent a score from counting even when the ball goes through the hoop, how many points one gets depends on where the ball is shot from, and so forth.

FASB sets the rules that determine how we keep score in finance, and also how the game ends up being played. In sport, knowing under the rules who won and by how much when the clock stops is simple. In finance, the clock never stops. Investors are trying to determine who is going to win in the fu-ture, not who has won at the end of the fiscal year, and FASB determines the limited information they can use to predict that.

Financial accounting treats human capital by the same standards that were created for physical capital. Most observers recognize that this is at best inaccurate, but because it sets such a powerful roadmap for running companies and because employees are such a big component of contempo-rary businesses, it creates huge distortions in the way those businesses op-erate. The fact that expenses and value of employees are treated so differently from physical capital is the main reason why there are now so many puzzling and seemingly dysfunctional decisions made about employment and work in general.

Consider, for example, having a trained and skilled workforce, which a typical observer would see as being a considerable asset, perhaps even a requirement, for success. It is not an asset for the purposes of financial accounting, though. If we try to learn something about the value of a skilled workforce from financial accounting information, we will get nowhere. The accounting rules say that items with value are assets, but crucially, they can only be considered assets if they are owned by the company. On that basis, slaves were assets and were considered as such on US plantations.[15] But employees cannot be.

There are no measures in standard accounting to tell us anything about the value of employees because companies do not literally own employees. Good employees often work for their employers far longer than the working life of any capital equipment. A majority of older employees, for example, have been with their employer at least ten years.[16] Yet they have no value on company balance sheets, nor is there information of any kind about them. This is the case even if employees are under contract to remain with their employer.

With a capital asset such as new equipment, financial accounting allows us to treat it as follows. First, we can use it to offset liabilities that we may be holding because assets have current value to us. Second, we can depreciate the value of that asset over its useful life so that it can be paid off slowly as it is used. For example, if we buy an expensive machine that we expect to last five years, we can allocate the costs across those five years, basically paying it off as we earn money from it. We don't have to pay it off at once. Periodic tax breaks allow companies to accelerate the tax deductions or front-load them to get the benefits sooner. For example, "bonus" depreciation policies allow a business to deduct as much as 50 percent of the costs of an asset from their taxes the year they buy it even though they may take many years to actually pay it off.

When we turn to the employee context, none of this applies. Consider what happens if we pay a lot of money—including sign-on bonuses—for a new hire who we believe will be very valuable to us for at least the next three years. Perhaps they are even under some contract that retains them for three years, including stock options and retention bonuses to help ensure that this employee stays with us. The cost of acquiring them still cannot be considered as an asset to offset liabilities. Nor can we "depreciate" those costs of hiring them by spreading them out across the next three years. For accounting purposes, the costs all fall in that first year when the employee is hired, and they count as an expense in that year, something that must be offset by income in that year. This is despite the fact that the real benefit of new hire employees is very likely to come further down the road. If we do not have enough income to cover that expense this year, the overall operations will appear to be losing money, which is a huge red flag for investors.

We might think that treating equipment or software as an asset and employees as an expense because we can own the former but not the latter is sensible, because employees can walk away while equipment and software cannot. But that difference is highly exaggerated because even though we may control a capital asset, its value can easily collapse unexpectedly. Equipment can break, software can fail to work, and markets and needs can change, rendering those assets useless to us. Even when that does not happen, it is difficult to resell them at anything like their accounting value.

Employees, on the other hand, can be managed in ways that retain them far longer than the value of most capital assets. More important, employees are one of the few assets that actually become more valuable with use, and they are infinitely more adaptable to new needs and requirements than equipment.

When we have capital assets, financial accounting essentially gives us a plan that reminds us and our investors that those assets are wearing out and will need to be replaced. We typically depreciate an asset over its working life, so when it is depreciated over ten years, we know when we get close to that period it is time to be replaced, and we should have saved money to pay for the replacement. We may have employees with extremely valuable IT skills that will also become obsolete over time in a predictable manner, but because they are not depreciated, we have no equivalent plan for them.

For the same reasons, we cannot invest in current employees for the purposes of financial accounting because the accounting rules say it is not possible to invest in something we do not own. Consider an employer that decides to send an employee to an expensive computer programming training program. The reason it makes that investment is because it believes the employee will be valuable for many years. But when they go to their accounting sheets, the cost of that training counts as an expense that has to be completely offset by additional income earned in that year. Although we talk about education, training, and development as investments, when it comes to accounting, they are just expenses. The cost of upgrading and maintaining equipment can count as an investment, as noted below, but not with employees.

There is no line item for training in financial accounting. It falls under general and administrative expenses along with items like office equipment. Are you spending a lot on training employees or on coffee? It looks the same to accounting. An inquiring investor will not know and cannot find out without digging into internal accounting, which they do not see.

Aside from payroll, which is typically the largest current expense, employee issues show up in one other place on the accounting forms, and that is on the liability side of the ledger in the form of future obligations. Many employee benefits, such as vacation time, retirement plans, and healthcare, have cost aspects that have to be paid in the future. These are liabilities that must be offset by assets. Liabilities are arguably worse than expenses on a balance sheet in that they continue into the future.

If we compare this to equipment, it may well be that we know there will be routine maintenance and future expenses associated with buying, say, a robot. Parts need to be replaced and components need servicing on a regular schedule, just like a car. If we engage in a contract with vendors in advance to provide that maintenance, it counts as an asset in our financial accounting.[17] Future-oriented expenses for employees, even ones that look exactly like maintenance and are paid in advance, like healthcare, count as liabilities.

If an employer had a choice of having a machine perform a task or employees perform it, and the operating costs of the two were identical, financial accounting would make the former look much more attractive: it counts as an asset that can also be depreciated over time, and its maintenance costs can also count as assets. Employment costs, by contrast, are expenses and liabilities.

If that were not enough of a burden, there is one more damaging financial assumption about wages and salaries. They are treated as fixed costs that cannot be cut if they are no longer needed. This notion developed in economics at a time when lifetime employment for white-collar employees and union contracts for blue-collar workers indeed made it very difficult or at least expensive to lay them off.[18] But the idea that employees are a fixed cost that cannot be cut would be news to the millions of employees who lose their jobs from layoffs every month. Even during the red-hot labor market of the postpandemic period when claims that there were simply not enough people to hire, roughly a million employees were laid off every month.[19] Why employment is considered a fixed cost is also a puzzle given that virtually all employment in the United States is "at will," which allows employers to end it unilaterally for any business-related reason, in fact, in the absence of explicit exceptions, for any reason. The fixed-cost assumption holds despite the fact that the average tenure in companies is less than four years,[20] capital expenditures often come with depreciation schedules much longer than that, and employers do not seem to have any difficulty in laying off employees when they feel the need.

Why other business expenses are not treated as fixed costs is equally puzzling. Contracts with vendors would seem to be fixed costs. Creditors have the ability to force employers to make payments even if the employer wants to end the contract, something that employees cannot do.

Public policy pushes the disadvantage of employment further by taxing the company for the amount it spends on employees with payroll taxes of various kinds, which makes it cost considerably more to use the employee even at the same internal accounting base cost as the machine.[21] I hear the capital/labor financial distinction from human resource executives when they say that it is relatively easy to get money from the CFO to buy software that promises to eliminate jobs even when that software may be quite expensive, but virtually impossible to get money for employment. A dollar is not a dollar in financial accounting. It all depends on where it sits.

To illustrate the priority that investing in physical assets has over investing in human capital, consider the results of the survey in Figure 1.1 from PricewaterhouseCooper (PwC) about the usefulness of new HR technology. In virtually all instances that means software intended to replace employees. The C-suite executives are 270 percent more likely to believe that it is very effective at reducing costs, increasing productivity, and improving a host of tactical outcomes than do the managers—line managers—who make use of the software and experience it. The reason for the difference would appear to be that the executives are focused on the accounting advantages of substituting software for people while the line managers are concerned about operating effectiveness.

Matthew Bidwell's study of a company's decisions as to whether to do IT work with vendors or to do it internally illustrates the pressure on senior management to cut accounting costs. In fact, they had quotas to hit for the amount of work that had to be pushed from employees out of the company to vendors. Remarkably, there was more slack allowed in meeting cost targets with vendors than when using their own employees. As one manager described the choice, "The buckets [for costs] are not the same, and the approval process and bureaucracy for a vendor is far less difficult than it is to bring on an employee."[22]

C-suite executives and business leaders are clearly focused on what investors think of their company's value and prospects, so specifically, what is it that the investors see? They see three sets of required financial accounting

■ C-suite
■ Middle management

50%

Increasing efficiency/
productivity

22%

42%

Reducing
costs

15%

45%

Improving the
employee experience

23%

43%

Attracting and
retaining talent

13%

50%

Providing
workforce insights

14%

39%

Changing
behaviors

13%

Q: Overall, how effective have your HR technology solutions
been in delivering the following outcomes? Showing results for
'very effective'. Base: Executive 175, Middle management 97

Figure 1.1 Management's Take on HR Tech Differs from Leaders'
Source: PwC's HR Technology Survey 2020

submissions: cash flow statements, which look at revenue; income statements
or "profit and loss" statements, which are revenues and expenses usually for
a fiscal quarter; and balance sheets, which report assets, liabilities, and shareholder equity.

What could they learn about employment? They would see expenses—
wage costs—in the income statements. They would see pensions and other

obligations to employees in the balance sheet. That's it. All that investors see about employees, arguably the most important attribute of an organization, is their costs and only those two aggregated measures of costs. Payroll costs are not only the largest component of operating costs in most businesses; they also appear to be the most "controllable costs" in the sense that managerial choices can influence them, in this context the opposite of the "fixed-cost" notion. A crude measure of how well an employer manages its costs is often therefore to see how low its employment costs are, especially compared to equivalent businesses. The goal of those choices is then to drive those costs down, relentlessly.

One type of employment that was the biggest target for squeezing was administrative expenses not neatly linked to revenue. These are often seen as part of overhead. Within administrative expenses, human resource departments and staff were targeted relentlessly. In 1980, the ratio of human resources staff to employment in a typical company was roughly one HR member for every 100 employees. By 2020, it was roughly one for every 150 employees despite more employment laws to administer and new employment priorities to manage such as those around diversity and inclusion.[23]

Squeezing employment costs can lead to many problems that affect business performance. But those costs do not show up in financial accounts in any discernable way. Consider, for example, the costs of turnover associated with high rates of quitting, widely seen as one of the more important problems in business. Those cannot be observed from financial accounts. Even a deep-dive into a company's internal accounting would not show those costs, as there is no line item where they would appear. They are spread across existing categories: more recruiting costs, severance pay if there is any, lost productivity due to standing vacancies, onboarding costs of replacement hires, and their training costs.

Peter Kuhn and Lizi Yu took a very careful look at these costs. They found that even in frontline retail jobs, two-thirds of the costs of turnover come between the time when the employee gives their notice to leave and before they actually depart. That happens in part because of negative effects on peers who remain, and in part because of the demands on them of recruiting, hiring, and onboarding replacements for those who left.[24] These costs are not being tracked even in the most sophisticated companies. Many smaller companies do not keep track of employee turnover at all, and even fewer companies try to measure those costs carefully. As another example, Saravanan Kesavan and Camilia Kuhnen found that changes in hours of work to better optimize schedules and cut headcount, an issue considered in more detail later, created variation and uncertainty in the earnings of those employees that then increased turnover and turnover costs while adding nothing to performance outcomes.[25] The effort to cut costs in one category—headcount—increased them in another—turnover. The difference is that investors see the former, and they do not see the latter.

The practice that receives the most attention is layoffs, getting rid of employees altogether. The cost-cutting appeal here is obvious because it leads to immediate and big cost savings. What is unstated is that layoffs also cut capabilities that are hard to rebuild. Restarting is difficult, as so many companies found when pandemic restrictions lifted in 2021 and they all tried to hire the same people at the same time. As described in detail in Chapter 4, the evidence shows that the harder and sooner companies cut back, the worse their financial performance was in the longer term because of the difficulty in restarting compared to peers that were more prepared to snap back. Recent evidence explaining why the US economy had the lowest productivity growth in history during the 2010 decade traces it to employers laying off proportionately more workers than in the past following the Great Recession in 2009 and the delays in hiring after.[26]

Liabilities from Employees

Returning to the liability aspects of employment costs, they are treated especially badly by financial accounting because they continue over time and, when they accumulate, they can be considerable. They have to be offset by assets, which represents a burden to corporate leaders. The enormous move away from pensions, or defined benefit plans, to defined contribution plans like a 401(k) is explained by this financial quirk. Pensions are future obligations and are actually a guarantee to employees. The standard view in economics had been that it was valuable for employees to have that guarantee and therefore much easier for a large company to manage that risk than for an individual employee, hence the pension arrangement. This benefited employers because employees were willing to have on balance less retirement income when it was guaranteed.

But pensions are also liabilities on the balance sheet going out for decades. They are sometimes the biggest liabilities companies hold. How to deal with this problem in financial accounting associated with pensions? Drop them and move to 401(k)s and defined contribution retirement plans. The company agrees to make contributions to them each year. The contributions may have been as great as with pensions. The difference, however, is that these plans are not a promise or an obligation, so they do not count as long-term liabilities.[27] Now they are simply an annual expense on the books, and the company's financial situation looks much brighter despite the fact that evidence suggests that defined benefit pension plans may have been cheaper.[28]

The new unlimited vacation craze from Silicon Valley and startups has the same theme. In most organizations, employees accrue or earn vacation days in line with their service, and the company owes that vacation time to employees. Sometimes employees are allowed to cash out the days, especially if they leave. Vacation time off is therefore a liability on the company books. If it moves to an unlimited vacation time policy, employees no longer earn or accrue the time off. It is simply a reasonably vague commitment from the employer. By moving from an explicit commitment to a vague one, the liability leaves the company's financial accounts, and it instantly becomes more valuable.

A reasonable person might have assumed that investors would be extremely worried about any policy that promised employees unlimited anything. In fact, the investment community cheered the move to unlimited vacations because they understood that this moved vacations off the liabilities accounts, and that there are many ways to prevent employees from actually taking excessive vacation time. No one is promising that your supervisor won't give you a hard time if you take time off or even that the company will not fire you if you do so. As we will see in Chapter 6, most employees don't take all their vacation time even under policies of accrued time off.

Efforts at Reform?

The fact that financial accounting is so limited in its description of what is happening inside organizations, and especially with employees, is not a new discovery. The subfield of human resource accounting developed in part to address that deficiency fifty years ago, although the focus was on measuring human resource–related costs such as turnover and internal accounting rather than addressing the issues of financial accounting per se. The recognition that traditional accounting ignored human capital was a popular topic again about twenty years ago when researchers started thinking about how much value management practices could create or destroy. They thought about alternative accounting systems for assessing human capital in organizations using calculations assuming that employees were assets.[29] Despite much discussion, these alternative approaches made no headway in financial accounting and remain on the fringe even of cost accounting.

In the late 2010s, groups of stakeholders pushed to secure changes in the financial accounting of human capital and employee issues to reveal more about the value derived from them while corporate officials pushed to block it. The Securities and Exchange Commission issued a modest and open-ended requirement in 2020 for companies to disclose human capital resources they believe are material to their business, something that the European Union had already done. But in the United States, companies decide what to report.

Ganish Pandit analyzed what companies have reported so far. My read of the results is that the information is all over the place—perfunctory statements of principles in some cases, a few statistics on topics like diversity—no consistency across the reporting and very little depth in any of the reports. Seventy percent presented no real data.[30] It is difficult to see how this would be useful to investors or anyone else. As this reporting is typically controlled by the CFO's office, it may not be surprising that they had little to say on human capital and perhaps little interest in doing so.

Other organizations are lobbying for more disclosure as well. The Sustainability Accounting Standards Board, a private organization advocating for a better understanding of intangible assets for investors and also for social and environmental sustainability, has set out its own reporting standards for companies on workplace issues, arguing that the workforce is the source of longer-term value.[31]

Investors themselves have pushed companies to reveal more about their workforce. They believe human capital decisions and practices matter in important ways to understand the business and that financial accounting limits their ability to even look at those decisions. There are now several organizations pressing for change.[32] The Workforce Disclosure Initiative, whose investor members controlled $8 trillion under management, recently asked 750 of the largest companies to report data on some workforce and employment issues. Only 20 percent responded to direct questions from their largest shareholders, illustrating the resistance that employers have to revealing this information.[33]

A reasonable observer might be perplexed at this point as to why employers do not want to report information that would show, for example, that some of their costs for expenses are actually investments in training. The reasons include slippery-slope explanations—once we give them this, they will expect it every year, it will open us up to more questions about that spending, and so forth. An earlier effort in the 2010s to set ISO 9000 standards and certification reporting requirements for the human resources function in the United States championed by the Society for Human Resources met a furious pushback from the Human Resource Policy Association, an organization of senior corporate executives in human resources. They raised these objections, as well as more general complaints about the administrative burdens such requirements would create.

The fact that employee turnover and difficulty in hiring caused so much disruption in business as the pandemic began to fade pushed investors to find other ways to get facts about the labor situation in the companies they follow. Justin Sagalini, who runs Fidelity Investment's $1.2 billion healthcare-services stock fund, noted his frustration in getting any of this information: "I'm looking for these data points, and they are not easy to find. There's no requirement for the companies to report the data."[34] The investment firm Neuberger Berman is using publicly available data on individual employees to try to estimate turnover rates across companies.[35]

Accounting requires standard measures so that we can make comparisons of the same operation over time as well as comparisons across operations. If companies can choose what they report and when, as is the case now, none of that is possible. It would be extremely helpful if companies could be required to report even a few simple metrics that would reverse the perverse incentives the current reporting creates. Top of the list would be annual employee turnover, separating voluntary quits from layoffs and dismissals, just as the Bureau of Labor Statistics already reports for the labor force as a whole. The percentage of vacancies filled from within would be another. Total employees broken out between full- and part-time would be a third. Employers should already have those measures. Beyond that would be total labor spending, including those leased employees and contractors in the liquid workforce. With those measures, the incentives to churn through employees, to hire rather than develop, and push work outside to the liquid workforce would all be reduced, because the actual and longer-term costs would be more apparent.[36]

What investors see about employees even in private companies is therefore just costs and only very broad categories of those. They would like to see all aspects of employment costs be lower—liabilities, costs associated with employment, and especially wages and salaries. They do not see all costs of employment, of course, in particular the penny-wise and pound-foolish costs that come when squeezing employees drives up turnover, for example.

GAAP rules that govern accounting in the United States do not dictate practices outside the country, where the International Financial Reporting Standards (IFRS) are more likely to apply. Those standards are more sympathetic to alternative accounting approaches. One place where they have had real influence on human capital is in professional sports. Not only are the players indisputably the main asset in professional teams, but the fact that players are traded and exchanged where monetary values are attached to them makes their asset nature abundantly clear. If we did not think about the asset value of the players and valued them the way we do public companies, we would think that the teams with the lowest payroll must be doing the best and that having great players under contract is of no value. European football teams use an alternative, asset-based approach to show the value of their teams, because employees are obviously the fundamental asset.[37]

Headcount Budgets

It is a little difficult to keep straight all the twists in the accounting interpretation of employment: it is perceived as a long-term or fixed cost even though it is neither by legal definition or in practice; long-term spending commitments can be treated as an asset when keeping equipment up-to-date, but it is a current expense when applied to training employees. Efforts to improve the performance of our capital stock are treated as investments, but efforts to improve employee performance represent a current expense. Unlike capital expenditures where continuing obligations can be counted as assets, employment also has liabilities attached to it.

To see how these negative implications of employment for financial accounting affect the practice of management, there is no better place to begin than with the budget-setting process in most larger companies. The continued operation of any unit or project group depends on getting their budget approved. That process requires making a business case as to what the money will be used for, typically in great detail, and what the company will get out of it. In companies with a dedicated finance function, it is common to require a separate approval from the CFO's office in addition to the division or functional boss.

In that process, it is also common now to have a second budget requirement, a special "headcount budget," a cap on the number of employees permitted, that is in addition to the overall dollar budget in proposals. What that means in practice is that the dollar budget has to be approved but also the employee component of that budget needs to be approved separately: the company might approve the dollar request but not the amount going to headcount.

Sophisticated companies have models that estimate how many employees are required to staff different projects or units, and the headcount budget of a proposal might be assessed against them. Vendors sell a variety of tools to estimate appropriate headcount. While the models can also help ensure that companies do not have too few employees, especially when new projects are being set up, clients seem mainly concerned about whether they have too many employees.[38]

Headcount budgets can lead to perverse outcomes, mostly because it is not possible to optimize on two different factors at the same time. If we were trying to simply spend as little on a project as possible, we would have one criterion: to minimize the amount spent on a given project. When we add a cap on headcount, it creates a situation where managers could actually do a project for less money but cannot. Adding a staff member above the cap to the project is cheaper than outsourcing it to a vendor, but the headcount budget requires that we go with the more expensive vendor option.

Headcount budgets exist because of the financial accounting imperative that hiring an employee is a more burdensome expense than buying a piece of equipment. An obvious consequences of this two-tier budgeting process is that it is easier to get a proposal approved if it has fewer employees in it. A smart line manager would look hard to see if there is some other way to get the project done with less headcount, and the liquid workforce of contractors and other nonemployees described in Chapter 3 is the way to do that.

At the C-suite level, consideration of staffing requirements may become more complex, especially when they involve moving jobs and employees across locations and countries. But they also understand the responses from the investment community, where adding headcount is seen as a minus and reducing it is a plus. As a colleague put it, "If you are in trouble, and you announce layoffs, Wall Street claps."

It is not just headcount where financial accounting priorities rule. CFOs typically have more control over compensation budgets and even workforce plans than does the human resources function. When Twitter introduced its new remote work policy, it was the CFO, not the human resources team, that met the press to discuss it.[39] The view among finance professionals is that the CFO office ought to manage workforce planning not only because that is where all the money goes, but because "HR professionals spend just 15% of their time managing labor costs." Their sense was that it should be their main task,[40] which suggests that they either have no idea of all the issues that HR departments must handle or they do know and do not care about them.

Office Space, the Pandemic, and the Continuing Cost Squeeze

The squeeze on costs associated with employees made it clear how much capital companies had tied up in warehouses and other locations.[41] That led to cuts in office space. The size of a typical office fell by about one-third from the 1970s through the early 2010s, and cubicles shrank in size by 25 to 50 percent in the ten years from the early 1980s.[42] Here the issue of relative size versus absolute size matters. Cutting the size of an executive office by half is not so bad when it starts out the size of a small airplane hangar. Cutting a small cubicle in half is another matter. Companies also redesigned their office spaces to make them more standardized and modular so they could downsize quickly and cheaply.[43] But empty offices were something else altogether. As long as I have an empty office—even a small one—the company appears to be wasting money.

Many jobs require that employees be in the field much of the time dealing with clients and customers. The development of laptops and mobile software made it possible to get rid of offices for those employees altogether. IBM claimed to have cut real estate costs by 75 percent in one division by cutting the offices of consulting employees and having them telecommute. This was the beginning of the joke that IBM no longer stood for "I've Been Moved"; it now meant "I'm By Myself," as corporate relocations gave way to telecommuting. AT&T moved 10,000 account executives to virtual status, taking back their offices; the business analytics company Dun & Bradstreet cut its Dallas office space by half with technology that allowed its sales force to work remotely. Ernst & Young cut its New York office by 40 percent by pushing its consultants out into the field and taking away their permanent offices.[44] This was permanent remote work, twenty-five years before the COVID-19 pandemic and its work-from-home requirements.

What about jobs where employees were away a lot but not all the time? This is the contemporary notion of hybrid work. Keeping an office empty costs about as much as one when employees are in all the time. The innovation here was the idea of "hoteling," temporary offices for employees like guests in a hotel. We allow employees to reserve it when they will be in town just like a hotel. If we get fancy, or we expect the visiting employees to need to see clients in that shared office, we allow them to personalize it with their own pictures, desk toys, and so on, which we bring out and set up whenever they are coming in.

No doubt many companies tried something like this, but Ernst & Young gets the recognition for doing it first in a big way in 1993 with its consultants in New York. The supply chain challenge here is not knowing how many employees will show up at the same time; there cannot be enough desks for all of them. Do you keep enough offices for the worst case—like Mondays before holiday weeks, when employees need to get a lot done—or the best case—like mid-week in August, when many people are on vacation? One way to do this is with optimization software to predict when employees will show up. Early on, Arthur Andersen borrowed software from the restaurant industry to predict and respond to demand for offices. Now there is a slew of vendors providing office space optimization software that acts like a restaurant reservation system, reserving offices, meeting rooms, and the like. For companies that lease space and can adjust their leases, the software also provides estimates as to the total amount needed.

Hoteling for office space faded quite quickly by the mid-2000s, leading more than one observer to wonder what happened to it.[45] In part it faded because employees with influence did not want to lose their offices. When I come into the office I want to be with my workmates, but in hoteling, I may not be near them at all. I could be in a different building. Research also found that, for many workers, office space was part of their identity, and the way they organized and decorated it mattered to them.[46]

Arguably hoteling faded because another, cheaper model emerged: open office plans. These are big, open rooms and common tables rather than individual desks. With no walls to build or office doors, costs are much lower, and space per employee can be squeezed down as well. There is no need for hoteling when there are open offices: just squeeze in another chair to the table.

The initial justification was that they would increase collaboration, based on research evidence that we tend to interact more with people to whom we are physically closer. But the extension of that argument—if we simply squeeze everyone together, we will have more interaction—proves not to be true. The general view is that employees hate them.

A widely quoted *New York Times* article from a decade ago pointed out the problems: everyone can hear your conversations, and they are annoyed by them.[47] The next problem is that employees then clam up and learn not to interact with each other to prevent irritating their neighbors. Then we all put on headphones to avoid being distracted so that we cannot interact easily with anyone in any case. We also put up personal barriers when there are lots of people in tight quarters, such that interactions actually fall by a lot.[48] Then there is the lack of privacy and personal space, all reasons why employees tend not to work well in open office plans. There are accommodations that can help—such as white noise machines to muffle conversations, more breakout rooms—but there is no evidence that open offices help with work-related interactions. Open-plan offices persist because they are so much cheaper than even cubicles, despite the fact that they do not work well; *New York Times* columnist David Brooks has described them as "the Immortal Awfulness of Open Plan Workplaces."[49]

Open offices were impossible to run in a pandemic, of course. The heightened concern about infections, even when it was possible to return to offices and when social distancing regulations eased, made it difficult to work in the side-by-side context of open offices. What we are hearing instead is a return to the earlier theme beginning in the 1980s of remote work.

In March 2020, when the work-from-home mandates associated with COVID-19 infections had just begun and were expected to be short-term, 74 percent of CFOs surveyed reported that they were already planning to move employees to permanent work-from-home status (one-quarter planned to move more than 20 percent) in order to eliminate their offices and cut those real estate costs.[50] Many of the leading tech companies—Facebook and Twitter early on, later Google and others—announced that a large percentage of their employees could work from home on a permanent basis, although what counts as permanent when companies so frequently change their policies is always in question. The expectation is that going to permanent remote work means losing an office, which is the big cost savings for the employer. At least part of the resistance by employers to hybrid models where employees keep their offices but work remotely part-time is because there is no real estate savings to it.[51]

The other important development with permanent working from home, at least in the Bay Area companies, is pay cuts. The argument is that we should pay based on the cost of living where you live, and if you move to a cheaper place, we should pay you less. Facebook and Twitter announced this policy early on in the pandemic. Stripe offered to give employees a $20,000 bonus if they would move to a cheaper location, and then take a 10 percent wage cut. The estimate is that the Silicon Valley companies were expecting employees to take about a 15 percent pay cut if they moved.[52]

There is no sensible reason to pay based on location for the jobs in question. When the Silicon Valley CEOs worked remotely from their homes in resort locations, I suspect their companies were rightly not expecting to pay them what local CEOs in Wyoming or New Mexico were paid. The kind of top tech jobs in these companies that could be done remotely are like consulting roles, and employers compete for them on a national basis, not in local labor markets. When we engage consultants, the location of their house does not come up as a factor in negotiating their rates.

In summary, the squeeze on all costs related to employment is widespread. If one wanted their business to look good to investors, it would be far better to lower the wage bill, which makes employment expenses look better, even if the costs of turnover that resulted exceeded the wage savings. Investors easily see the former but not the latter. It is also appealing to use nonemployees— including employees of a vendor—as opposed to one's own employees even if the total cost of vendors is greater because it reduces the apparent employee costs. Nonemployees, which includes employees of someone else paid the same amount, working for the same time period, and operate under a contract, are seen as a variable cost. Why a contractual arrangement can be seen as a variable cost while employment is a fixed cost represents one of the mysteries of accounting. For whatever reason, shifting work away from employees will improve profitability estimates and share prices based on financial accounting.[53]

As we will see in Chapter 3, the arrangements for workers who are not employees can become very complex. In an extreme example, employers can engage employees to work for them and then transfer the employment arrangement to another, specialized organization, a professional employee organization (PEO). The PEO literally becomes the legal employer of those workers and then leases them back to the original employer. About 3.7 million workers are employed by PEOs.[54]

The punchline from this new approach is straightforward. Employers in public companies and other types of companies are pushed by the influence of financial accounting to squeeze up-front employment costs at the expense of costs elsewhere—minimizing hiring costs but making more bad hires, holding down wages at the expense of turnover, using nonemployee workers to shift costs from the employment column to the other expenses column, and hiring talent rather than developing it because training cannot be accounted for as an investment. The description of these practices as suboptimal reflects the incentive system under which they operate. Research confirms the long benefits of an alternative approach: if you bought shares in companies that manage their employees better, you would not only make money, you would beat the market average now and in the future. In other words, because investors don't believe this relationship exists, you can beat them by investing in it.[55] We cannot blame practitioners for not recognizing those relationships in the past, as they were only revealed by careful analysis. We shouldn't ignore them now.

2

Beyond Financial Accounting: What Drives Leaders

Other developments on the management side reinforced the incentives from financial accounting and the shareholder value push to squeeze employment. Some of these have to do with business leaders themselves.

How Business Leaders Became Different

Before the 1950s, the professional managers who led large companies tended to be lawyers and bankers. But that soon shifted with the post–World War II engineering focus. By the 1950s, a study conducted at Virginia Polytechnic Institute found that one-third of the largest corporations were headed by executives who had graduated with engineering qualifications; another at Columbia University at the same time found that 40 percent of all the managers in industrial companies were trained as engineers.[1]

As one observer noted, engineers were "frequently bewildered" by executive positions because those jobs were about overseeing people, and people were hard to understand, especially if your training had been in technical fields like engineering. One consequence of the movement of engineers into the executive ranks was a big demand for training and development in the area of managing people. The corporations met this by creating new organizational development departments, which taught management skills and advised the businesses on how to manage employee problems.[2]

By the 1960s, engineering began to fade and marketing became the pipeline to the top. No matter where they started in this period, however, CEOs were grown through the ranks, going through management training and leadership development where they learned—or at least were forced to consider—ideas about the advantages of paying attention to human needs and managing employees carefully. If they were not capable of managing people, it is difficult to imagine them advancing to the top jobs.

The rising power of investors—hostile takeovers, activist investors, and shareholder lawsuits—meant that the skill and ability to manage them became the new priority in the 1980s. Shortly thereafter finance replaced marketing as the most important function, where it remains now, as the preferred path to the CEO suite. Depending on the population of CEOs used, 47 percent of top CEOs came out of finance.[3] Where the CEO did not come out of finance, they were joined at the hip with the CFO. Half the CFOs, in turn, came from public accounting.[4] As the executive search firm Korn Ferry concluded, those CFOs from public accounting backgrounds "are typically very compartmentalized, seeing things in black and white and focusing strongly on managing risk."

The power of investors and investment banks also mattered because of their importance as role models. By the end of the 1980s investment banking was the super-lucrative career, and the leaders of those banks were typically far wealthier than the CEOs of the companies they advised. Banks, and especially investment banks, have long had their own stripped-down models of managing employees, where high pay compensates for burdensome workloads and a general lack of attention to the lives of junior employees who toiled in up-or-out models, chasing ever higher levels of pay. Roughly 24 percent of US public companies had board members from banking,[5] and the views of investment bankers—especially investment analysts—had special influence when evaluating the finances of companies.

How a banker who grew up in a system where individual competition was ruthless and encouraged, where supervision was largely absent, and where the well-being of employees was a secondary concern would look at a company that made employee needs a priority and spent money doing so is worth considering. Edward Lambert at Sears and Jeff Bezos at Amazon offer examples, as we see below.

Nelson Flightstein's account of corporate evolution provides some of the underpinnings of that transformation and the associated shift within business from seeing corporations as mainly production operations to seeing them more as investors operating within a business context. With that shift executive decisions became even more governed by financial criterion, and the executive and finance function became of singular importance, influencing all operating decisions.[6]

The CFO role is a relatively recent innovation, growing out of the more traditional and stodgy position of corporate treasurer, essentially an accounting function. The waves of inflation along with more aggressive anti-trust legislation in the 1970s threatened the way conglomerate corporations made money. Figuring out how to add value, or at least keep it from eroding, became a prime concern. More sophisticated finance executives stepped in to show a way forward that involved not just accounting but guiding business decisions. One study found there were no CFO positions or function in 1964; by 1980, 80 percent of large US corporations had them.[7]

That CFOs and their new office came out of the rule-based field of accounting was consequential. Accounting was its own profession with a long learning curve, which meant that it was difficult for someone in that track to have much experience outside accounting. It attracted different kinds of people as well. Although CFOs are not as routinely appointed to CEO, as many suspect, it does appear to be the most common field where most CEOs begin their careers.[8] That initial grounding no doubt affects the way they see the world. On average, CFOs see the world differently than CEOs, even acknowledging the fact that many of the latter were previously the former. Researchers have found, not surprisingly, that CFOs were more likely to make decisions based on rules and logic and were less patient with people and people issues as compared to CEOs.[9]

Post-1980

The nature of who the leaders were became more important after the 1980s when the CEO role began to change. Before then, business leaders had important administrative roles overseeing committees and functional experts who made recommendations that guided the companies. They got to these top jobs slowly, after decades of being marinated in the company's values and practices, rotated across its operations, and running smaller parts of the businesses. The notion of being administrators in no way suggests those jobs were easy, as the organizations they ran were enormous and incredibly complicated, especially once they became conglomerates spanning unrelated businesses.

The immediate pressure to staunch the bleeding from the 1981 recession, at the time the worst downturn since the Great Depression, combined with deregulation across a range of industries and new competition from Japan, demanded a different approach. That appeared to require different leaders with different skills.[10] The first actions were to cut, including, for the first time, layoffs of white-collar workers and the dismantling of some of the deep administrative functions. Faced with new and effective competition for the first time, the pressure to "do something" at industrial companies as well as service companies like IBM was palpable.

If there was a model as to how to respond, it arguably came from Lee Iacocca, who took over the bankrupt Chrysler Corporation in 1978, secured government loans to keep it afloat, and returned it to profitability three years later. He became a relentless pitchman synonymous with the company (the name "Iacocca" was said to be an acronym for "I Am Chairman of the Chrysler Corporation of America") and was seen as a hands-on manager making decisions personally, including bet-the-company actions like introducing the minivan that previously would have been developed slowly through corporate departments.[11] He also developed the role of CEO as celebrity, which continues today.

After Iacocca, CEOs were expected to be the public face of their company and take the same kind of hands-on approach to restructuring their companies. Or, more pejoratively, have their fingers in everything. Before then, it would have been extremely unusual for a CEO to initiate new policies or procedures ("I want to see wellness programs!") or even to intervene directly in projects before they were finished. Proposals worked their way through committees with all the details pinned down before the CEO would see them, if at all. Now it is common for the CEO to initiate proposals themselves in all levels of decisions, and also for leaders in the functions to get the thoughts of the CEO before even starting an initiative.

I remember in the 1990s when a head of human resources gave what was then the novel advice on how he succeeded in that role by saying, "I do whatever my CEO wants." That may sound obvious now, but at the time, it was unusual for a CEO to have distinctive thoughts about human resources that the company would be expected to enact. In our executive programs at the Wharton School, it soon became common for companies organizing executive classes here to run the content of individual class sessions past operating leaders, including the CEO, to get their approval before beginning the program, sometimes even at the level of reviewing faculty slide decks. The idea that tasks like these should be delegated to experts or that the CEO might have more important things to do seemed passé.

As the power of human resources declined with the need to deal with unions, the executives in human resources sought a new mission. Thomas Kochan and Lee Dyer described how its attention shifted to the CEO and CFOs. A former head of human resources at GE, Frank Doyle, described the new role as being "the perfect agent" of the CEO, executing whatever they wanted.[12]

That became easier to do when corporations flattened. Harvard professor Julie Wulf documented the change in the organization chart after the 1980s. Corporations got flatter by cutting out layers of management. Rather than pushing authority from the very top down, however, she argues that it increased the span of control or responsibility of the CEO, concentrating even more power at the top, as the chart in Figure 2.1 suggests.

CEOs had twice as many direct reports at the end of the period as compared to the beginning. In other words, more power appeared to be concentrated at the top, in line with making the CEO directly responsible and accountable for everything going on in the company.[13]

The high-water mark for this hands-on approach from the CEO to human resources may well have been Jack Welch, who took over from Iacocca as the

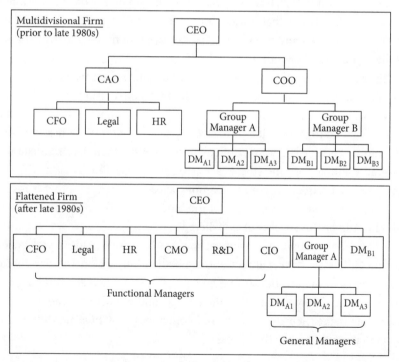

Figure 2.1 The Flattened Firm (Illustrative Example for Large US Firms from 1986 to 2006)

Source: Julie Wulf, "The Flattened Firm: Not as Advertised," *California Management Review* 55, no. 1 (2012): 5–23

most famous leader in business. As David Geddes argues, he was the leader who laid out how to operate a company in ways that pleased the investment community, among other things, by cutting headcount, driving down administrative costs, and managing earnings with GE's new financial arm in ways to make sure that it always hit its targets.[14] He pushed GE to continue and even expand efforts to develop managers and business leaders, but he also advanced the practice of forced rankings. Forced rankings had been around since World War II, but Welch extended their punch by requiring that the company dismiss the bottom 10 percent of performers as measured by those rankings every year. The justification for this was his famous "A Player, B Player, and C Player model" where "C" players were bad: get rid of them; "A" players were good: try to hire more of them; and "B" players were mediocre: push them up if you can or out.

The people we bring in are not necessarily going to perform better than the ones we let go, especially given how poorly we hire, as Chapter 3 indicates.[15] But GE adopted it, Welch actively advocated it, and on the basis of his advocacy, other CEOs saw that it was adopted in their companies as well, at one point covering as many as one-third of US corporations. GE quietly dropped it the year after Welch retired.

The most likely explanation for the continued belief in this model is a bias familiar to psychologists called the fundamental attribution error. The idea is that when we see someone behaving in a particular way, such as being difficult, we tend to explain it to ourselves by saying that it is the result of who they are as a person (they are a difficult person) rather than the circumstances around them at the time (there is a crisis going on). One reason why this bias may be particularly common among successful people is that it is self-justifying: my success is because of me, not because of any circumstances, and I would be this successful anywhere.[16]

CEO-driven people management matters because the ideas and beliefs of the CEO now have a direct and immediate impact on the day-to-day practices of human resources and how employees are managed. A long history of research documents that the background of business leaders affects how they make their decisions,[17] and contemporary CEOs are different in ways that matter a lot to their ideas.

Their Background Changed

The education of CEOs and other business leaders began to change when the MBA degree became a much more important gateway to top corporate jobs. Monika Hamori, Rocio Bonet, and I have been tracking the attributes of the top ten executives in the Fortune 100 companies since 1980. By 2011, 63 percent had some advanced degree, and by 2021, 43 percent had an MBA degree. In the bigger group of Fortune 500 companies, 40 percent of CEOs had an MBA.[18]

The curriculum in MBA programs is dominated by microeconomics, accounting, and finance and operations courses, all of which rest on the same optimization assumption that there is a single best way to solve business problems, that individuals are rational, and that shareholder value is the numeraire. At the Wharton School, for example, the required courses in the MBA curriculum in 1990 included 1.5 full-semester courses on managing people. Now it is down to 0.33 courses and a weekend simulation. The Harvard Business School had a required course on human resources that was pulled from the core in the mid-1980s. It also stopped teaching the stakeholder theory of governance shortly thereafter. A recent study of CEO behavior traces differences in how they managed their business to changes in the curriculum that different age groups experienced as MBA students. The finding? Course content matters.[19]

The special importance of the CFO comes from the fact that they are at the center of all business decisions. But finance was not the only area making inroads into the executive suite. A startling one-third of CEOs have engineering degrees and backgrounds despite representing only about 6 percent of all college graduates.[20] Another study found that 17 percent of the CEOs of Fortune 100 companies began their careers in engineering, particularly surprising because many of those companies have few engineering operations.[21] LinkedIn reports that when looking at all CEOs in its worldwide database, which admittedly includes companies as small as fifty employees, the most common educational background is computer science, followed by economics.[22] All these fields share a focus on optimization. When we combine it with the dominant role of finance in public companies, which share that focus, we have a seismic event in business leadership.

Along with the shift toward leaders with this focused academic background is the decline in management training and development programs, which is where most corporate leaders had learned about the psychology of individuals and the principles of management. By the mid-1950s, virtually every large company had a management development program designed to create supervisors and staff the entry level of the management pipeline. A survey of large employers in 2007, just before the Great Recession, found that only about half of US companies offered any training for new supervisors, let alone a dedicated program of development. Just a few years later, 58 percent of managers reported in a Lou Harris poll that they had received no management training whatsoever.[23] There is no reason to think that this training increased after the cost cutting of the Great Recession. If we look at leadership development programs designed to help develop executives, 60 percent of corporations had put them in place by 1955, a figure that declined by half, to 31 percent, by 2019.[24] They didn't get management material in school or in corporate training. They weren't going to get it on the job now either, as our study of Fortune 100 top executives found that cross-functional experience associated with job rotation development programs has been in decline since 2001.

Another new development came from the rise of tech companies and Silicon Valley. Their explosive growth and eye-popping financial returns made them the new role models for business. The famous founders of those companies—first Bill Gates at Microsoft and Steve Jobs at Apple, and then a new generation like Larry Page and Sergey Brin at Google and Elon Musk—had no prior business experience as employees (Jeff Bezos spent eight years in investment banking before founding Amazon, which offers intensive finance experience but little in the way of management). Most startup companies begin without structured management practices and any human resource expertise. What is different about these companies, and perhaps many startups today, is that they intended to keep working that way. For example, when Wharton began an executive development program with Microsoft about twenty-five years ago, the company was already the biggest corporation in the world in terms of market capitalization. It had done no employee development before, and the head of human resources was a computer programmer who had been moved over to that role.

We can see this footprint in the famous competition between Silicon Valley and Route 128 in Boston, where the latter approach failed almost completely. This difference was often attributed to lack of traditional corporate models in the startups, although whether those structures drove the wrong business strategies chosen by Route 128 firms is certainly not clear. Arguably the high-water mark for the most extensive and sophisticated (if you liked it) or bureaucratic (if you did not) human resource policies was Route 128's Digital Equipment Corporation. It faded in the 1990s and was acquired and absorbed by Compaq in 1998, which itself was absorbed by HP. Perhaps the most important difference with the Silicon Valley firms is that even when they got bigger, they hired talent from outside rather than growing it from within—a radical development at the time only made possible by the depth

of talent in that local market. Those companies had none of the human resource practices associated with employee development or career management. They also relied heavily on contractors and outsourcing, presaging the
liquid workforce.[25]

Beyond those startup-based practices lie what might be thought of as uto-
pian ideas about how to run organizations, or in some cases dystopian ideas.
Dan Lyon's description of work life in Boston-based company HubSpot is full
of quirky practices that apparently seemed reasonable to the founders but
not to people who experienced them, such as treating employees as players
who are in competition with potential replacements in the outside labor
market to keep their jobs and having celebrations for those who are pushed
out.[26] His detailed description of Silicon Valley tech firms documents how
practices like open office plans and constant restructuring are driven by optimization ideas and a lack of awareness of the unpleasantness of actually
working under those practices.[27]

No matter what their industry, startup companies now almost uniformly
believe they should adopt that "no bureaucracy" model even as they grow
and that it is somehow a failure if they do not. Catherine Turco's account
of living in the startup world reveals how persistent the myth is that it is
possible to run companies with no formal management systems.[28] The
startups that have become big companies all eventually adopted more
standard human resource and management practices, but the myth that
we can manage large organizations without any systematic management
practices continues to permeate the tech and startup world and to some extent influences investor views as to how little management should actually
be required. One consequence is that as they get bigger, those companies
persist without clear or sensible management practices far longer than arguably makes sense.

Business Leaders Are Managed Differently

Beyond the fact that business leaders have different experiences is the evidence that we manage them quite differently now. The foundational book
The Modern Corporation and Private Property, by Adolf Berle and Gardiner
Means, described the important separation between ownership and control
that created an incentive for the new managers to pursue their own interests
at the expense of the owners.[29]

How to address that issue initially focused on voting rights and other legal protections to prevent problems once they were recognized. The financialization approach after the 1990s tried to get executives to think and act like shareholders by giving them more and more compensation based on equity. Doing so changed the nature of those top executive jobs.

That process accelerated when companies began to hire executives from the outside. Those relationships began with negotiations between the candidate and the company as to what the arrangement would be. The terms and conditions were then turned into contracts. Questions of executive pay then drove other issues and broader contracts: What happens to my equity if the company is acquired; can the company ever push me out before I can receive the payments; how will the board of directors assess my performance to decide how much equity to give me? Over time, the contracts grew to cover more issues and more executives.

It is difficult to get information about the extent of executive contracts because they are not all reported in any consistent place. But there is little evidence that they were common before 1980, and the exceptions were limited to issues like change in control if the company was acquired. By 2000, about half the CEOs in S&P 500 companies had employment contracts.[30] By 2019, the figure was closer to two-thirds. Roughly that same number of employers also had contracts with named officers or the top five highest-paid executives, roughly matching the authority hierarchy of the companies.[31] How much deeper they go into the organization now is unknown because contracts below that level are not reported to regulators.

The most important aspect of executive contracts has to do with compensation and the contingencies on which it is based. In 1993, 35 percent of CEO compensation came from financial incentives that were contingent on some kind of performance goals. By 2014, it was 85 percent.[32] The only part of their pay not based on some kind of formula is salary, and that declined from 12 percent of total compensation for S&P 500 CEOs in 2009 to a trivial 4 percent in 2018.[33] There are many components to contingent compensation, some of which are tied to achieving specific performance targets on business operations and tend to be paid annually. The contracts also specify a time limit for the agreement, after which it either ends or must be renegotiated.

As described in more detail in Chapter 6, the scale of executive compensation now is so great, with their pay leveraged onto shareholder returns, and the gap between their total compensation and all other employees is so huge, that it is difficult to pretend we are all in this together. The short-term financial stakes for the executive are so high—drive up the share price during your term and even your extended family can retire—while regular employees need a long career just to meet much more modest goals. We used to believe that the big divide in the workplace was the legal one between white-collar and blue-collar, exempt from the Fair Labor Standards Act or nonexempt. Now the biggest division is between the executives, the very top ones, and everyone else.

Despite being employees, executives now are managed mainly via these contracts. They are negotiated in an adversarial context with their employer—attorneys working on both sides—where they are seeking an advantage in the form of greater protections from dismissal, higher compensation, and lower targets needed to achieve it. This process assumes that the interests of the executives are not aligned with those of the organization. These agreements are also time-limited, like a contractor, and most everything relevant to their employment, down to the level of individual perks, is laid out in the contract. Executives are managed almost completely against formal performance metrics set out for them in advance. A standard employment contract for executives has nineteen separate topics ranging from what they are permitted to do outside work to what happens when they leave the organization.[34] There is a very large literature demonstrating that executives change their behavior to conform to these contracts.[35]

Stewart Schwab and Randall Thomas did a deep-dive into corporate filings to see what was in them and in particular how far they went in governing the working relationship between the executive and their nominal employer, the corporation. The agreements go quite far. They found, for example, that only about 7 percent of the CEOs appeared to be "at will" employees who could in principle be terminated the way typical employees are. Even those 7 percent give the CEOs special rights if they are terminated, limiting, for example, the criteria for which they can be dismissed.[36]

These contracts specify in great detail, running sometimes hundreds of pages, how they will be paid, how they will be judged, how they can be pushed out, and virtually everything about their working life, down to the value of perks, office size, and so forth. Equity grants are especially complicated because there are so many varieties—nonqualified stock options, stock appreciation rights, restricted stock unions, outright grants. Then we come to the vesting requirements associated with them and rules governing the exercise of their options. The agreements also spell out what activities the executive is allowed to engage in outside of work.

Drafting these contracts is a huge exercise. The executives have their own attorneys, their employer has its attorneys, and the executives and the HR departments they oversee have their own executive compensation consultants, while the board of directors have their compensation consultants to check on the company's consultants. When executives leave on bad terms, the departure invariably goes to litigation over whether their contract was violated, and the fights can go on for years.

The top executives and especially the CEOs are the leaders of the employees in the company and shape in all important ways the experience of those employees. They shape the culture and set the norms, execute the practices that build relationships with employees, and try to secure commitment and engagement from employees. The irony is that their own relationship with the organization is based on a contract that has none of those attributes. They are managed like contractors, where the arrangement is set out in a legal contract for a fixed time period—rather than open-ended—where performance requirements are specified in advance—rather than adjusted to circumstances—and where financial incentives are the most important and possibly even the only tool to manage their behavior. It is hard to believe that their own experience being managed this way does not affect how they see and manage their own workforce.

We can see the low priority that corporations give to people management issues by the fact that financial incentives are not attached to them. A study of the FTSE 100 companies, most of which operate in the United States, reports that employee issues like recruitment and retention were among their biggest risk factors, but only one-third of them had performance targets or incentive pay tied to any employee-related outcomes.[37]

This finding relates to the broader issue as to whether corporate leaders think that managing employees well really matters. A recent Conference Board survey of CEOs from around the world reported, for example, that they saw recruiting talent as more important than developing talent internally. In an article discussing Elon Musk's broader view that MBA-type management practices are not useful and that an informal "kicking-the-tires" approach is the way to go, investor Dan Rasmussen supported this view, asserting that what is important is "rewarding doers rather than focusing on airy concepts such as management."[38] In other words, it's just about incentives.

To summarize, the long-run trend running back to the 1970s saw the CEO becoming much more of a hands-on leader, taking direct and personal control over administrative functions. The background of the CEOs also began to change after the 1980s with financial experience becoming the norm, though engineers have made a surprising comeback in the CEO ranks as well. What all these backgrounds have in common is a focus on optimization: that there is a single best approach to business challenges that can be determined by experts and then executed by their organization, and that top executives are held accountable for their success against financial outcomes, not necessarily operational ones. This orientation requires something to optimize against, and in business, financial accounting provides that measure.

To see what this change in approach to management looks like, consider the shift in direction away from employee involvement and engagement at Sears. It was bought by Edward Lampert's hedge fund, ESL Investments, in 2005 with him as chairman and visionary and since 2013 as CEO, while still running ESL. He had no prior experience operating a business, and his experience as an employee was in finance, when he left Goldman Sachs at age twenty-six to start ESL. It had roughly thirty-five employees. Sears, which he merged with Kmart, had 300,000.

The company ran very much in line with the approach of optimizing financial performance, including cutting back hard on measurable employee costs. It ran lean—critics would say starving the stores—and invested much of its available cash in stock buybacks to aid investors. None of the employee first and service practices from the 1990s that made Sears a leader in management were retained. Lampert operated as a top-down, hands-on manager, responsible for essentially all decisions. He instituted the unique approach of carving up the company in 2008 into thirty separate profit and loss centers with each executive having to make a business case pitch to him and the leadership team to get operating funds. In other words, the company operated like an investment bank.

Sears closed stores and lost money at a fast clip and went to bankruptcy in 2019, with Lampert and his hedge fund being sued by Sears Holdings Corp for siphoning off corporate assets. Then, in an only-in-America sequence, he reacquired the company from bankruptcy at roughly half the price of the original acquisition, reducing its footprint in 2020 to 182 stores down from 425.[39] Along the way, he made many "Worst CEO" lists.[40]

Data Science Gives Optimization a New Push

The fact that businesses were so focused on cutting employment costs made that question ideally suited to the optimization approach, or data science under the broader heading of artificial intelligence. It is driven by a new wave of entrepreneurs and their companies who quite quickly muscled aside the industrial-organizational psychologists and their behavioral models in favor of far simpler optimization concepts. They came from engineering, specifically data science, which is to statistics what engineering is to science: deriving very practical solutions from more abstract principles that do not necessarily build on established theories. At present, they are virtually all algorithms derived from machine-learning programs—sets of equations that optimize the fit between attributes we can observe in job candidates, staffing requirements, marketing decisions, and the outcomes we desire.[41]

Any time we need to make a prediction about what will work and where it is possible to see what worked in the past, we can try to build a machine-learning-based algorithm. It will then tell us how closely any individual or situation looks like what was successful in the past. Machine-learning algorithms are agnostic about which variables work or why they work. Measures that have never been tried may be useful, and ones that have never worked before may contribute something when used together with other variables. The more the merrier: the algorithm throws them all together and produces one model from those separate measures, giving each applicant a single, easy-to-interpret score as to how likely it is that they will perform well in a job.

Frankly, it was not very hard to push the psychologists and their models out of the way because the answers they provided to workplace questions were not very satisfying, especially to the newer generation of financially oriented managers who did not assume that the older models were effective. Consider their likely response to arguably the core management question "How do we get employees to perform better?":

A: Get them motivated. Motivated employees perform better.
Q: How much better?
A: Could be a lot.
Q: How do we get them motivated?
A: A bunch of things—incentives, empowerment, goal setting, and so forth.
Q: How do I choose which ones to do?
A: Try them all.

Q: What will this cost?
A: Probably not much.
Q: How much of it should I do?
A: More is better.

It may well be that those answers are the most realistic that we can provide. A CFO used to hearing a traditional pitch for money where actions, costs, and returns are spelled out clearly, even if they weren't necessarily right, would find their head exploding. Then along comes the data scientist with a simple model that says, "This much of x leads to that much of y," and it is clear which one wins that contest, even if the latter model is largely a guess. The marketing from vendors selling these solutions is impressive, and by some judgments duplicitous.[42]

To get a sense of how big this development is, industry analysts estimate that in 2020, there were already 4,000 software-based tech vendors using data science to sell solutions to human resource departments.[43] A 2020 survey of 10,000 companies by PwC reported that 74 percent planned to increase their spending on HR technology and that 39 percent intended to use a larger number of vendors in the future, adding to the complexity of their management tasks.[44] Recent surveys suggest that roughly 17 percent of US employers were using algorithms to make employment decisions in 2019, as noted earlier, with plans for expanding their use rapidly.[45]

The good thing about these machine-learning algorithms is that they can make better predictions, especially in areas like hiring, which we see in the next chapter. A bad aspect is that they reduce the role of managers and supervisors, which weakens relationships with employees and ultimately hurts the effectiveness of management in fundamental ways. These algorithms are increasingly used to take over tasks that employees had been performing with some success, undercutting the benefits of empowerment. These consequences are described in detail in Chapter 5. It is difficult to see that the goal of optimizing the level of employment, which is what these algorithms do, is worth those costs.

The Underlying Values and Ideology of the New System

Optimization and employment cost minimization are unlikely to get as far as they do unless they are consistent with widely accepted assumptions and guiding principles. These assumptions are all consistent with the idea that people are rational in the sense of being focused on rewards and punishments, that dispositions matter more than management, and that hiring the right people and dumping the wrong ones is the key task. One could easily conclude from these assumptions that management really does not matter very much. Leaders can focus their time doing the high-profile and high-value-added tasks for shareholders, like clever financing and mergers and acquisitions.

A great example of this attention problem comes from a recent story about Boeing's post-2015 restructuring and how it contributed to its current travails with its 737-Max jetliner. The company's lean production-like program, where engineers were encouraged to find process improvements, had been something of a hallmark for quality and cost effectiveness at the company. When the new management team headed by then-CEO Dennis Muilenberg announced that it was cutting funding for that program, an engineer involved in it objected in a town hall meeting, pointing out how much money the program had saved. An executive responded dismissively "The decisions I make have more influence over outcomes than all the decisions you make." In other words, employee engagement and other workplace issues are just rounding errors in total outcomes compared to executive decisions, so why should we bother supporting them?[46] In the end, though, no one had to walk back those puny decisions made by the engineers, but the decisions made by top executives continue to plague the company.

Readers with a historical bent will recognize how the optimization approach with its focus on cost minimization looks like the Theory X approach Douglas McGregor made famous, in contrast to the Theory Y view that took human behavior seriously and the importance of managing it carefully.[47] The Theory X approach requires a lot of time and energy from leaders and from line managers. Making employees believe that they should care about the business requires a continuous effort of a kind that is neither learned in business functions nor necessarily appreciated by financial analysts. Northwestern University's William Ocasio argued persuasively that the scarcest and most important asset in running modern businesses is the time and attention of their leaders.[48] Given this, we can see why CEOs are attracted to optimization approaches because they can be delegated, executed by decision rules, and conform to ideas that make CFOs and analysts happy.

There is also a clear feeling among managers that businesses are constantly in flux, that the key to a successful strategy is to generate new capabilities to go after changing markets, and that the best way to do that is to churn: out

with the old staff, in with the new. It is responsible for the constant restructuring of organizational charts that most corporate employees experience
and the idea in talent management that we need and will be able to find
someone doing precisely the job we need to fill somewhere in the outside
labor market, ideally working for an organization we respect.

Whether it is actually true that the best way to compete is to generate new
capabilities as opposed to finding new markets is not clear, nor is it obvious
that the best way to generate new capabilities is to churn the workforce. But
this view contributes to the reality in the corporate world that employment
relationships are extremely unlikely to be long-term: the company is not
looking after your long-term interests—career, healthcare, retirement—and
that reduces your willingness to look after the company's interests, especially
when they conflict with yours.

The financial accounting priority to drive down employment costs has
been reinforced by a new generation of business leaders who come to their
roles with an optimization perspective and much less knowledge and experience in managing people than their predecessors. The optimizing perspective of cutting employment levels is pushed further by the new tools of data
science and are reinforced by pronouncements from vendors and consultants
to the extent that it becomes the smart thing to do, despite a lack of evidence
that it is more effective. As we will see in Chapter 5, these approaches undercut the role of supervisors and their relationships with employees, which
may be the most important factor shaping employee performance. They also
undercut employee involvement practices, arguably the most important and
successful management practices of the modern era, returning to a top-down
approach that fits the optimization story. These have been tried in the past,
and failed. We consider those consequences in Chapter 5.

From here, we look at the consequences of the financial accounting and
optimization-driven approach to management, starting with perhaps the
most important one: how we hire.

3

Hiring

Arguably no single management decision has more impact than who gets hired—or not hired—for which jobs. It affects who gets access to the resources that come with good jobs as well as the people who make fundamental decisions governing important organizations. For similar reasons, hiring—or talent acquisition, as its rebranding is known—is the more important decision that employers make. It is now ranked as the number-one issue in importance for corporations because we now do so much less training, development, and promotion from within, so most all talent needs are met by looking outside to hire. Hiring creates turnover at competitors, which drives a further need to hire.

Even though hiring is so essential by almost any measure, the way we do it has become increasingly worse in the past two generations. The priorities of financial accounting play out prominently, cutting the up-front employment costs associated with hiring—which means headcount—while creating significantly more work for line managers. We shifted from standardized and often elaborate processes based on research evidence about what predicts good hires to unstructured and informal approaches full of biases.

The most damning aspect of contemporary hiring practices, especially for those who want to believe that companies always push to be efficient, is the problem of the measures used to assess success. The two measures that companies track most often about hiring outcomes are time to fill positions and cost per hire. Incredibly, few employers track whether their processes produce better hires. The Society for Human Resource Management's benchmarking survey on hiring found that only 23 percent of the seventeen hundred or so firms surveyed in their report measured the quality of their hires.[1] LinkedIn's review of the twelve most popular metrics for assessing hiring finds that none of them are about the quality of candidates hired.[2] A different survey of employers found that 60 percent of companies reported that their top challenge for the coming year was hiring quality employees, but only 26 percent even had a method for defining quality.[3] Another survey found that less than a third had the data that could answer that question.[4]

A different survey found that the "quality of hire" was the eighth-most-used metric in assessing how well recruiting and hiring worked.[5] Employer responses about their future priorities in hiring are virtually the same: improve efficiency and costs, time to hire, and candidate experience, where the latter is a way of saying "convert more of those possibly interested in working for us into actual candidates."[6]

How could it be that the hiring function tracks the costs associated with hiring but not the outcomes of hiring? Wouldn't one think that bringing in good employees is the point of the hiring process? Because the priority of financial accounting is different, and that is to minimize the headcount and employment costs of the hiring process. Doing that means squeezing staff, including recruiters, but also the people who could track the quality of hires. Cost-per-hire can be done by the CFO's office, and time-to-fill by applicant tracking software. Ask yourself what we would expect to see if, say, a restaurant tracked cost per meal religiously but not the quality of food: McDonald's would win the best restaurant every year. What you would expect to see in business when we track cost-per-hire but not quality of hire?

Contemporary Practice

Hiring talent not only remains the number-one concern of CEOs in the most recent Conference Board Annual Survey, it also is the top concern of the entire executive suite.[7] PwC's recent CEO survey reports that concern about talent and skills is the biggest threat to their business.[8]

One thing is clear: no one seems happy with the way hiring is done now. It's taking longer to hire. A proprietary measure based in part on data from the US government's Job Opportunities, Layoffs, and Turnover Survey found that vacancies have stayed open longer every year since the bottom of the Great Recession in 2009.[9] A survey of large companies found that the time to fill positions rose by 62 percent from 2010 to 2015. For white-collar jobs in those organizations, it increased by twenty-six days.[10] This is despite the fact that time to fill vacancies is the second most commonly tracked measure of hiring outcomes, and this period was not a tight labor market where it was difficult to hire.

There are many delays in the process, many more steps than in the past with many more players involved, and the use of vendors has exploded, which creates handoff and integration issues. Candidates are increasingly ir-ritated by the hiring process.[11]

Employers also spend a ton of money on hiring: the Society for Human Resource Management estimates $4,129 for the average job in the United States, but that is just for the administrative costs, which does not include performance losses while positions are vacant, the productivity losses while new hires learn the ropes, or, as we saw in Chapter 1, the time and distrac-tion other workers now spend in hiring replacements. It is many times that amount for managerial roles,[12] and the United States fills more than 70 mil-lion jobs per year in an economy with roughly 160 million total jobs. Overall, employers in the United States spend almost $300 billion each year to hire new employees just for those out-of-pocket costs.[13] The single biggest cate-gory for all the spending on vendors related to human resources by employers is to help them hire.[14]

For a recent example of how the focus on minimizing the up-front costs of hiring creates bigger and more expensive problems in other areas, con-sider the huge hiring challenge that companies reported just before the pan-demic in 2020. The COVID-related shutdowns beginning in March of 2020 were expected to be short-lived, and it was presumed that businesses would be back open just a few months later. Despite that, 20.5 million people were pushed out of work. Presumably the expectation was that the employers could rehire them or find new workers when the shutdowns were lifted. At least in the first few weeks many employees were furloughed—not being paid and not working, but still officially on the books.

Even more surprising, many employers also gutted their recruiting staff, because that so obviously restricts the ability to restart the busi-ness. Tech companies in particular—who were complaining the loudest about staff shortages—began slashing their recruiting staffs in the first weeks of the shutdowns, by 80 percent in some companies. Zip Recruiter, one of the recruiting vendors, cut its own staff by 39 percent.[15] What would they do when business picked back up? Nothing, until they hired recruiters.

The assumption that we could just hire who we want when we want had already started to fade with the tighter labor markets of the late 2010s, but with the sudden restart of the economy when pandemic restrictions lifted in the spring of 2021, it was gone altogether. As with previous very tight labor markets, the hardest jobs to fill were recruiters. Stories about lost business because of unfilled jobs were legion in the press and persist more than a year later. As is always the case, we blame workers for somehow not being available when employers want to rehire them rather than the employers for waiting until the last minute.

Hiring in the Golden Age of Corporations

Management candidates were whisked away to corporate headquarters for as much as a week of interviewing and testing that included a battery of psychological tests, "in-basket" assessments of simulated work problems, and interviews with psychologists. In some cases, candidates were also sent for medical tests. Here the goal was to make sure they were going to live long enough for the massive investments the companies were planning to make on them to pay off.

One might argue that because companies are in a more or less constant re-structuring mode—building new capabilities by hiring and pushing out old ones with layoffs—they may not care as much about spending the time and money to make good hiring decisions because they are unlikely to last very long. The counter to that argument is that what they are doing now is not cheap, and having bad employees for a short period of time is only a plus if you can replace them with better hires: a stream of bad employees is still a nightmare. If the process leads to bad hires in the first place, it is likely to do so the next time as well.

There are two reasons why we are so hiring-centric now. The first, as described in more detail in Chapter 5, is that we no longer fill positions in-ternally through promotions, lateral assignments, and retraining for new ones. We moved from filling 90 percent of positions from within in large corporations before the 1980s to a fraction of that amount. A 2017 survey from the Society for Human Resource Management put the figure at only 11 percent of vacancies filled internally.[16]

The second and related reason is retention. Virtually all hiring is backfilling jobs that employees have left. In the pandemic year of 2020, the United States still filled 70.4 million jobs even though the total number of jobs in the economy fell.[17] These were filled by outside hires. Only 28 percent of talent acquisition leaders report that internal candidates are an important source for filling their vacancies.[18] Less than one in three employers require that managers look internally before hiring from the outside.[19] This is despite the evidence suggesting that internal candidates are better and cheaper and that filling openings from within,[20] especially by promotion, reduces the turnover of others in the organization. LinkedIn data indicate that the most common reason current employees have for considering a position elsewhere is career advancement, which is surely related to the fact that employers are not promoting to fill vacancies.[21]

There is no evidence whatsoever for the rationalization that turnover is high because "kids today are just job hoppers." Young people have always moved a lot. As noted in Chapter 1, the average fifty-year-old worker in the United States has already had twelve different employers, and young people in recent years actually changed employers less often than older cohorts at the same age. Outside hiring creates a retention problem for other employers. When employees see vacancies filled not by promotion but from outside hiring, they get the idea that opportunities elsewhere are the key to advancement.

The major change in hiring from earlier generations is that the focus then was on selecting the best candidates from among those who apply. Now the focus is almost entirely on recruiting candidates to actually apply and more or less flipping coins as to which ones get hired. For lower-level retail jobs in the big chain stores and restaurants, it is a commodity-based approach of getting as many candidates as possible to apply and screening them quickly and cheaply with simple tests. Elsewhere, and especially for white-collar jobs that are less standard, hiring is a wildly idiosyncratic process.

The Hiring Funnel

A simple way to get oriented to how hiring works today is with what practitioners refer to as "the hiring funnel," or the flow of individuals through the hiring process. Glassdoor data gathered from employers suggest that typical corporate job openings before the pandemic attracted 250 applicants. Out of those, roughly five make it to the interview stage, and only one of those will get a job offer.[22] In other words, the base rate probability of an applicant getting a job offer was about four-tenths of a percent. In smaller companies the odds were better, with roughly 1 percent of applicants being offered jobs.[23]

Even with this simple overview, a surprising conclusion is just how many applications there are for a typical job opening, even in tight labor markets. It is not surprising that famous companies like Google or Goldman Sachs attract thousands of applications, but given the complaints from employers at the time about not having anyone to hire, it is revealing to see how many applicants they were getting. It is true that many of those applicants are applying to many jobs, which suggests they are not truly available to be hired, but the vast majority of offers appear to be accepted when extended. That suggests that applicants are serious.

Electronic Hiring and Recruiting Candidates

How has hiring become like processing packages down an assembly line? It began with job boards, basically websites with job ads and Monster.com in 1999. It was like a classified job advertising page at your local newspaper except that it covered the country and eventually jobs outside the United States as well, and it was cheaper and easier to put job ads on these job boards than to go city-by-city with newspaper ads. For candidates, it was now possible to see jobs across the country all with a click of a mouse. It also devastated local newspaper publishing by cutting the job ads that had been their most important source of revenue.

The additional innovation of the job boards was to allow candidates to post their resumes so that employers could also look at candidates without having to do any expensive recruiting. That made possible what we now call "passive search": candidates who are not looking for a job but are found by someone who is hiring.[24]

The initial response of employers to their employees posting their resumes was to find out who they were and fire them.[25] As the labor market tightened their approach changed, and human resource employees known as "salvagers" tried to find out who was posting resumes and persuade them to stay. Most employers in this period said that they wanted to get better at outside hiring *and* get better at retention, something that was impossible for all of them to do. Although job boards have become less important, one of them alone, the job board Indeed.com, now delivers roughly one-third of all hires in 2021.[26]

Employers wised up to the fact that employees who wanted different work could do so far faster by going to the job boards and getting another job at a different employer than they could finding a different job in their own organization. Their smart response was to bring job boards inside their companies, even engaging Monster.com to build them. We consider this development in Chapter 6.

When the labor market tightened in the late 1990s and employers found it difficult to hire, they made it easier to apply for jobs, in some ways extremely easy to apply: everything could be done electronically, everything could be done quickly. Candidates did so, sometimes applying for hundreds of jobs at a time. When the labor market shifted from tight to slack during the 2001 recession and thereafter, employers found themselves overloaded with applications. To handle the scale of the challenge, they moved to automation and applicant tracking systems (ATS). These were simple software systems that would scan resumes, or later standard application forms, to look for key words. If a job required a college degree, for example, then an application that had no mention of the candidate having that degree would be omitted from selection.[27]

If, say, half the candidates have the required degree, then that "switch" would cut out half of the applicants. If we added another requirement such as years of experience that half the candidates might have, that would seem to cut out half as well (if the attributes were uncorrelated). The fact that candidates need to get through both switches could mean that only 25 percent get through. If we have just five of these requirements, only 3 percent of the applications will get through. The Great Recession in 2008 magnified the problem as applications went up enormously. My favorite example came from someone in human resources who reported that they had 25,000 applications for a reasonably standard engineering position, and none of those applicants made it through the ATS screen.

How could this happen? Hiring decisions are now pushed onto line managers, and their first task is to figure out what the requirements of the job and of candidates should be. Unless there is some discipline in that process— and there will not be when recruiters are taken out—there is no pushback to adding more. This is especially likely because we involve more people in the hiring process. Then we end up in this costly situation where we cannot fill positions caused by cutting recruiters and pushing their work onto line managers.

Another way to get a sense of the amount of automation involved in the hiring process is by considering how little human effort goes into reviewing a typical application. To get a sense of how involved recruiters are, consider their workload. The typical metric is the number of "requisitions" or vacancies that have been authorized to be filled, and the process is underway for each recruiter. Survey results from the Society for Human Resources Management suggest that the mean number is thirty to forty depending on the size of the organization. Imagine being a recruiter in charge of filling as many as forty jobs *at the same time*. If we assume, as described below, that there are roughly forty applicants for each position and an average time to fill a vacancy of thirty days, then the typical recruiter has forty new positions to fill and sixteen hundred new applications to track every month.[28] It is hard to imagine anyone being able to handle that workload with any kind of care without considerable assistance. A study by Korn Ferry showed that the average recruiter spent only six seconds looking at each resume. As described in more detail below, that help comes from vendors, from decision rules as to which applications should get priority, and also from the line managers who now do more of the hiring work. A survey of talent acquisition managers found that the biggest increase in their priorities from 2017 to 2021 was to prepare to automate the process of hiring.[29]

We can learn a lot about how hiring actually works from the 14 million or so applications in the applicant tracking system of Jobvite.com.[30] The results are not always identical to other sources, but they have the advantage of reporting on the wide array of hiring channels and doing so consistently.

Most of the applicants come via job boards like Indeed.com, and most of the actual hires come from the company's own career site or website, but the effectiveness column tells us which are the favored paths. If a candidate comes in via the hiring manager, they get the job almost a third of the time, by far the most likely path to getting hired. An applicant coming in from a job board, by contrast, has about a 0.06 percent chance of getting hired. Is it possible that professional recruiters, who get 11 percent of their candidates hired, are only one-third as good at spotting talent than are hiring managers? It is far more likely that hiring managers have power, and they just hire the applicants they want.[31]

Bo Cowgill and Patryk Perkowski at Columbia University hired professional recruiters to see how they would screen candidates with different attributes. Perhaps not surprisingly, those from elite colleges and well-known employers disproportionately made the cut to be sent to hiring managers for interviews. The most interesting finding might be that even when it was possible to predict which candidates were unlikely to accept the job if it was offered, the recruiters did not appear to factor that in, arguably leading to wasted job search and interview time for clients. The recruiters were trying to play to the preferences of the hiring managers, and so they disproportionately selected such candidates for shortlists—alumni from elite schools and experience with big-name companies—even when they were reasonably sure the candidates would not accept the jobs.[32] Even the professionals play into biases.

Referrals

While job boards produce most of the applications and the company's own career site accounts for the most hires, referrals from current employees are typically reported by employers as the preferred channel for hiring. In the data in Figure 3.1 referrals account for a third more applicants than do the employers' own recruiters, and a greater proportion of them get hired than the recruiter's candidates. It would be quite something if current employees with no training and little guidance could pick successful candidates better than professional recruiters and the traditional application process, but that is typically what we believe.

There are reasons for thinking this isn't right. We pay referees an incentive bonus if we hire someone they recommend, but there is no cost if we do not hire their referral, so why should referees not pass along everyone, good or bad? A clever study by Emilio Castilla at MIT found

Source Name	Hire Count	Hire Percentage	Applications	Application Percentage	Effectiveness
Career Site	69.502	28.93%	4.993.677	34.93%	0.83
Job Boards	45.928	19.12%	7.060.680	49.38%	0.39
Entered by Recruiter	31.172	12.98%	280.870	1.96%	6.61
Referral	29.458	12.26%	376.594	2.63%	4.66
Internal Mobility	19.242	8.01%	74.273	0.52%	15.42
Agency	9.425	3.92%	201.341	1.41%	2.79
Hiring Manager	6.425	2.67%	19.760	0.14%	19.35
Email Campaign	778	0.32%	20.212	0.02%	2.29
Custom Campaign	362	0.15%	2.569	0.02%	8.39
Federated Search	237	0.10%	3.233	0.01%	4.36
Resume Search	102	0.04%	1.924	0.01%	3.82
Notifications	97	0.04%	1.587	0.01%	3.64
Social Media Shares	57	0.02%	600	0.00%	5.65

Calculating "Effectiveness"

Effectiveness looks at the Hire percentage by source in comparison to its Application percentage.

$$= \frac{\text{Hire \%}}{\text{Application \%}}$$

The higher your Effectiveness, the better the Source is at driving Hires.

Figure 3.1 Recruiting Funnel by Applicants and Hires
Source: Jobvite

that at least on paper, the referred candidates did not appear to be better than those who came in through other channels. Referees are not super recruiters who do a better job finding good candidates, and referrals are not cheaper than other sources of candidates, especially if we include the bonuses. Why do they seem to be so popular? They are probably easier to manage for overwhelmed recruiters. Company recruiters report that they spend on average about thirteen hours trying to identify candidates for each open position, and that includes the fact that they may get help doing so from vendors and others in finding candidates.[33] If they give automatic preference to referrals, that drives screening time down enormously.

Castilla did find that referred candidates performed better on the job, although only if the person who referred them was there to mentor them. In other words, the better performance comes because the referee looks after them as new hires and helps them succeed. We might achieve the same results simply by assigning any new hire a "buddy" who will help them acclimate to the new environment and gets a bonus if the new hire succeeds. Referred candidates were also more likely to accept jobs when offered than those coming through virtually all other sources (face-to-face selling by the referee seems to matter), and that certainly makes things easier and cheaper for the recruiters.[34]

A contemporary downside to referrals, of course, is that the people we know tend to be like us, and hiring through referrals means that the workforce in the future will look like the one we have now, including demographic attributes. This matters greatly for organizations interested in diversity, because recruiting is virtually the only avenue allowed by US law to increase diversity in a workforce.

Passive Candidates

The textbook description of hiring is that employers pitch job ads out into the universe and wait for candidates to apply—what some call the "spray and pray" approach. A more targeted approach, made possible by computer power and the internet, is to identify individuals who might be good candidates and pitch jobs directly to them. A survey of fifteen hundred working adults by Zogby Analytics found that 69 percent of the respondents said they had received a text message from a recruiter about a job they hadn't applied for. Ninety-eight percent of those messages are opened, versus 20 percent for email, which is why recruiters are shifting to the texts.[35] Another national survey found that 18 percent of employees got their current job from an employer contacting them.[36]

One idea motivating the interest in passive candidates is that there might well be something wrong with active candidates who are looking to leave their current job, even if it is to work for us. This is like Groucho Marx saying that he didn't want to join any club that would have him as a member. One problem with that view is that finding someone who doesn't want to move is difficult: surveys of employees find that only about 5 percent do *not* think about moving.[37] As economist Harold Demsetz is alleged to have said when asked by a competing university if he was happy working where he was: "Make me unhappy." The right offer will make most anyone interested in moving.

Nevertheless, the interest in these passive candidates is huge. Perhaps the most stunning statistic about hiring in that regard comes from Census data showing that a majority of people who changed jobs were not actively searching for a new position in the period before they were hired away.[38] Someone or something came to them and persuaded them to apply for a new job. Chasing down these candidates has been around at least since Silicon Valley's boom, but it accelerated with the internet. Cisco Systems was famous for identifying people searching its libraries for technical information and then pitching them job ads, and for asking potential candidates to describe their ideal job and then assigning a current employee buddy doing similar work to help persuade them to apply. Their best moment was arguably inserting a little button at the bottom of their job applications that said, "Oh no, my boss is coming!" in case you were filling it out at the office. That would minimize the Cisco application and pop up a new screen that said "Gift Ideas for My Boss."

The interest in these passive candidates accelerated since then, albeit with less humor. Sixty-nine percent of US employees report that they have received an unsolicited contact from a recruiter about a potential job.[39] In total, 18 percent of US employees in 2020 had been hired into their position by their employer initiating the job search.[40]Employers spend a vastly disproportionate amount of their

1. budgets on recruiters chasing individuals who have to be persuaded to become candidates.[41] I know of no evidence suggesting that passive candidates become better employees, let alone that it is cost-effective. Fascinating evidence from a LinkedIn survey found that self-identified

passive job seekers searching for new jobs are different from active job seekers, but not in the way we might think.[42] The number-one factor that would encourage those passive job seekers to move is paying them more money, while for more traditional active candidates, the top factor is better work and career opportunities.

Active job seekers also report being more passionate about their work, more engaged in improving their skills, and a majority report being satisfied with their current job. They seem interested in moving because they are more ambitious, not because they are struggling.[43] Yet recruiters report that finding new ways to get at passive candidates is their most important priority. "Recruiting passive candidates" actually beat out "recruiting highly-skilled talent" as a priority for recruiters.[44]

An additional source of hires that is typically not mentioned in these reports is the liquid workforce. Thirty-five percent of leased employees of staffing firms are offered permanent jobs by the clients where they are working.[45] This may be a sensible way to hire, but it is not cheap: clients pay the staffing firms a fee to hire one of their workers of roughly 20 percent of the worker's annual pay. These fees do not show up as employment costs that CFOs want to minimize. They are tacked on to the administrative business expenses of the staffing agency.[46]

All this suggests that contemporary hiring is a two-class system, each with different funnels. The lower class, which we might think of from the perspective of the applicant as the equivalent of traveling coach, is where everything is handled electronically and cheaply. Although 85 percent of applicants enter there, the chances of any individual getting hired through that path are close to zero, less than 1 percent. Given that, it is difficult not to see electronic hiring from the perspective of an applicant and as a low-cost way of warehousing applicants who have little chance of being hired. First class, by contrast, involves the personal touch and human contact. Those at the front of first class have personal connections, either referrals from peers or the hiring manager. The rest are the passive candidates contacted by targeted searches.

Phantom Jobs

A quirky but revealing issue on the recruiting side is job advertisements for jobs that do not actually exist. With electronic hiring it costs nothing to post job openings on your company website, which are then also scooped up by online companies like Indeed.com and pushed out to potential job seekers around the world. Because there are so many social media sites now for distributing job advertisements, employers no longer pay to place job ads at all. The job boards now play the role of aggregators, finding job ads no matter where they are and getting them in front of candidates.

Given that, some employers go fishing for candidates even when there is no job to fill ("Let's see if there is someone out there really great, and if we find someone, we will create a position for them"). Often job ads stay up even when the position is filled, sometimes to keep collecting candidates to fill vacancies in the future and sometimes just because it takes more effort to pull the ad down than to leave it up. And sometimes truly fake ads are posted by unscrupulous recruiters looking to gather resumes to pitch to clients elsewhere. Economists James Albrecht and Susan Vroman conclude that these "phantom job" ads are a significant factor in the labor market. Among other things, they make the labor market appear stronger than it is, that there are more jobs than in reality, and that vacancies appear harder to fill.[47]

As the labor market tightened, employers became more concerned about their marketing to and handling of candidates, what they refer to as "the candidate experience." This led to a focus on new measures such as page views per applicant (i.e., Do visitors to our career site actually apply?), percentage of applications abandoned (i.e., started and not completed), and percentage of offers accepted. It also helped identify a new development in the tight labor market around the ghosting of recruiters by candidates. That means that an applicant has given up on their application, including not returning a recruiter's calls even when a job was being offered.[48] The Job Seeker Nation survey in 2020 found 10 percent of respondents saying that they have ghosted a recruiter.[49] This development falls under the heading of "what did you expect?" Employers routinely ghosted job applicants when jobs were scarce. When jobs became more plentiful, applicants adopted the same practice.

Selection: Sorting Out the Applicants

As described earlier, the big shift in hiring over the past generation or so has been on the recruiting side, gathering big pools of applicants in coach while at the same time having an express lane for preferred candidates. We still have to find ways to sort them out, beyond simple applicant tracking systems.

Arguably no topic has been studied as long or as thoroughly in the social sciences as how to find the right candidates to hire. Those studies began in a rigorous way at least since World War I in the United States, with a parallel literature in Europe.[50] Despite that, practitioners are to a remarkable extent unaware of or ignore its conclusions.

Sarah Rynes documented the great disconnect between what practitioners believe research in hiring and related areas shows and what it actually demonstrates.[51] One hundred years after psychologists began testing to predict which candidates would be good hires, the notion that testing candidates might help predict hiring is still described as a new idea.[52] Only 40 percent of employers do any tests of skills or of general abilities, which includes IQ. Seventy percent of employers do drug tests, however, which include testing for marijuana use, and most companies that tested for it in states where recreational use is now legal still seem to do so.[53]

Economists Mitchell Hoffman, Lisa B. Kahn, and Danielle Li found that even when companies use objective tests, hiring managers often have the power to ignore them.[54] When they do they get worse hires, so just doing the tests is not enough. Psychologist Nathan Kuncel and colleagues found that even when hiring managers use objective criteria and tests and are required to pay attention to them, if they can apply their own weight and judgment to those criteria, they picked candidates who performed worse as employees than if they had used a standard formula across all candidates.[55]

A straightforward conclusion, which applies to virtually all decisions, is that having processes in place and sticking to them works better than allowing each individual to go their own way. So why are we doing the latter? The consequences of cutting back on employment costs meant cutting recruiters, relying instead on technology, and pushing hiring decisions onto line managers. Because it is an additional burden to their more important roles, HR does not have the authority to ensure that line managers are trained in how to hire or follow standard procedures. So, line managers hire who they want.

In fairness to the practitioners who would like to know what to do, the personnel psychologists who examined employee selection were much more interested in testing general hypotheses than maximizing the ability to make good hires. That made it difficult to boil down the research conclusions into clear recommendations. Economists have now gotten into the act, and begin by asking the much more basic question: Are traditional recruiting and selection practices better than doing nothing? These studies show, for example, that we can predict reasonably well what attributes make better teachers, even though employers do not use that information in hiring;[56] they also show that good recruiting practices do lead to better hires but that companies don't use them for lower-paid jobs, apparently because they don't think it matters.[57]

Even the recruiters have limitations, though. One explanation as to why recruiters—who we think should know better practices—do not make more use of formal processes like standardized tests, despite evidence that they work, has to do with concern about the perception of their bosses. Individuals who use systems and tools seem easier to replace than those who appear to use personal expertise and judgment that is unique to them.[58] Scott Highhouse concludes that this is one reason why recruiters resist structured practices like tests and even structured interviews, because they want bosses to believe their personal expertise matters. That is easier to pull off when success is not measured and assessed against the reality of hiring outcomes. Intuition seems to be what rules the day.[59]

The Role of Interviews

Given the reluctance to use standardized tools and that nonexpert line managers increasingly make selection decisions, as well as our common overconfidence bias in assuming we can spot the good hires, it is not surprising that the most important practice by far in selecting employees—but perhaps the least effective—is interviews. One reason is that anyone can conduct them, regardless of whether they do them well. Many employers appear to believe that interviews *are* the selection process. As we describe below, we almost never check to see how accurate our interviews are.

Interviews per se can be a very useful selection device. But to do so requires discipline in structuring them—for example, asking everyone the same questions to make comparisons reliable—so that we focus on the candidate's past behavior in work-like settings that may reveal something about their future behavior at work, and that we prepare in advance so that we know not only what is a good question but what is a good answer. Hence the term "behavioral interviewing." Few other questions reveal anything useful about future job performance. As with the famous question "If you could be any tree, what would it be?," most other questions do not have answers that reveal information that is valid and reliable, even if after the fact we can imagine in individual cases that they were useful.[60] Unfortunately, generic behavioral questions don't work—such as "tell me about a time when you had a conflict and how it was resolved"—because most candidates have prepared for them and have self-flattering responses.

One way we can see how seriously employers interview candidates is in reports from a quarter-million job candidates submitted to Glassdoor about their hiring experiences with particular employers (see Figure 3.2). Specifically, did the process push them? How difficult was it? We might expect a typical normal distribution, as many people saying that their job interview was difficult as those saying it was easy. Given that interviewing for a job is often stressful, we might also expect the results to be skewed toward "difficult" responses.

What we find, however, is that they disproportionately report that the process was easy, which would be consistent with the employer not investing much time or energy in it. At least ten times as many respondents gave their experience the easiest rating, as opposed to those giving it the most difficult rating.

Despite the sense that employers were not putting much effort into this process, they are spending more time on interviews. It has almost doubled since 2009.[61] Glassdoor's interview data suggest that the interview process in the United States takes on average twenty-four days.[62] How much of that increase just represents delays in setting up those interviews is impossible to

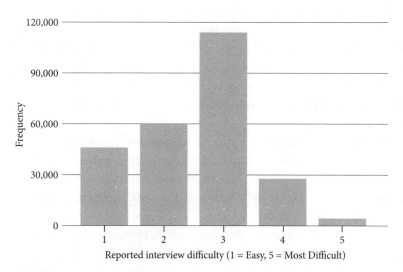

Figure 3.2 Job Interview Difficulty in Glassdoor Reviews
Source: Glassdoor Economic Research

tell, but it does represent at least a partial answer as to why it takes longer to fill jobs and get through the hiring funnel.

Why is interviewing taking longer? The high-water mark for attention given to unstructured interviews, along with the fact that they were sequential (many interviews one after the other by different interviewers), was arguably at Google in the early 2000s, where they had something like a crowd-sourcing view of the process that more opinions about candidates were better. Candidates in this period would have fifteen or more interviews, including with senior executives.[63] Much to their credit, Google checked to see if it was really true that all these interviews led to better hires. They found no benefit to multiple interviews—after four interviews, there was little if any gain in predictive power—and they eventually stopped the process. I asked one of the people who had been on the Project Oxygen team doing this work why it was that they believed all these unstructured interviews were useful, given all the prior research to the contrary.[64] They said that the team knew that research, but the leaders believed that Google was special and therefore the research results did not apply to them.[65]

One explanation is that as line managers take on more of the responsibility for hiring, they give their work group more of a role in it, as Peter Kuhn and Lizi Yu's study in Chapter 1 found for retail settings. Especially where there are teams, many people might be interested in having a say as to who joins their group. When we have more employees interview each candidate, the time involved is a considerable expense, and we do not track it.

As noted earlier, the most basic step in interviewing and a necessary condition for making the results meaningful is to standardize the process, beginning with asking the same questions to each candidate: what are known as "structured" interviews. In practice, unstructured interviews, asking whatever you want even if it differs across candidates, appear to be the common approach.[66]

Interviews, and especially unstructured interviews, have another problem in that biases can easily show up because the interviewers can decide on the fly what to ask of whom, and how to interpret the answer. Everyone knows some executive who is absolutely sure that she has the unique question that really predicts good candidates ("If you were stranded on a desert island . . ."). Sociologist Lauren Rivera's examination of interviews for elite occupations, such as those in professional service firms, indicates that hobbies, particularly those associated with the rich, featured prominently as a selection criterion there. There is no reason to think they predict anything about job performance, but they reflect the aspirations of the interviewers and presumably the people with whom they would like to be associated.[67]

Amazon introduced a modification to the typical interviewing process by inserting a final interview with an employee from outside the hiring group, known as a "bar-raiser," who has been trained in interviewing techniques. That employee has veto power over the candidate and is focused more on assessing "values" than on skills.[68] This is certainly an improvement over the traditional process, but why not have a professional recruiter play that role, as was common practice a generation ago? They are likely to be cheaper than the line managers per hour, and because it is all they do, they are likely to be better at it. And why not do it at the beginning of the process, rather than wasting staff time interviewing candidates who will eventually be turned down? A simple answer is that those costs do not show up in financial accounting because they are just added to the tasks that traditional employees perform. But using a recruiter, on the other hand, adds an employee to our cost structure.

Professional recruiters are not necessarily objective, of course. David Pedulla's account of how recruiters view applications that have nonstandard work experience—gig jobs, marginal jobs, and the like—suggests that they rely on stereotypes to develop stories about what the applicants are like. Those stories may well differ for individuals who appear otherwise similar, and they shape what happens to the applicants in the hiring process.[69]

The issue of bias comes up most clearly with the hiring criterion of "fitting with our culture," which is the number-one hiring criterion employers report using.[70] It is also one of the squishiest attributes to measure because few organizations have an accurate and consistent view of what their own culture is, and even if they do, understanding what attributes represent a good fit is not straightforward. For example, does the fact that an applicant belonged to a fraternity reflect experience working with others, or does it reflect elitism or possible bad attitudes toward women? Should it be irrelevant altogether? In the absence of any guidance, unstructured interviews allow hiring managers and recruiters to impose their own view on what the culture is and their own view as to which attributes fit. Another way to describe this is simply bias.

On a more mundane level, 77 percent of recruiters say that applications will be rejected because of typos; 35 percent say for having an email address name that is unprofessional; and 25 percent say that text with long paragraphs will do it.[71] It is difficult to believe that anyone has checked to see if these criteria actually predict who will succeed in jobs, but it is a quick and cheap way to sort out candidates.

Vendors and Outsourcing

As with most other aspects of management, we push tasks out to vendors in order to cut headcount. About 40 percent of US companies outsource at least part of the recruiting and selection process to vendors.[72] The Recruiter Nation survey found 7 percent of companies reporting that they were increasing their use of outside recruiters in 2017, and by 2020, it had risen to 23 percent. PwC conducted a massive survey of corporate hiring, and the 10,000 respondents reported that on average they were already using an average of nine vendors to help them hire. Forty percent reported that they planned to add more tech vendors in the next three years.[73]

Recruitment process outsourcing (RPO) is arguably the most important vendor development, because it takes over virtually the entire process of hiring for employers. Although these companies are not themselves huge, their influence in the labor market is. Consider, for example, the largest of the US RPOs in terms of jobs filled, a company called People Scout. It fills 300,000 jobs per year. To put that in perspective, all branches of the US Armed Forces combined take in only 180,000 recruits per year. The RPO industry itself claims to fill more jobs in the United States than the entire Fortune 500. It is common for RPOs in turn to outsource much of the process to smaller subcontractors, typically in India and the Philippines. They scour LinkedIn and social media to find potential candidates for the client and sometimes contact them directly to persuade them to apply for a position.

Sometimes these vendors negotiate in advance with applicants over the amount of money they are willing to accept, especially for "leased" employee jobs. The recruiters get paid an incentive if they negotiate the amount down. To hire programmers, for example, these vendors can scan websites where programmers might visit, trace their digital exhaust from cookies and other user tracking measures to identify who they are, and then find out what their curriculum vitae looks like. From there, software can identify where they live and generate the cost of a relocation package based on typical housing costs to move them to another employer.

If we think about the basic steps in contemporary hiring, every part of that simple process has now been disintermediated into a market of separate vendors. "Candidate discovery" is now the segment that helps identify passive candidates; "candidate engagement" are the vendors who manage career websites and provide other services to move curious job shoppers into becoming candidates; "candidate processing" are the ATS providers and other automated systems that manage the applications; "candidate verification" vendors manage credit checks, references, and background investigations; and "candidate assessment" manages the selection process.

Each of those segments can be broken down into further market niches. Candidate discovery, for example, includes these segments just on the internet channel: job boards (like Career Builder); job aggregators that scoop up and organize all the job ads on the internet (like Indeed.com); social media sites (LinkedIn); programmatic ads that target sites where desired candidates might see them; job post distributors that push the ads out to networks of sites; and job post optimizers, consultants who help their clients get their ads seen.

As an example of the niches served by these specialized services, consider karat.com, a vendor that will interview engineers on your behalf and assess their technical knowledge and capabilities. As a counter, websites like blind.com allow individuals to ask and answer about how to score well on those interviews and others like them in order to impress the recruiters. Lloyds Bank took a different approach and with a vendor developed a new, virtual reality–based assessment of candidate potential that it used as an employee selection device: gamification. Shortly thereafter, the JobTestPrep company offered to teach potential candidates how to do well on it. Especially for IT and technical jobs, cheating on skill tests and even video interviews (where colleagues off-camera give help) is such a concern that specialized vendors like eTeki.com help employers figure out in real time who is cheating.

The financial accounting focus on doing things cheaply has driven the explosion of interest in AI—more accurately, simply machine learning—in hiring decisions. Machine-learning-derived algorithms have made considerable progress in identifying relationships with previously intractable problems, such as when a given machine will break down. In the context of hiring, however, we already know a lot about what predicts good hires and what doesn't, and these algorithms ignore that.

Machine learning does that by building models with many predictors that together, often in complex, nonlinear relationships, correlate with individuals who have performed well in a given job. The more a given candidate's attributes look like those of the high-performing individuals, the better their scores on the algorithm are. One of the earliest examples of success was when the Evolv company found that the expected commuting distance for a candidate to their call center job predicted turnover very well. It just wasn't clear why.[74]

There are literally thousands of vendors claiming to offer AI solutions to hiring. Almost none of them seem credible in the sense of having developed serious, machine-learning-based algorithms. These models require huge amounts of data to build, and few employers have the scale to do that, even if they kept the information on who they hired and could merge it with performance data and applicant characteristics. Large vendors could aggregate data across employers to get the scale to build these models, but models that fit one company are unlikely to fit another unless things are incredibly similar. To fend off concerns about the discriminatory impact of hiring practices, we need to show that whatever algorithms we are using predict who will be a good hire in our own organization.

The appeal of these models is the financial one of squeezing down hiring costs, especially reducing the number of employees in human resources. Amazon's infamous hiring algorithm was developed with the explicit goal of reducing the need for recruiters. "Everyone wanted this holy grail," as one of the insiders noted. "They literally wanted it to be an engine where I'm going to give you 100 resumes, it will spit out the top five, and we'll hire those."[75] They abandoned it when it proved too difficult to sort out its bias against women candidates.

A Summary of Contemporary Hiring

What can we conclude about the process of hiring? First, it is difficult to see contemporary practices as anything other than a mess. Compared to the process decades ago, where professional psychologists administered standardized tests, checked to see what worked, and hiring managers were trained to play their limited role in making decisions from a short list of candidates, the current process is chaotic, redundant, and quite likely more costly. The fact that we have cut recruiting staff, who are cheaper, and pushed hiring decisions onto line managers, who are more expensive, is the exact opposite of traditional notions of efficiency. But it does serve the financial accounting purposes of cutting headcount. This burdensome task has not increased the number of line managers, however, as it just added to their workload, and they can do it badly with few consequences.

In contrast to earlier periods where little attention was paid to recruiting and much more to selection, virtually all the attention now is on finding candidates. There is understandably little interest in potential among candidates, in part because there is so little interest in internal development. The goal is to find people who can step into quite specific roles with little or no training. Despite the investments in technology, a hugely dispropor-tionate percentage of candidates are hired through personal connections, and despite the move to informal selection practices, the time required to fill job openings has been going up for more than a decade.[76] While some economists have been inclined to see that as a sign of labor market tight-ness, a simpler explanation confirmed by surveys of employers is that more steps have been added to the selection process, such as drug tests and more interviews.

There is also a big gap now between the time a candidate is offered a job and when they start working. Getting permission from the CFO to actually start paying someone can take quite a while. It is common now for candidates to be told that their actual offer is on hold because of a budget freeze; often the company is not hitting their quarterly numbers. Again, the problem is driven by the fact that employee compensation and employment costs are current expenses that cannot be paid off over time. If we delay every offer by one quarter, we cut wage and employment costs for those jobs that year by 25 percent. The process of approval is so uncertain that some line managers begin the hiring process without having the budget approval to hire, and only when they find the candidate they want do they try to get the budget to pay for it.[77]

Here as well there are costs to these delays that are not easy to observe, mainly the lost opportunities from leaving positions unfilled and work un-done. Candidates walk away when they are asked to wait. Then we have to go back to our shortlist, see who is available, possibly dig up new candidates, and so forth. A study by Indeed.com found that the more hurdles and delays are added to the hiring process, the fewer applicants complete it.[78] These delays may actually play to financial accounting's priorities: slowing down hiring cuts the expenses that it cares the most about minimizing, wages and salaries, and the associated costs of doing so are not apparent in our financial accounting records.

"Dear Applicant J742B, We regret to inform you that you have been eliminated from consideration for the creative-director position, prior to the final round of deliberations (Round 19). . . . While you have excellent credentials, your Round 4 'sixty-second video bio-pic' did not fully sell us on the concept of 'you.'" This was your chance to wow us with your uniqueness! Yet, despite our recommendation, you neglected to hire a film (or even television) director to realize your vision. However, we did enjoy the skydiving scene, and we gave you credit for doing your own stunts. We hope that your tibia heals soon."

The part of this scenario that does not ring true is following up with a candidate and explaining why they did not get the job.

Source: Sasha Stewart, "Re: Our Hiring Process, " *The New Yorker*, July 6, 2020.

4

The Rise of a New Industry and
the Liquid Workforce

Another development created by the factors described in Chapters 1 and 2 is the rise of an industry of vendors that lets companies shift work away from current employees in order to reduce the wage and salary components of their expenses.

After the 1981 recession, companies began cutting administrative expenses as a means of becoming more responsive and competitive. There was a special focus on cutting human resources, especially in practices associated in growing and developing talent for lifetime careers, as the priority had shifted to cutting talent. A phrase that became popular at the time in human resources was being a "corporate hero": someone who participated in cutting their own budget in aid of overall corporate cost cutting. Writers like Ben Harrison pointed out early on how these practices squeezed employees.[1]

But the cutting had a more fundamental purpose than just reducing expenses. It was pushed along by an important change in ideas in the business world: focus on what you were truly good at and get rid of everything else.[2] Some of this had been underway for some time. The payroll processing pioneer ADP performed that outsourced work for companies and was already a billion-dollar company in 1985. An even bigger business was managing retirement plans, with their complex actuarial and compliance requirements. Some of this is literally outsourcing—the tasks go out the door—as David Weil's *The Fissured Workplace* describes.[3]

To what extent the outsourcing move was driven by the push of cutting fixed costs (human resource staff) versus the pull of an industry of vendors ready to take it on is an open question, but by the 1990s, one HR task after another went out the door. These tasks might not have been particularly big functions in companies, but when they were aggregated across all companies, they became huge new industries all on their own. Consider the following:

- The size of the industry that manages or services employee benefits in the United States is $215 billion.[4]
- The US staffing industry, which finds employees and workers for clients, was a $152 billion business in 2019.[5]
- The human resources consulting industry is now a $31 billion operation and accounts for 10 percent of the global market for all consulting.[6]
- Although every measure of training we have is down, US organizations still spent $83 billion on external training providers and expenses in 2019.[7]
- The "human capital management" industry, which just covers the software used to help manage human resource practices, was a $17.6 billion operation in 2020.[8]

This list does not count everything spent by US employers on human resource–related vendors, and it does not include what employers still spend internally. It still adds up to half a trillion dollars per year. To put this in perspective, this is close in size to the entire US construction industry, and the top two hundred or so companies in the business of human resources in the United States made $13 billion in profits in 2019.[9]

This development might well be a good thing for efficiency and performance precisely because the vendors are better and more efficient at performing these tasks than are companies themselves, especially smaller companies. In terms of company financial accounting, however, the advantage is obvious: it cuts headcount. As with all outsourcing, it moves jobs from companies with diverse functions and complex internal labor markets (the clients) to companies with much simpler structures, typically flat organizational charts, and far fewer opportunities for advancement (the vendors). Much of this spending pushes the tasks across the corporate boundary into outsourcing. Staffing that provides clients with workers who are not on the client's payroll but do the same work as the employees of the client is not outsourcing per se.

One consequence of pushing so much human resources work out of the company to vendors has been that it reduces the capabilities of the client company dramatically, especially its ability to do analyses. If a company wants to learn how well its hiring practices work, for example, the difficulties start with the fact that the hiring data sit with the recruitment process outsourcing company that does its hiring; the performance data lie with the vendor whose software manages performance appraisals; and its industrial psychologists, who in the past analyzed that question, left long ago. Assuming the client could get the data from both, it would have to turn to consultants to get it done, incurring new costs that have to be approved by the CFO.

The most important long-term result of this outsourcing of human re- source tasks, however, is that it created a huge and influential industry whose interests are not identical to those of the clients they serve. These are for- profit operations whose goal it is to make money, and they do that by sell- ing more services. If they can create demand through marketing, that helps achieve their goals. Demand is created by offering solutions to problems, of course; by highlighting existing problems; and, more perniciously, creating the perception of problems even where none truly exist.

The marketing support company Avos described how these vendors could gain influence. First, find a topic that is trending in the news that relates to your product. By definition, that will be some workforce-related issue. Second, develop some report on it that has links to other reports and news items. Third, get your report in front of those with an interest in the issue.[10] The typical HR vendor spends between 5 and 10 percent of its oper- ating budget on marketing.[11] In a $500 billion industry, that represents a lot of money, from $25 billion to $50 billion spent to influence the market. There are no prizes for thinking that no reports produced by the vendors ever say, "Nothing to worry about here."

In the mid-1990s, for example, some of these vendors began to argue that the United States was facing a real labor shortage because of the smaller "baby bust" cohort of young people in the labor force. This was despite the fact that the United States had never had anything like a labor shortage in modern times, and the projections of the US Bureau of Labor Statistics showed no such thing. The cohort behind the baby bust just starting to enter the labor force was even larger than the baby boom itself.[12] Of course, there was no labor shortage, but many companies nevertheless went through resource- intensive exercises to prepare for it.

That was followed in the early 2000s by the creation of the "millennial" notion, the idea that younger people were somehow wired differently than those who came before them and had to be treated differently. The National Academy of Sciences completely debunked this idea. It pointed out that these claims from consultants were typically just confusing the fact that this age group was simply younger than the older individuals to whom they were compared, and would change as they got older.[13] Yet consulting projects to understand millennials and training programs to somehow accommodate them persist undaunted.

After the Great Recession, the consulting companies supported and advanced the suspect notion that there was a "skill gap," a shortfall in people who could fit current jobs, despite the fact that unemployment was high and that the current jobless had just filled those jobs: employers actually had a simple labor market problem of trying to pay too little and ask too much of candidates.[14] In 2018, the fixation on robotics that self-driving trucks were about to replace truck drivers, driven by consulting company reports, led the HR departments of many companies to start planning how to handle their unemployed truck drivers. Within three years, the big complaint was a shortage of truck drivers.

The vendors supported the idea of cutting employee costs and spending the money on vendors instead, making companies appear more flexible. The fact that client companies are now so bare-bones that it is difficult for them to execute on their own has led the vendor industry to shift away from giving advice to taking over tasks completely. Companies that were solely in the HR consulting business have largely disappeared as independent businesses, mainly subsumed within organizations that take over tasks by outsourcing, especially managing employee benefits.[15] The largest IT firms like Accenture and all the major accounting firms that exist on outsourcing now all have substantial practices dealing with human resource issues, especially replacing employees with software.

The Liquid Workforce

Thirty-five percent of leased employees of staffing firms are offered permanent jobs by the clients where they are working.[16] They appear to represent roughly 2 percent of corporate hires.

These two choices also echo the famous question about what constitutes the boundary of a firm: what should be done inside and outside. There is no doubt that in recent decades, we have moved in the direction of the latter. Among large corporations, for example, it was reasonably common for them to fill all vacancies from within except a few entry-level jobs for school leavers. That amounted to 90 percent or more of all vacancies. Now the evidence from company-hiring software and other sources puts that number closer to 33 percent. That is an enormous shift.

The focus here is on something short of outsourcing, where the work is done by the client. The difference is that a large proportion of the workers are not employees of the clients where they work but they are likely employees of someone else—not contractors and not gig workers. The work remains inside, but the workers are outsourced. The phrase often used to describe this arrangement is "leased" employees: workers employed by a staffing firm while their work is directed by the client.

Why this might be useful is not immediately obvious. It does not appear to cost less per hour: in addition to paying the workers, the leasing company has its own overhead and profit targets to hit (which they seem to be doing nicely). The big appeal is the sense that the client can "dial down" the number of workers if the need for them falls or "dial them up" if demand increases. The ability is the liquid workforce idea, like a faucet: turn up or down the supply we need. That ability isn't free, of course, and it is priced into the contract with the leasing company. Nor does it appear that employers have great difficulty in dialing down their regular employees with layoffs, as noted earlier.

What the liquid workforce does do is manifest the financial accounting goal of having wages and salary expenses appear to be as small as possible, as described in Chapter 1, even if doing so simply shifts the costs somewhere else. It gives the appearance of flexibility only in accounting terms, because we have moved from employees (fixed costs) to workers under contracts (variable costs). That flexibility suggests the ability to optimize the number of employees—never pay more than you need at any point in time. Finally, it reduces the need for employee management, which is done by vendors and is otherwise time consuming at best for leaders.

To get a sense as to what the new liquid workforce looks like and what it means, it helps to consider its origins.

The Early Days of Open Labor Markets

Outsourcing is as old as the notion of corporations. Well into the twentieth century, for example, companies like DuPont did none of their own sales or distribution. Independent agents did the marketing and selling, often for more than one company at a time, and some of those agents were large enough to have their own employees. The fact that car dealers today are independent businesses and not owned by their brand began with the founding of the auto industry, where all sales were outsourced to independent dealers.

Companies brought outsourcing inside with a model known as inside contracting, where independent contractors worked side by side with employees. As many as half the workers in US manufacturing operations in the early 1900s were actually contractors, some of whom brought along their own employees.[17]

Employment itself was a pretty casual affair. Turnover rates of 300 percent or more were common in manufacturing operations. Labor historian Sandy Jacoby described how informal staffing decisions used to be, using the example of the Baldwin Locomotive Works, one of the better employers in the Philadelphia region and at the time, operating the largest manufacturing complex in the world. Each supervisor would come into their shop in the morning and see how many workers were missing. Then they would go to the gates of the factory where there was a crowd of men looking for work. If a supervisor needed two men, he might throw two apples into the crowd; another one needing three men might throw three pears out. If you caught an apple, you went with the first supervisor, if you caught a pear, you went with the second. It was the essence of a "just in time" workforce.[18]

No doubt many factors helped change these arrangements, but one of the more important came with the rise of the assembly line and the creation of semiskilled work where mistakes involving expensive machine tools became much more consequential. It became costly to try to slot an inexperienced outsider into existing jobs.

Ford Motor Company, one of the first to experiment with the assembly-line idea (taken from meat-packing plants), found that the quality of cars coming off the new line was terrible. The idea that this had to do with high turnover spawned a number of innovations: exit interviews to see why employees were quitting (hating their bosses was a common complaint), the creation of a new function to oversee the management of employees (the department of industrial sociology), and tenure-based pay practices to improve retention.[19] Most famously, Henry Ford announced that he was raising pay to five dollars a day "so that employees could afford to buy my cars." The real reason was to cut turnover. It fell quickly, from roughly 300 percent to about 50 percent as soon as these practices were in place.

The lesson here is that relatively few jobs could be done well by simply pulling someone in from outside to perform them.

A similar shift took place in the management ranks, where outside hiring soon gave way to internal development. It is perhaps not surprising that when corporations did something for the first time, they went outside to find experienced managers to lead it. When starting a new railroad, for example, the smart move was to hire from the Pennsylvania Railroad, one of the largest and most sophisticated operations in the world at that point. The new company got an experienced leader and the practices of the Pennsylvania Railroad. By the 1890s, job hopping across railroad companies was a common affair.[20]

A related approach was to acquire executives by acquiring companies. This was perhaps most important at the DuPont corporation, when Pierre du Pont took over the company and created the first multidivisional organizational structure with a separate operating division for each type of product the company produced. Because the divisions operated with considerable autonomy, the job of running them was quite different from typical management roles at the time and more like an owner than an administrator. DuPont acquired sixty companies between 1902 and 1907, and the leaders of the acquired firms, almost always their founders, typically became the executives in the new, and larger, merged corporation. When Louis Chevrolet sold his car company to General Motors, he stayed on to run the new Chevrolet division. Standard Oil did much the same thing. As George B. Corless, one of its executives, noted: "Mr. Rockefeller Sr. recruited many of his executives by buying successful companies and then giving jobs to the former owners."[21]

The Standard Oil Trust also generated new types of corporate jobs that were unique to the company. Because the organization was a collection of separate oil companies, common and collective tasks were run by the trustees of the companies through a series of committees. Each committee had a permanent staff of workers to support and execute the committee's work, and these staff members became middle management, handling the important tasks of coordination between the various committees. As the trust grew in size and complexity, the top trustees themselves eventually became full-time employees and executives in the company. They needed people to support them, and created new headquarters and corporate staff jobs.[22]

The approach of acquiring experienced talent was not sufficient when corporations began their explosive growth in the 1920s. After World War I, companies began to establish entry-level positions in functional areas such as sales or engineering, hiring high school and college graduates and training them along the way. William H. Whyte, in his famous book *The Organization Man*, describes his own experience as a new hire in the Vicks company's sales training program in the early 1920s: new recruits were taken out in the field, given a short orientation, and expected to start selling Vicks products immediately.[23] The young employees had first to prove themselves in a functional area—in his case, sales—before they might be given the opportunity for development and advancement elsewhere in the company. The company was not particularly worried about attrition, perhaps because its investment at that point was minimal: thirty of the thirty-eight people in Whyte's cohort were dismissed soon after being hired.

These new practices coincided with the flowering of the welfare capitalism movement, which began in Europe a generation before and came to the United States as an approach in part designed to stave off interest in unionization by production workers, in part as a general effort to fight the rise of socialist inclinations among employees and society, and in part as a precursor to a moral argument that employers had social obligations beyond simply making money.[24] At least some of the practices associated with welfare capitalist efforts included stabilizing employment, creating career paths for advancement, and providing some benefits that helped retain employees. The Great Depression wiped out many of these paternalistic practices, but as Sandy Jacoby concluded, some of the practices would become part of standard personnel practices used from then on in large companies.[25]

The situation changed sharply during World War II, when the government mandated planning practices for all government contractors and began teaching them operations research practices. The shortage of managerial talent after the war led to a wave of mergers at those companies that had lost leadership, the creation of executive search firms to help clients find management talent at competitors, and a great deal of company hopping. But it was simply not enough to meet the needs of business.

Austin S. Ingleheart, president of General Foods, noted how the Army tried to give officers a broad understanding of its operations through stints at its War College. He applied that to his own company, arguably beginning the idea of rotational assignments for developing executive talent. Other companies also borrowed lessons from the Army. The most important document guiding those companies was "Personnel Administration at the Executive Level," produced by the US Naval Institute just before the war and based on practices drawn from fifty leading firms before the Great Depression. The replacement charts identified who steps in when an officer goes down. Many companies used this document to build their own development programs.[26] So leading practices from the 1930s, which in fact were created in the 1920s, came back to become the leading practices for the 1950s.

By 1955, a Conference Board study showed that 60 percent of companies with 10,000 or more employees had a program in place to develop executive talent. Twelve years before that, the Conference Board could not find enough companies with development programs to conduct a study on them.[27]

Not every company operated this way, of course, because the fixed costs required to set up training programs and high-potential programs, even to create workforce plans, required scale to be effective. Smaller companies might function by peeling away a few trained and disgruntled managers and production workers from the big corporations. But 40 percent of all US workers were employed by only one-half of 1 percent of all the enterprises in the country then. These companies grew ever larger in part by mergers and acquisition, with roughly half of all the industrial companies in the United States being involved in a merger or acquisition every year in the 1950s and 1960s.[28]

In short, the rise of the new model was not so much because companies decided that outside hiring was a bad idea. It was because it was just not sufficient to produce the amount of talent companies needed in the fast-growing corporate settings.

The Lifetime Employment Model

Meeting the talent management challenges after World War II—identifying what skills the organization will need, filling those needs internally, and planning to meet future needs by growing talent—were big, complicated exercises because all talent came from within. On the white-collar, managerial side of the organization, the internal model was even more elaborate. Mabel Newcomer's study of corporate executives across the generations found that half the leaders of large businesses had been hired from outside their corporations in 1900, but by 1950 that figure was down to 20 percent. In 1950, 47 percent of executives in Newcomer's sample retired in office, as opposed to only 11 percent in 1900. Of those who retired in office, 40 percent had been with their firms more than forty years in 1950, in contrast to 21 percent in that category in 1925 and only 5 percent in 1900.[29] Companies would hire engineers and technical employees out of college and put them into "test" engineer positions, a term created by General Electric, where they were trained and given experience. The other hires were put into management development programs.

The needs of the business were reasonably predictable in what was then a highly regulated economy with little foreign competition, although not perfectly so, and the human capital requirements followed in a reasonably mechanical process from business needs. If one department was growing faster than another, the staff for it would have to be trained for the new skills and moved over to it. The current staff there would have to be promoted faster to fill in new management positions. All the talent had to be built.

When big changes happened in business, they required massive retraining and redeployment. One reason companies did not want to get rid of even poor-performing employees is that they never knew what their needs would be in the future, every employee was seen as a long-term option, and there were no replacements unless they were grown from within. It was worth it to rehabilitate ones who were struggling, because that was all you had.

The companies did not do this just to be nice to managers. It was in aid of securing their commitment. They knew it would be easier to get them to move to a new town, to change fields, and so forth if the managers knew the company was going to look after them. IBM in particular articulated the view that the way the company could adapt quickly to new circumstances was through these loyal and protected employees.

These are the tasks associated with the general talent management challenge, and are still laid out in contemporary textbooks.

Workforce Planning

By the mid-1960s, 96 percent of the larger companies surveyed had a dedicated workforce planning department that began with economy and business demand forecasts and then derived staffing requirements from them. By the end of the 1960s, a math-based modeling tool called MANPLAN could predict staffing needs at the department level, factoring in estimates of employee turnover based on individual-level psychological assessments and career stage.[30]

By 1978, sophisticated modeling had come to workforce planning. Regression models predicted turnover and workforce needs in 30 percent of these plans, and Markov Chain models that predicted transitions, such as from employment to retirement or how promotion to a new position creates vacancies down the job ladder, were used in 22 percent of companies. At the simplest level, these plans tackled questions such as: If we plan to grow by 5 percent next year, how many more middle managers, supervisors, and frontline workers will we need? At the level of individual projects, it can be much more complicated: we are moving into a new line of business. What skills will that require, and how many of them do we have internally?

Once the need was determined, then the task of meeting it was mapped out. In a steady state there was always a mix of hiring, virtually all at the entry level, and development and promotion for those who would be advancing to fill the ranks of the retirees. When expectations for growth changed or when something new was required, then it was a scramble to adjust the model and the flow of workers.

Figure 4.1 shows what it looked like to move from a discussion of the challenge in the abstract to a solution. In this case, General Electric laid

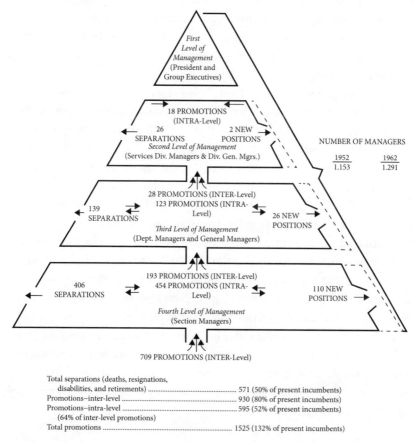

Figure 4.1 Analysis of Managerial Manpower Requirements for Section Manager and Higher Positions, 1952–1962
Source: *Professional Management in General Electric Book Three: The Work of a Professional Manager* (New York: General Electric Book Company, 1954), 99

out in 1952 the workforce plan for the top four levels of management in the company over the next ten years: there would be 138 new positions, 709 employees would be promoted into the lowest level (tier four), 193 of those would be promoted into the third level, 28 fortunate souls would go onto the second level, and from there the different process of succession planning would take over and determine how many advanced to the very top. A total of 571 members of the overall group would leave the company in this period, presumably almost all via retirement.

To make this model work required hiring candidates who could grow in the organization. Chapter 1 described the process of hiring in this earlier period and the fact that great care was taken with that process, as it was a lifetime decision. Companies like GE hired new college graduates with the plan of developing them into managers. While they did hire new graduates with specialized degrees to assign to industrial sectors—chemists, electrical engineers, mechanical engineers—the idea was that managers would be grown from within.

The first degree mattered relatively little in management careers.

Who got promoted and to what job was a decision of high drama in these corporations. The people in charge of that—at least managing the process and making recommendations—were in human resources. William Whyte noted a survey done in the early 1960s asking executives which business function was the most "glamorous," and the answer was human resources. Why not? They were the kingmakers. The person in charge of the group managing these promotion decisions was typically referred to as "the chess master," because they moved the managers and executives around like pieces on a chess board.

The process used to determine who got which job was succession planning, something that at the highest levels had as much intrigue and consequence as succession events in monarchies. One difference is that in corporations the process extended down, well into the administrative ranks.

The idea that any company today would even try to guess something as de-tailed as how many people would be promoted from one level to another ten years out would be seen as a fool's errand. The reason they did a generation ago was that they did not see any better way to operate, given that all their talent had to come from within.

The Decline of the Lifetime Model

The change in approach started with the downsizing waves that came out of the 1981 recession.

Three things were new. The first is that layoffs were permanent. The US Bureau of Labor Statistics did not even keep track of permanent job losses until 1984, because the assumption was that layoffs would be temporary, during recessions, and that those laid off would return as soon as business picked up again. That is, layoffs had meant what we now call furloughs. Hourly employees were actually paid while on layoff by company-funded supplemental unemployment insurance programs, negotiated first by unions and then applied more broadly. When they were recalled, they went back to the same job with the same level of seniority and the same pay that they had before.

The second development is that the layoffs now hit white-collar jobs, starting most publicly with IBM's initial increase in the number of such employees who were fired or dismissed for low performance and then moving on to regular layoffs. In fact, the evidence suggests that into the mid-1980s, workers in those roles were more likely to lose their jobs than were production workers, a stunning development.[31] These job losses were not just clerical positions. They went up at least through middle management with the process of reengineering.

The third development was that layoffs became disconnected from the business cycle. The idea of restructuring meant basic changes in business that cut jobs and workers in one area even when companies were growing in order to improve efficiency there. There were layoffs in one part of the company but hiring in others. Implicit in this approach was that the companies were no longer relocating or retraining employees in roles that were seen as obsolete to take over new positions.

Budget cuts in 2013 eliminated the Bureau of Labor Statistics program tracking mass layoffs associated with large employers, and it had only begun tracking them in 1996. But we can see from that limited data that layoffs actually rose as the economy improved in the late 1990s. In 2000, 846,000 employees lost their jobs from these mass layoffs in the private sector, and that year may have had the strongest overall job market since the 1960s.[32]

When there have been recessions, the evidence suggests that, over time, companies have responded to downturns by cutting jobs sooner and by cutting them harder than in the past. That was certainly true in the 2008 Great Recession when roughly one out of every six workers lost their jobs, and the 2020 pandemic recession was literally off the charts in the amount of job cuts. Many additional workers were furloughed—involuntary time off without pay—in addition to those who permanently lost their jobs. Recent evidence suggests that the astonishingly low level of US productivity growth from 2010 to the pandemic years—the lowest on record—can be attributed to the fact that employers delayed hiring for so long, deferring to investor concerns about keeping costs down, that it crippled their performance.[33]

Understanding the effects of layoffs on organizational performance is not straightforward, as we can see in Figure 4.2, because companies are already in trouble when they decide to lay off employees. Assessing the effect of the layoff is difficult. A standard approach compares shareholder returns before and after layoff announcements. Despite the widespread view in business that investors applaud layoff announcements, studies show on average a negative effect on share prices. There is some evidence that the effects improve over a longer period, although not all studies find that result. The effects on other measures of performance, such as productivity and profitability, are decidedly mixed. In short, there is no agreement that firms benefit from layoffs except from short-run cost cuts, which can be necessary. Otherwise, cutting early and hard, a standard "best practice" assumption in the investment world, is associated with negative effects on longer-term performance.[34] Companies often find themselves losing ground when recoveries come because they do not have the capability to ramp up quickly.

The *Washington Post* did an assessment of the fifty most valuable corporations in the United States in terms of their market capitalization and their layoff practices during the 2020 pandemic year. Virtually all of them—forty-five—were profitable that year, and twenty-seven had layoffs. Most of those layoffs were of this third approach, disconnected from business cycles,

Seasonally adjusted, 1990–2020
Numbers in thousands

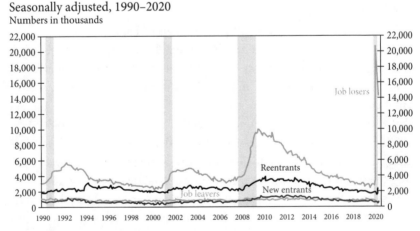

Figure 4.2 Job Losses and Worker Flows
Source: US Bureau of Labor Statistics

in that they were hiring and laying off at the same time. The only surprising part of the story was how many companies that laid off had also promised not to conduct layoffs because of the hardships already in place from the pandemic. In fairness to the companies, when they made those promises in the spring of 2020, the expectations were that the state regulations closing and restricting businesses would last only a few months at most.

Still, the juxtaposition between the public pledges not to lay off employees and the layoffs, which often came quite quickly, were bracing. The assumption in the story was that the companies felt the opportunity to save money was too great to delay further. Few companies tried to explain their change in direction. One that did was Phillip Morris, which said "prolonging it further would be unfair to everyone." The laid-off employees might not agree.[35]

Even in the tight labor market of late 2021, when unemployment was below 4 percent and there were more than 10 million vacancies, and the biggest concern seemed to be keeping employees from quitting, employers were laying off employees at the rate of more than 10 percent per year.[36]

It may seem puzzling why careful academic research, which is done with much greater rigor than business consultants use, finds no advantage to layoffs and yet the investor community still applauds them. Investors may be unaware of that research, or perhaps it is the fact that layoffs target a specific issue that investors care about greatly—reducing wages and salaries and doing it quickly. The longer-term effects on overall financial performance are quite possibly the next generation's problem.

An important beneficiary of the shedding of talent was startup firms, especially in technology, who could now easily find experienced and skilled candidates to hire, putting together new businesses in the same way that existing companies were assembling new competencies by hiring from the outside. A good example of this is the disk drive industry, where one could argue that alumni from IBM more or less created the startup companies that drove it.[37]

What Happened to Workforce Planning

Workforce planning collapsed when companies moved from growing talent to dumping it with layoffs. Workforce planning is the first step in talent management: assessing future needs. A Conference Board study concluded that workforce planning had fallen from 96 percent of companies with a dedicated department in the mid-1960s to 19 percent of companies that did any work-force planning at all by the mid-1990s.[38] The 30 percent of companies that had used regression modeling in 1978 fell to 9 percent by 1985; the 22 per-cent of companies using Markov Chain models fell to 6 percent. A survey of CEOs at large companies in the early 2000s found that only 25 percent had any kind of talent planning past two levels down from the CEO, that is, below the senior vice president level.[39]

To the extent that workforce planning happens at all, it is for large-scale, predictable jobs such as call center work, and the plans are really calculations of staffing needs if one knows what the demand will be. The Society of Workforce Planning Professionals—yes, there is a professional association just for this task—offers a calculator using strong assumptions that nothing changes in the future and basic arithmetic, a sharp contrast to the Markov Chain and regression models of the previous generation.[40]

It is extremely difficult to get a sense of how much workforce planning ac-tually takes place now and what it means. But much of what goes on under the heading of workforce planning appears to be annual budget planning, where the CFO needs to approve the financial plan for the next year or so and needs estimates of workforce changes for that to happen. In fact, CFOs are already deeply involved in developing workforce plans, as noted earlier, and arguments from the investor community suggest they should be even more involved due to the high costs of labor.[41]

To illustrate how primitive workforce planning is now, a recent survey of companies that actually reported doing workforce planning found that only a minority did a gap analysis—here is what we have, here is what we will need—or provided estimates of future needs, presumably past the current budget cycle. There is no planning without this. The fact that the cycle for these plans is typically shorter than a year means it would be difficult for programs to respond internally to changing needs.[42] In short, it seems little real planning is going on.

Evidence of Churning the Workforce

There is no doubt that layoffs are disruptive and damaging for employees. Employers and the investment community view them as helpful to busi-ness and necessary. No doubt that when demand collapses for a long pe-riod of time, it would be difficult for businesses to survive without cutting employees. But most layoffs are not of that kind. In 2021, for example, with the economy in full rebound mode, employers still laid off about 12 percent of their workforces.

A different and more basic question is whether US employers are churning through more workers now—keeping fewer for shorter periods of time and then filling vacancies from outside. A simple way to check would be to see if there are more vacancies in the economy now, because if positions are filled from within, there is no reason to post a vacancy.

If we look back to 1950 and 1960, for example, the reported data suggest that there were only 14,750 vacancies in 1950 and 18,150 in 1960 outside of agriculture in a labor force of 62 million and 70 million, respectively. That would be an incredibly small 0.00025 percent or so of all jobs, which suggests strongly that not all vacancies are being captured.[43] In 2019, where the data are more valid and reliable, the figure is closer to 0.03 percent. That could suggest a huge increase, but it is also likely that vacancies were not measured accurately in earlier periods.

Katherine Abraham was among the first researchers to notice a shift taking place in the number of vacancies. Studies relied on counts of job advertisements first in newspapers. Using various ways to address that problem, she concludes that there was a substantial change in vacancies after the 1970s.[44] In 2000, the Bureau of Labor Statistics began the Job Openings and Labor Turnover Survey (JOLTS), which offered a much more consistent approach to measuring vacancies. More recent reviews looking out over longer periods and including the JOLTS data confirm that change after the 1970s.[45] Since 2001, using the JOLTS data, vacancy rates and hiring rates have remained reasonably stable compared to earlier periods, which is consistent with the idea that there was a break after 1981.

Particularly for economists, the measure that was most important for assessing whether the employment relationship had changed was tenure, or the amount of time employees stayed with their employer. For an individual, tenure stops when they leave an organization, so either quitting or being laid off will lower levels of tenure. Layoffs go up in economic downturns and quits go down, however, and in upturns, the reverse is true. Those two events tend to offset each other. It is also the case that changes in average tenure could have many causes, such as disproportionate quits among one age group or layoffs disproportionately among another.

Robert Hall examined employee tenure in the United States and concluded that while most jobs are short-term, once a job lasted five years, there was a very good chance that it would last for most of one's working life—twenty years or so. Even though the US labor market had a lot of short-term churn, it was quite likely that workers would settle into a lifetime job.[46] If we look from 1983 to 1996, however, we see a big change. While tenure rose for married women with children, as they no longer had to quit and more of them continued to work, it fell for everyone else. For men, it fell for every age group, especially for men age fifty-five to sixty-four, where it fell by one-third.[47] Henry Farber's encyclopedic review and assessment of the research on job tenure from 1973 until the Great Recession concluded that for men, tenure declined sharply in the private sector while actually rising in the public sector for all ages, and longer-term jobs in particular declined. Job loss did not seem to be the cause, which suggests that voluntary quitting driven by lateral hiring may be the explanation.[48]

A surprising finding for people who think that kids today are job hoppers is that baby boomers had about six jobs by the time they were twenty-four and more than twelve by their mid-fifties.[49]

A more recent study of tenure shows that declines in tenure are largely accounted for by declines in the largest companies. Those are the ones that had provided special security for employees and arguably better opportunities for internal advancement. Tenure fell from an average of fourteen years for employees in large firms in 1979 to ten years in 2008. In smaller firms, it either rose or stayed roughly the same.[50]

When we look inside the largest corporations and the executive ranks, where the lifetime employment model was most likely to persist, the change was dramatic. The percentage of the top executives in the Fortune 100 who had never worked anywhere else was 53 percent; by 2001 it was 43 percent; by 2011, it had dropped to 30 percent.[51] We also found in other data on a much broader group of executives that average tenure in their company was only about four years, as other studies found as well. Most tellingly, we found that when asked by executive search firms whether they would be interested in being a candidate for a role that was not specified in another company, half the executives said yes.[52]

The giant natural experiment of the pandemic and the tight labor market it created with the sharp reopening of businesses in 2021 did create some temporary change in behavior. During the January 2022 Omicron surge in infections, many companies were expecting downturns in business and were otherwise expecting to lay off employees, even though the expectation was that they would have to hire replacements again reasonably soon. Mickey

Levy, chief US economist at Berenberg Capital Markets, explained why they did not: "With such an extraordinarily tight labor market, businesses just didn't want to lay people off because the cost of searching around and finding new employees is very high."[53]

Tenure has not continued to decline in US organizations, however, but neither has it increased. It has ticked up slightly for the workforce on average solely because workers under the age of twenty-four have done less job hopping in the 2000s, possibly because there had been fewer jobs for them to hop across.[54] There is no evidence that employers are trying to rebuild long-term employment relationships, but neither is there evidence of it collapsing further. The big changes happened after the 1981 recession but did not accelerate after that. Something else is afoot.

The Liquid Workforce

When we look at corporate practices, Charles Handy in 1976 described a model of a flexible workforce where there was a core employee group that was protected from the ups and downs of business needs (and layoffs) by a periphery of contractors and nonemployee workers whose ranks would rise and fall with changes in demand.[55] In 1984, John Atkinson broadened the story by noting that while it was possible to be flexible in the manner that Handy described—numerical flexibility—it was also possible to be flexible by redeploying cross-skilled employees to meet changing needs.[56] When my colleague David Neumark and I looked at what US companies were actually doing, we saw them pursuing both aspects of flexibility at the same time.[57] That included not only retraining and using temps, but also layoffs of regular employees, which did not go away as these periphery models suggested they might.

Then came Uber and its business model that allowed for numerical flexibility on a permanent basis. Uber became a phenomenon with the business community far beyond the ride sharing industry. Here we had a liquid workforce that was only paid when there was something that they needed to do. Otherwise, they waited, with no pay, and no cost to Uber.

The origin of the word "gig" is the short-term engagements that musicians and other independent contractors have. Consulting firms now use the term "gig" to cover all kinds of arrangements, including contractors, outsourcing, temporary help, and part-time work, which is how they come up with eye-popping statements like "one-third of the workforce are gig workers." The term "contingent" work also has dual meanings, and is often used in research to measure nonemployee workers.[58]

Despite the gig hype, the number of people working as contractors has been reasonably stable since 1995, when the Bureau of Labor Statistics first set out to measure them in a serious way. Just under 7 percent of the workforce are independent contractors when last measured carefully in 2017.[59] But there are prominent examples where the level of use is high. Google famously has more contractors—129,000—than employees, something that is common among tech firms.[60] Contract work is at the core of sharing business models like Airbnb, the obvious ride services Uber and Lyft, and also the rash of new delivery services like Deliveroo and Amazon's new flex delivery service. FedEx's Ground Service has had this same model of contractors doing the actual delivery for decades. A 2020 Conference Board survey on COVID-19-related changes found that C-suite executives expect they will have fewer employees and more contractors after the pandemic is over.[61]

One way employers moved toward gig work, especially initially, was to push the legal boundary between employees and contractors hard, basically engaging workers as contractors but treating them like employees. The boundary between the two is set by the common-law employment test, which has several components. One is that contractors should not be at the core of businesses' operations, which they clearly are in many sharing models such as Uber and Lyft. The best-known criterion is that clients should not be supervising contractors and directing their work. Contractors working through electronic platforms are directed not with supervisors but electronically, through measurement and incentives. They monitor exactly where the drivers are, plot out turn-by-turn routes for them to follow, and require performance standards to remain as contractors. At Amazon, the standard for on-time delivery is an impossible 999/1,000. Uber's infamous surge pricing that raises rates when demand is high is an incentive plan to get drivers to meet that demand.

To get a sense of how valuable the independent contractor model is to ride sharing companies, consider what happened in the 2020 California election after the state legislature passed a 2019 law requiring that gig workers be treated as employees. Uber, along with Lyft, pushed for a proposition on the ballot in 2020 that would exempt them from that law. Some estimates suggest that $200 million was spent in the campaign for Proposition 22, although the California secretary of state reports that Uber officially spent just under

$54 million. The proposal passed, and in the period just after the election, Uber's market capitalization rose by over $20 billion. That would make the return of that investment 38,371 percent, an eye-popping gain that would rank as one of the most profitable political actions of all time. Lyft did only a little less well, spending $28 million on the campaign and gaining $3.5 billion in market capitalization, for a return of 11,887 percent.[62]

The attractiveness of the independent contractor model for the ride sharing companies is arguably more about the drivers providing their own cars, handling their own maintenance, securing their own insurance, and so forth than about the driving tasks handled by independent contractors. Taxi companies have long had independent contractors just driving cabs owned and maintained by the cab companies,[63] though not as successfully as the ride sharing companies. For other businesses, the fact that workers did not receive any pay when there was nothing to do was the key.

It violates employment laws to treat contractors like employees, but it happens with great frequency, by some estimates a stunning 30 percent of the time. Laws are changing, especially in Europe and in California, New York, and Illinois in the United States, to limit the use of contractors in roles that had traditionally been filled by employees, including drivers in ride sharing companies like Uber.

Companies use intermediaries to protect themselves against legal challenges and other complaints when using gig workers. The most controversial of these arrangements involved teleworkers who perform their jobs from home as independent contractors brokered by other agencies. Companies like Arise and Liveops provide brokerage arrangements and promote the arrangement to potential workers as an opportunity not only to work from home, but also to be an entrepreneur.

An investigation by ProPublica uncovered the business model. These broker companies have contracts with their clients, who include the biggest names in corporate America. The individual contractors will present themselves to customers of the clients as if they are employees of that client. The broker companies in turn typically require that the potential contractors themselves incorporate to have their own businesses, so that the arrangement between the broker vendor and the contractor is clearly a contract between business entities. The original client requires training before a contractor can begin working for the broker on behalf of the client, and the contractor pays for the cost of that training themselves, including other costs, such as background checks. Then they begin work, but there is no guarantee as to how much work they will get and when it will come.[64] They are essentially like on-call workers, except that they have no employment relationship either with the client or the broker who has engaged them. We will see similar stacking of contractual arrangements in other aspects of the liquid workforce below.

Each engagement of a contractor supporting an individual client comes with its own contractual performance requirements. The one in Figure 4.3 was for AT&T. Failure to meet these standards in handling calls leads to a breach of contract, which can end the relationship with the contractor. It is difficult to imagine an employee being supervised any tighter.

It is not possible in existing companies to move completely to contractors even with these broker arrangements, but the idea of keeping employment and wages down, and making up the inevitable staffing gap with Uber-like workers who did not get paid when there was nothing to do, sounds extremely attractive. Recruitment process outsourcing vendors jumped on that model. They use the term "full cycle engagement" to describe their ideal arrangement, where they manage the balance of hiring, layoffs, and especially

Service Level Requirements	
30 Day Repeat %	≤ 30%
ATT Next	≥ 90% of upgrades
Average Handle Time (AHT)	Between 400 and 740 seconds
Average Hold (in seconds)	< 30 seconds
Caller Disconnect/Caller Not Present	< 5%
Calls with Credits (Number of calls before a credit is issued)	15.0
Clarify Call Disposition Rate	Between 95% and 130%
Clarify Text to Confirm (T2C)	> 85%
Commitment % (% of commitments made/total calls handled	≤ 0.5%
Credits/Adjustments (Avg Per Call)	< $2.50
CTI Transfer	> 90%
Digital 1st (2–30 days)	> 85%
Invalid Cases	< 1
Login RONA% (Default AUX)	< 4%
myATT Zone	> 20%
Outbound Aux %	< 5%
Payment Arrangements/ExpressPay	≤ 2% of the calls
Release Ratio	< 10%
Schedule Adherence	≥ 95%
Short Calls	< 1%
Snapshop Secondary Clicks	≥ 50%
Tech Guide Utilization	> 90%
Terminated Sessions (calls that are answered but have no saved interaction in Clarify)	< 5%
Tools in 10	100%
Willingness to Recommend (ACE–WTR)	> 35%

Figure 4.3 Contractor Job Performance Requirements at AT&T
Source: ProPublica

nonemployee workers to ensure that the client has the minimum required number of workers required to get the work done each day.

The overall goal for companies was to cut employment costs as low as possible and optimize—more specifically minimize—the number of employees needed. The new liquid workforce model relies heavily on nonemployee workers. If you threw a dart into any large organization, there is a good chance you would hit someone working there who was not an employee. They could be individual independent contractors, employees of a vendor who has taken over some function like running the cafeteria for the client on a long-term basis, or most likely employees of staffing firms working for the client on a contract, something that is a new development. An important aspect of this new liquid workforce is that it does not look at all like a typical workforce, but neither does it look like gig workers at Uber.

The Liquid Workforce Infrastructure

The main manifestation of the liquid workforce involves using workers who are employees of other organizations, such as staffing firms or vendors. It is possible and arguably necessary to have employees rather than contractors because the overall need for employees is predictable, despite all the discussions about the need for flexibility. The number and type of workers that we truly need to "dial up"—we need them right now, and we know we won't need them shortly—is a small percentage of the typical workforce and has been declining. A proxy for the need for flexibility comes from looking at changes in the rate at which new jobs are created and old ones terminated. We should see these figures rising if there were changes in business that demanded changes in jobs and workers. From the mid-1990s through the 2010s they fell sharply, by some measures by half.[65] The need for flexibility would seem to be falling.

In any case, most organizations need the bulk of their labor from the predictable workforce of people who have been there for a while and will be there for a while longer. The best way to get that—other than through your own employees—is with leased employees, the term used by the Bureau of Labor Statistics for those employed by vendors but working at a client's location for at least a year. Paul Osterman finds that 11 percent of all people working are now leased employees under contract.[66] The size of the overall liquid workforce of non-employees is even bigger. In 2001, we asked employers in a Census survey how many people who were not their employees were working in their establishment on a peak day that week, and the answer was already about 20 percent.[67] More recent estimates come from a variety of sources and suggest a substantial increase since then. For example, a survey of corporate budgets found that nonemployee workers accounted for 32 percent of the total budgeting for labor.[68] A survey by Kelly Services found that 27 percent of their clients' workforces were made up of these workers,[69] while Ernst & Young's client survey reported businesses expecting it to be 30 percent of their workforce in 2020.[70] If we look at one vendor that provides liquid workforces in food services and hospitality, Aramark, it has contracts covering 89 percent of the Fortune 500 companies and two thousand health-care facilities using over 2 million workers to do so. But it has only 215,000 of its own employees.[71]

Negotiating, monitoring compliance, and enforcing individual contracts for almost one-third of workers would be a huge amount of work—so organizations turn to vendors to do this for them. This is where the liquid workforce becomes remarkably complex, and the administrative challenges of navigating through it would appear to be quite challenging to the players.

The best-known of the vendors are temporary help agencies with prominent names like Adecco, Randstadt, and Manpower. This industry had only twenty thousand employees in 1956, and they were focused on clerical and factory jobs, stepping in for workers on vacation or who were out with illnesses. By 1990, it had 1 million employees—1 percent of the labor force, 2 million by the end of that decade or 2.7 percent of the labor force, where it has more or less remained.[72] Outside the United States, the numbers are much bigger. This does not count the fact that individual companies have their own temp operations—on-call workers who are employees but who only work on demand—that are equal in size to the temp industry. This is still only about 5 percent of the workforce, so it will take a few more steps to get close to 30 percent of the corporate workforce. But before getting there, it is useful to review temp work as the basis of this new workforce.

The temp industry appeared to play some role in buffering regular jobs, in that cuts there came sooner and steeper in the downturns after 1990 than in regular jobs. Temp work also climbed up the hierarchy of skills over time, featuring in more managerial and professional jobs.[73] Its expansion, starting in the 1980s, appeared to be driven by keeping labor costs down; temp workers then were cheaper than the regular employees of clients. Now that situation has almost reversed, as the wages of regular employees have been held down while temp worker costs, including the charges from their agencies that cover their administrative costs and profit margins, continued to rise with the outside labor market.

While clients of temp agencies stopped reporting that temp work was cheaper some decades ago, they can still keep wage costs down, especially in tight labor markets where it is hard to fill positions. Rather than raising wages to attract applicants to fill open vacancies, the clients engage agencies to fill their vacancies with nonemployees who can be paid more without raising the wages for all employees.[74] In other words, it's price discrimination: we have a small group of employees who are mobile, and when they find a higher-paying employer, they leave. We have other employees who are much less likely to move. We fill the jobs of those footloose employees who leave with higher-paid temps. We have two wage scales, one for the employees who are embedded in the company and the other for workers who move across employers to staff vacancies, typically facilitated by agencies.

This happens frequently with nurses, where hospitals and other health-care providers routinely use "travel nurses" who come in to staff long-term vacancies. Estimates put the revenues of travel nurse companies at $5.3 billion, a nontrivial amount. The average gross profit margin of those companies was 26 percent despite paying travel nurses significantly more per hour than staff nurses.[75] Why don't healthcare providers just raise their wages to fill their vacancies, rather than keep paying the higher costs of travel nurses? Because they want to avoid raising wages for all their nurses, which they would likely have to do. Similar arrangements are in place for doctors, IT professionals, and indeed any standardized job where an experienced person could walk in and perform it proficiently.

An analysis within individual companies found that where temporary help was more expensive than employees—as with travel nurses and doctors—it did prevent the employer from having to raise wages for all employees in those roles in order to fill standing vacancies.[76] Temps could be paid more than regular employees and still hold down average labor costs. This is clearly not a good outcome for employees and it creates costs in other areas, but it does keep wage costs down, which is the goal in financial accounting.

The fact that nurse wages did not rise enough to meet demand while the travel nurse business paid a huge premium led to a pretty obvious problem: more and more staff nurses left to become travel nurses. When they left, they created vacancies at their previous employer, which increased the demand for more travel nurses.

The Sandoval Regional Medical Center illustrates the problem. One-third of its nurses left to become travel nurses employed by vendors during the pandemic. Although it has a total staff of 580 employees, almost half of its entire payroll now is going to pay just sixty travel nurses in 2022.[77]

The Plethora of Vendors

The liquid workforce idea only begins with staffing agencies. The chart in Figure 4.4 illustrates how the companies that began in temporary help have branched out to offer different ways to get labor for clients. Professional firms in the chart have a white-collar focus, such as accounting, while commercial firms provide a full range of workers to clients. These vendors in the talent acquisition segment account for almost half of the roughly $500 billion human capital industry, as noted earlier. The biggest of the staffing companies that provide temporary help, leased employees, and in some cases direct hires, like Adecco and Manpower, have gross profit margins of 25 percent[78]—not bad for a reasonably simple business.

The chart in Figure 4.5 shows the percentage of clients who use each of these vendor services.[79]

Among the lesser-known categories, managed service providers (MSPs) may be the biggest player in the liquid workforce. This arrangement sounds

	Commercial	Professional	More common among...
Human resources consulting services	27%	9%	Commercial Firms
Payrolling/indepedent contractor classification	50%	34%	Commercial Firms
Direct hire/perm placement	98%	84%	Commercial Firms
Recruitment process outsourcing (RPO)	30%	17%	Commercial Firms
Temporary help	98%	89%	Commercial Firms
Human resources outsourcing (HRO)	11%	3%	Commercial Firms
Ongoing services outsourcing (e.g., janitorial, landscaping)	8%	1%	Commercial Firms
Master supplier	14%	15%	--
Direct-to-consumer (e.g., home healthcare, repairmen, etc.)	3%	4%	--
Human cloud/online staffing (similar to UpWork, Freelancer.com, etc.)	0%	3%	--
Managed service provider (MSP)	19%	23%	--
Retained search	21%	25%	--
SOW/solutions (your firm responsible for deliverable)	13%	35%	Professional Firms
Median number of services offered	4	3	-
N	120	235	

Figure 4.4 Frequency of Offering Selected Services, by Primary Staffing Firm Skill Set

Source: Staffing Industry Analysts, North American Staffing Company Survey, 2022

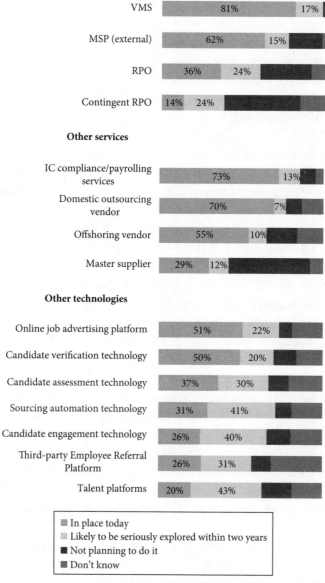

VMS/MSP/RPO

- VMS: 81%, 17%
- MSP (external): 62%, 15%
- RPO: 36%, 24%
- Contingent RPO: 14%, 24%

Other services

- IC compliance/payrolling services: 73%, 13%
- Domestic outsourcing vendor: 70%, 7%
- Offshoring vendor: 55%, 10%
- Master supplier: 29%, 12%

Other technologies

- Online job advertising platform: 51%, 22%
- Candidate verification technology: 50%, 20%
- Candidate assessment technology: 37%, 30%
- Sourcing automation technology: 31%, 41%
- Candidate engagement technology: 26%, 40%
- Third-party Employee Referral Platform: 26%, 31%
- Talent platforms: 20%, 43%

■ In place today
■ Likely to be seriously explored within two years
■ Not planning to do it
■ Don't know

Number of respondents ranged from 106 to 109

Figure 4.5 Use of Services/Technologies, 2022
Source: Staffing Industry Analysts, Workforce Solutions Buyer Survey, 2022

like outsourcing, except they are vendors on premises, doing the work at their client locations. The work they are doing could not be more central to their clients' operations, and they work extremely closely with the clients' employees. MSPs are vendors who take over functions, typically in IT. They differ from what is now referred to as "on-demand outsourcing" in that they take over the responsibility for the service, whatever that may be, while the latter provides services as requested and bills for those services. To illustrate, a company that uses outside legal counsel might have an arrangement where the outside law firm responds to requests from the company and bills the client for that work, an on-demand outsourcing model. If the client has the outside law firm on retainer, however, the firm does whatever legal work the client requires for one set fee and is a managed service provider model. This is similar to health maintenance organizations (HMOs) in healthcare—you pay one fee, and they take care of all your health needs. Another difference from the retainer model is that the MSP is typically in your work location, working side by side with other functions.

Although the MSP industry is mainly in IT and fields that intersect with IT, it is a big industry with more than $250 billion in revenue. IBM appears to be the largest provider, but five of the ten largest of these companies are based in India, and much of the work is offshored there.[80] (It is not a coincidence that those five firms also dominate the list of H1-B visa users in the United States.) It is not a highly concentrated industry, however, and beyond the top ten, it is unlikely that anyone outside the IT industry will have heard of the next 500 in size. IT work in many and perhaps most companies is now deeply integrated in the finance function, customer relationships, and supply chains. Starting with enterprise resource planning systems, IT is also seen as the backbone of companies because it integrates so many parts of the operation. This crucial task is now done onsite by workers employed by another organization. Their employer and their supervisors are elsewhere.

Do jobs that are this central to the business purpose violate the common-law employment test? Fortunately for the vendors, there are several other parts to that test, but the clients inevitably become "co-employers" in order to be able to supervise the leased employees. It would be difficult for them to interact with the other employees in a flexible enough manner to get work done otherwise. What is the advantage to the client of using this approach, if they end up with most of the obligations of being an employer and are paying top dollar for the service? It is true that they do not now have to completely manage a functional area that they may not understand. But they also get to shift these expenses off their employment category and cut their headcount.

Statement of work providers (SOWs) are vendors who manage specific projects and the contractors who perform them for clients. A master supplier or master vendor, by contrast, takes charge of all of the nonemployee workers, often subcontracting out to other vendors who supply the contractors, temps, and individual workers. Think of them like a general contractor at a building site.

"Payrolling" is similar to professional employee organizations (PEOs), where the vendor becomes the employer of record, except in this context it is directed at seasonal workers, contractors and project-based work, and direct-hire temps rather than one's own employees. "Direct to consumer" arrangements are what are most appropriately referred to as gig work, where there is an electronic platform like Uber that matches contract workers to clients, taking a fee in the process. Aside from Uber and Lyft, the vendor Task Rabbit may be the best known of these arrangements. They match providers and clients for household tasks and handyman projects, like fixing window screens.

The biggest of these gig operations by far, however, are in the domestic support business—home healthcare, housecleaning, or babysitting. The largest of the platforms, Care.com, claims 34 million members, evenly split between clients and individual providers, yet it is an extremely decentralized industry with thousands of platforms.[81] Collectively, these gig companies dwarf the ride sharing industry.

These human capital vendors have moved into hiring regular employees for clients as well. Most temp arrangements allow clients to pay a fee and hire the temp workers into permanent jobs, essentially trying them out first— temp-to-perm or contract-to-hire. They are an important source of regular employees. A recent survey of companies with more than 1,000 employees found that 10 percent of their temp agency workers were turned into regular, full-time employees.[82] These "direct hire" offerings operate like a retained and contingent search where the vendor recruits candidates, and the client makes the hiring decision. Finally, recruitment process outsourcing is where vendors take over the entire recruiting function.

Even a startup client with little or no human resource function can quickly jump into this world of alternative work, dialing up a solution to a project, bringing in a work group this week to handle a new task and a different group next week to handle that one. Behind the scenes there can be a stack of vendors—a master vendor overseeing a statement of work provider who manages one-off projects, a payrolling firm that manages long-term temps, a sea of small temp agencies providing the temps—just as we saw with hiring in Chapter 3. Vendors in this industry are now advertising a "worforce-as-a-service" business, where the client needs virtually no employment infrastructure, no human resources of any kind. They just ping the vendor, who delivers the type of workers needed, perhaps going a step further and scoping out for the client what workers and how many the client needs, and then delivering and managing them.[83]

A new development tracked by Staffing Industry Analysts is the "hiring platform" model, a kind of automated staffing firm in the direct hire market. These vendors maintain a database of candidates, much like an executive search firm might, that provides assessments of candidates and vetting of them that clients might want. Data science–driven matching algorithms tell clients which candidates are the best fit for their openings. Like executive search firms, they charge a fee based on the annual starting salary of a candidate they place. The big difference is that the process is automated and so much cheaper than recruiters.[84]

The PEO Model

As already noted, it is also possible to outsource your own employees. PEOs will take over the legal obligations for your own employees, becoming the employer of record, leasing your own workers back to you. About 3.7 million workers are employed by PEOs,[85] which makes them larger than the temp industry. Initially, PEOs were a regulatory dodge: if your regular employees were technically employed by someone else and leased back to you, it was possible to give much more generous healthcare and retirement benefits to those who remained, mainly the executives. That loophole was closed in the 1980s, but other advantages remain.[86] They were also a way to avoid litigation costs. If the government took legal action against you, or indeed if your employees sued, the PEO as the employer of record was liable, not your company. Many PEOs were small operations. If they were hit by a big lawsuit, they would simply fold up into bankruptcy.

The PEO takes responsibility for most of the administrative aspects of employment, such as payroll processing, managing benefits, and filing employment taxes, and may be more efficient at doing so than the original employer.

That employer, now the client, would not have the authority to supervise and direct those workers, who are now employed by the PEO. But they typically decide to become a co-employer along with the PEO in order to do so. With that decision, they share liability for employment-related violations and litigation. The remaining advantage of using them is to shift the employment costs of workers from the employment category to a services expense and improve the appearance of their finances to investors.

The main benefit from using PEOs for the client, according to its industry group, is that it eliminates the need to hire HR people. It shifts that cost from the employment column to current expenses. On the other hand, the clients are still paying for HR, just not one they control. In the process, the client loses control over practices such as what the benefit and pay packages will be, what policies will be on vacations, discipline, and so forth.

It also reduces the ability to solve many workplace issues before they become worse. For example, if an employee has a problem with their boss in a normal work environment, a good HR person might talk to both parties, see if any misunderstandings could be cleared up, and become the third party in the middle to try to resolve the issue with less conflict. It is also possible that the supervisor was in the wrong, sometimes involving issues of sexual harassment or general inappropriate behavior. It is difficult to see how anything like that could happen with a 1-800 phone number to a call-center handling HR issues for a hundred companies. It is just not possible in that circumstance for even an experienced representative to know enough about the culture of an organization or the history of the relationship between supervisor and subordinate to work out the problem.

If we think it is important to have a distinctive culture, let alone distinctive ways of competing, then it is important to have management practices that support that culture. If we are outsourcing the management of our employees, then we lose the distinctive ways of managing our employees— and it is hard to do that if someone else employs them. In doing so, it is very difficult to get them to perform differently. That undercuts any unique way we might have found to compete.

Is This Really a Better Approach?

The original idea that outsourcing something to real expert vendors makes it easier and cheaper to do bumps up against the complexity of the provider market and the transactions within it. To manage vendors, clients have had to create a new administrative function, vendor management. It has its own industry certifications for managers tasked with handing vendors and its own professional associations to help those managers keep pace with what the vendors are doing. Perhaps not surprisingly, there are now vendors to whom you can outsource the management of the other vendors to whom you have outsourced the actual work.[87]

Most clients now have software to assist this process, vendor management solutions (VMS). The main task of the software is to take a client's work needs—for example, we need five workers with these attributes—and distribute them across the various vendors with whom it works to see who can fill them. The software is most useful where clients do not have master supplier contracts and are pitching needs to many vendors at the same time. The software keeps track of who has delivered what, which requisitions are unfilled, and provides data and analysis measuring the performance of different vendors, mainly the time to fill vacancies.

Vendor management is far from a perfect solution. An Ernst & Young survey finds that the respondents in 21 percent of the organizations surveyed say they do not know who has primary responsibility for recruiting their liquid workforce, and 25 percent do not know who has primary responsibility for managing them. For those who do know, only 20 percent say that HR is responsible.[88] Vendor management functions typically negotiate the contract with the vendors, but line managers seem to be responsible for managing the contracts: the IT department is responsible for its nonemployees, the finance department for its nonemployees, and so forth. Their managers have to specify how many, what kind, and when they are needed—and, of course, someone has to manage these workers from outside.

One of the conclusions about managing vendors and this liquid workforce is that, at a minimum, the notion that vendors are a simple replacement for having one's own employees do the work is not true. Lauren Weber's account in the *Wall Street Journal* of what is required just to manage one type of contractor—programmers—in the computer gaming industry should give one pause: each contract, and therefore each individual contractor, has to be managed by a current employee to make certain that person actually does what needs to be done.[89] That task is typically added to the list of things that regular employees have to do. It well may make sense to have the managers responsible for the work manage those nonemployee workers, but this arrangement hides much of the administrative costs of using them.

Then consider the mass of contracts involved in a typical liquid workforce. In a typical arrangement, a vendor management function negotiates the contract with a vendor. Here the focus is mainly on costs. The arrangement may well be a master supplier agreement with a big vendor, the equivalent of a general contractor in construction, who will in turn engage a number of statement of work subcontractors to find particular sets of workers with unique skills, just as the general contractor engages subcontractors in construction. The statement of work vendors have their own subcontractors, often overseas firms scanning LinkedIn and other online sources to find contract workers or potential leased employees.

Each one of these contracts and sets of vendors has its own principal-agent incentive issues, and each has its own infrastructure and administrative costs. At the extreme, vendors often find that it is not in their interest to meet the demands of a particular client—something bigger comes along and demands their resources—or they may find that a deal is not profitable and want to renege on it. My colleagues in the construction management business, which oversees architects and general contractors, who then in turn oversee their own contracts with subcontractors in an arrangement very similar to the liquid workforce model, say that big projects inevitably end up with some or all of the parties in court claiming contract violations.

The big issue behind contract disputes of all kinds is typically interpreting the requirements of the contract. This is a much bigger challenge in the liquid workforce model because what is being delivered is workers, and they are about as nonstandard as one could get. Clients have an interest in getting the very best workers sent to them by the vendors—experienced, conscientious, easy to work with. Such workers also cost the vendor more to engage. The vendors have the opposite interest: to deliver workers who are cheaper for them to hire, other things being equal, that improve their margins, and those workers tend to be less experienced, less conscientious, or more difficult to work with. Then there is the quirky issue of fit. A client may not like a worker sent to perform particular tasks, but if they want them replaced, the vendor has to find something else for that worker to do as well as find suitable replacements. They do not want to have workers just sitting on the bench waiting for an assignment. Even if the vendors want to deliver exactly the workers the client wants, those workers may not be available when the client wants them.

But unlike in construction, legal fights among the hierarchy of contractors in the liquid workforce appear to be relatively rare. Some suggest this is because they take extra time to hash out extremely specific contracts. It is also the case that these parties hope to be together for many years, much longer than a building project, so their interest in fighting over disputes is muted. It is also easier to fix problems: "you sent me worthless workers" is easier to resolve (replace them) than "you poured the wrong type of concrete." Nevertheless, these issues all have to be negotiated.

Next, we come to the purported flexibility of the liquid workforce, specifically that it is easy to dial up and down the size and composition of the workforce. While vendors may have that capacity, it costs money to do so: dialing down the workforce means that the vendor takes back employees and finds something else for them to do, the same problem that regular employers would have. Dialing it up on short notice means finding additional workers from someplace else in their system or through their networks. Those costs have to be paid for, and the fact that the financial performance of the vendors has been so strong suggests that they are not simply absorbing them. It costs clients to do this.

The first constraint in making adjustments is that everything is subject to the contractual operating agreement: if the adjustments are not outlined in the agreement, any change has to be renegotiated. Renegotiations have costs, and not just the time and effort to engage them but hold-up costs: if your vendor is in the middle of a project and you want to change it, the option of starting over with another vendor is unpalatable, so your vendor can charge you a lot to make changes. It is the same problem one faces in making changes to an agreement with building contractors working on your home. When we have a hierarchy of vendors, each of which has operating costs that have to be paid for, each one having a contract that has to be negotiated, the administrative costs will be considerable. In other words, the more flexibility the client wants to secure, the more they have to pay for it at the beginning of the agreement.

All this does not seem like a set of arrangements that simplifies the workplace. If anything, it seems like a full employment plan for contract lawyers.

What we know about organizational effectiveness is that it takes time for groups to learn to work together, even if the individual participants are skilled and experienced. The idea that we can throw a group of strangers together and get a well-functioning team is simply not true. Especially when we are performing similar tasks repeatedly—building hospitals, writing particular insurance, dealing with the same customers—we get better at it over time. These are the conclusions from organizational learning, especially about the tacit knowledge that comes from experience, and that knowledge can be very specific. Surgery teams, for example, develop knowledge specific to the pairings of individual doctors and staff: change them up, and outcomes get worse. Established teams will therefore beat new teams, other things being equal. The idea that we can change up vendors, bring in new workers, and just expect them to be effective sounds like an assumption necessary in optimization models, and it is a myth.

Ironically, the notion described in Chapter 1 that financial accounting sees employees as fixed costs actually applies much more to the nonemployee workers of the liquid workforce than it does to the actual employees of the organization. With regular employees, they can be redirected at a moment's notice to do whatever the employer wants. The liquid workforce workers are governed by actual contracts that do have fixed costs to change them. Oliver Williamson's Nobel Prize–winning work outlined why organizations would not want to operate this way because of the costs involved in all these negotiations, especially for workers whose skills are idiosyncratic and their performance not a given. The flexible nature of employment is much better suited to flexibility demands. So why is this liquid workforce idea happening?

Once again, the best explanation leads back to financial accounting. Shifting jobs from employees to vendors moves costs from the wage and salaries category, which investors punish, to a services category. When headcount falls, our performance per employee goes up. With respect to internal accounting and actual costs, many of the costs of the liquid workforce are hidden. If we added, say, 30 percent more employees to our organization, the human resource administrative costs would rise sharply, but if we move 30 percent of our jobs to nonemployee arrangements, with vendors setting them up, it appears that our administrative costs decline. Those costs show up elsewhere, in business services, but not in wages and salaries. Some of the costs are pushed onto existing employees—the administration of the contracts and the direction and monitoring of the nonemployee workers.

One of the best of the surveys asking companies why they make use of a liquid workforce was done by the Economist Intelligence Unit.[90] The survey focuses specifically on gig workers, where the definition is a little imprecise, but it seems to include nonemployee workers of all kinds, and there may be differences in the US (75 percent of the respondents) and UK employers (25 percent) who responded to the survey. But flexibility leads the explanation, as one might expect (see Figure 4.6).

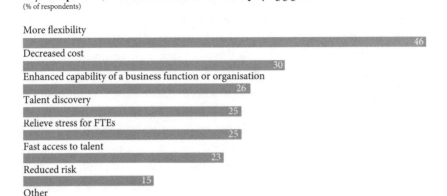

In your experience, what are the main benefits of employing gig workers?
(% of respondents)

More flexibility

> 46

Decreased cost

> 30

Enhanced capability of a business function or organisation

> 26

Talent discovery

> 25

Relieve stress for FTEs

> 25

Fast access to talent

> 23

Reduced risk

> 15

Other

> .1

Figure 4.6 Benefits of Gig Workers
Source: The Economist Intelligence Unit

But what did respondents mean when they said that flexibility was their motivation for using these practices? A revealing statistic is that 32 percent of respondents agree that their company cannot meet its strategic objectives without these gig workers, and 20 percent disagree (the remainder are unsure or neutral). Strategic objectives are plans for the future, which means that these companies are building plans that require these alternative workers. In other words, they are not used to meet unforeseen demands. The companies are setting their own staffing levels below what is necessary to operate their businesses, which creates the need for a permanent, alternative workforce.

Whether this approach is actually cheaper is a very difficult question of internal accounting for the companies to answer, as it depends on what is included in the costs. The respondents reported unique problems with using these workers that were not present with their own employees. Eighty percent of the respondents in this survey reported that it required a different approach to manage these nonliquid workers than their own employees. They also agreed that using them took more management resources (58 percent) and involved more risk (55 percent). Twenty-nine percent of the respondents report that the benefits of using these workers were offset by the additional administrative costs versus 23 percent who did not agree; 31 percent said that the benefits were offset by the additional risk versus 26 percent who did not agree (in both cases the remaining responses were "neutral" and "don't know"). The leading drawback, shown in Figure 4.7, is that these

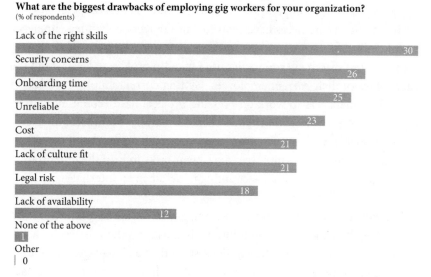

What are the biggest drawbacks of employing gig workers for your organization?
(% of respondents)

Lack of the right skills

30

Security concerns

26

Onboarding time

25

Unreliable

23

Cost

21

Lack of culture fit

21

Legal risk

18

Lack of availability

12

None of the above

1

Other

0

Figure 4.7 Drawbacks of Gig Workers
Source: The Economist Intelligence Unit

nonemployee workers lack the right skills, which is typically seen as one of the main reasons for using them, to get skills quickly that one could not otherwise have.

Remarkably, given what we know about the difficulty in making teams work and the need for them to be together for some time before they function well as a team, 71 percent of the respondents report that they bring in these gig workers as individuals and then assemble them into teams managed by their own employees. Paul Osterman's study of workforce training notes that roughly a third of leased employees get training from the client, as opposed to about half for regular employees.[91] Employers are not necessarily saving much on training by using them. The fact that employers train these leased workers moves them closer to being the actual employer of those workers under the common-law employment test described in Chapter 1.

There is nothing inherently more flexible about laying off workers and hiring new ones, or contracting with vendors to give us new employees and take the others away, than there is in using one's own employees. It may be more accurate to say that we now do a very poor job of rearranging talent internally because we don't pay to relocate them, we don't retrain them, and we don't invest in cross-training to meet short-term changes in demands.

For example, few companies have a good sense of all the competencies that their individual employees have: who are our Francophones, for example, or people with C++ programming knowledge. It is something of a joke but nevertheless true that many companies use LinkedIn profiles to learn about the capabilities of their *current* employees. Getting current employees released from their managers to work on pressing projects has become more difficult in recent years, as authority has been decentralized and local managers are accountable for their own profit and loss, which means that it costs their performance to release employees from their tasks to help the organization with its tasks. This is another accounting issue, albeit an internal accounting problem.

Matthew Bidwell's study of a single company's decision as to whether to do IT work with vendors or to do it internally illustrates these issues in detail. He describes a web of complicated interests of the local managers, including compelling arguments for doing it internally, which project managers usually preferred because it gave greater control over the work, reduced the risk of it failing, and simplified management. The pressure on senior management, however, was to cut accounting costs, and they argued for using vendors. In fact, they had quotas of work going out to vendors to maintain. Pushing the tasks out to vendors created more work for the local managers. The higher-end system integrators they used were actually more expensive than their own employees.

Bidwell describes at the local level how the financial accounting control systems played out. The accounting constraints were much tighter around doing work internally than using vendors: remarkably, there was more slack allowed in meeting costs targets with vendors, who were governed by legal contracts, than there was in using your own employees. One manager described the accounting rules in exactly the same way as our earlier discussion in Chapter 1: "The buckets [for costs] are not the same, and the approval process and bureaucracy for a vendor is far less difficult than it is to bring on an employee."[92] There was no sense from this account that pushing work out was overall better for the organization.

There are two bodies of research evidence on the effects of using these alternative workforces: one with a psychology base, and one with an economics base. Of course, they disregard each other, but they reach a quite similar conclusion. Do they help? The answer is no, at least on the admittedly limited dimensions being measured. The complication in knowing is that the decision to use temps or staffing firms is not random. Something about companies causes some to use them and some not, so sorting out the effect of that decision per se on outcomes is quite difficult. The psychology studies look within companies, which gets around that problem a bit. They uniformly find negative effects on the temps themselves—that is, being second-class citizens in their organizations.[93] More interesting are the results that using temps depresses the job-related attitudes of regular employees, such as commitment to the organization by making them see themselves more like temps. Turnover rises as well.[94] We found in a similar study that this mechanism also reduces overall productivity and service quality of stores.[95] The research in economics finds negative relationships with productivity[96] and declines in innovation.[97] Finally, a recent study undermines the notion that getting rid of temps is easy, showing that even when temps come to the end of their contract—when they and everyone knows they are leaving—their departure still has negative effects on organizational performance.[98]

Effects on Employees

As noted earlier, where vendors are the employer of record of the liquid workforce, the workers onsite for clients are only partially responsible to the client even when the client is a co-employer. All the practices that employers can use to motivate and engage their regular employees, from compensation and benefits to organizational culture to effective supervisors, are largely off the table with the liquid workforce. In practice, this means the organization where these workers do their jobs has largely given up on managing them. The borrowed servant doctrine in employment law allows the client to direct the work being performed by those liquid workforce workers, but that does not include the broader practices of management, such as rewarding employees, setting performance targets, and measuring them.[99]

What it means for employees to have these split authority structures is not well known. An older literature on boundary spanners, such as sales employees who spend more time with clients than with their own employer, highlights the difficulties when obligations conflict; an equivalent literature on dual allegiance for unionized employees who had obligations to their union and to their employer shows similar tensions. What it means—especially for the leased employees who work full-time and for more than a year onsite for a client but are employed by an organization that arguably has more power over them and who they see less—remains unexplored.[100]

Assuming the liquid workforce model means the transfer of some jobs from one organization to a vendor, the net effect depends on what the jobs are like in each organization. For some tasks, such as accounting, law, and management consulting, outsourcing means pushing those jobs to professional service firms. It is true that doing so eliminates the possibility that accountants, lawyers, and strategic planners will ever get to be operating executives in those corporations, but they may well be better paid accountants, lawyers, and consultants with more autonomy than they would have had in the corporations.

The changes that get the most attention and that involve more employees are at the bottom of the corporate pay scales—janitors, food service workers, gardeners, and so forth. In corporations, employees in those jobs had similar benefits to other employees, in part encouraged to do so by IRS regulations and laws like the Affordable Care Act, which prohibit having better health-care benefits for some employees than for others. As others have noted, a janitorial service that only does that work might be less likely to offer benefits like healthcare to its employees or have compensation systems that tie janitor pay at least in part to the pay of higher-paid employees. When a bank or other large corporation outsources its janitorial work, it is quite likely that the individuals doing that work will have lower pay and less access to benefits than janitors employed by the bank would have.

The other consequence is that their career paths become more limited. It was possible to work one's way up from the shop floor at companies like UPS when virtually all positions were filled from within by people who began as loaders or drivers. But even if every manager position was filled that way, there are so many lower-level employees and so few open manager positions that it was hard to describe it as a reasonable career path. As a contemporary example, Walmart fills 75 percent of its store manager positions from the hourly workforce, a commendable number. But there are roughly 470 employees per store manager, and given turnover rates, the base rate probability of any new store associate becoming a store manager is likely more than a thousand to one.[101]

The liquid workforce model also creates clear path dependence that makes it difficult to go back even if circumstances change, an irony for the cause of flexibility. Consider a company in the late 1980s that made a decision to bring in workers from a staffing agency to take over clerical tasks in a division. To get the cost savings, once it makes that move, it cuts the recruiters, trainers, and HR staff from that division to recognize some immediate savings.

Suppose years later it decides that the cost gap between our internal pay and what we are paying the vendors has disappeared. What do we do to go back to having employees? We would have to bring back some recruiters, some trainers, develop and put in place management systems for the employees, and hire human resource people to run them. These are switching costs that make it difficult to change back. Given our financial accounting system, they would all need to be offset by revenue the year they are incurred because they count as current expenses, even though they are an investment in the future. A thoughtful observer might wonder whether some of those costs could be outsourced. It is possible. For example, RPO firms could staff the business for us, but the more parts we outsource, the more we defeat the reason for moving back to employees.

Public policy also facilitates the liquid workforce approach with immigration practices. There are at least twenty-three different categories under which foreign workers can come to the United States for temporary work, bringing in about 1 million workers per year on temporary assignments. These include separate programs to bring in fashion models, which Melania Trump made famous; entertainers and athletes; and the best-known, H1-B (for college-level jobs) and H-2B (for shorter or peak-load employment) visas. Employers interested in accessing these workers have to promise that they will pay market wages, and they have to assert that they could not find US workers for these jobs if they hope to bring in foreign workers permanently.[102] Although these workers are employees, they are not like US employees in that the employer who sponsors them can make them pay a penalty if they quit, in which case they must return to their home country unless they can find a new employer to take them on before they leave their original employer.

Virtually all of the H1-B visas are for IT workers, and most all of those bring in workers from India. Although they are sometimes confused with the super-smart temporary workers (those are O-1 visas), these workers typically perform mid-level tasks that hundreds of thousands of US workers are also carrying out. The biggest employers are disproportionately Indian firms, or those with Indian outsourcing operations where the H1-B temps perform tasks for US clients and then continue to do so when they return to India. Cognizant Technology alone employs roughly 10 percent of all H1-B workers.[103]

There are many issues about these programs—is it really true, for example, that employers could not find workers to do these jobs even in the Great

Recession? But perhaps the biggest is that they hold the US labor market back from adjusting. In the 1960s, for example, the program was used mainly to bring in nurses. As a result, nursing wages did not rise, and fewer students became nurses.

Why Has the Liquid Workforce Become So Popular?

It would be a considerable internal accounting exercise to get a sense of what the real costs and benefits were of moving away from employees toward the liquid workforce model, and there is no evidence that companies have the willingness to do that. It became popular at least in part because it sounds right, especially from an optimization perspective. If the goal is to use as little labor as possible—and that sounds obvious—being able to dial it down when it is not needed seems like the straightforward thing to do. It also fits with a worldview where labor is a commodity and driving employment levels down is the goal, where employees are seen as fixed costs while vendor costs are seen as variable. If we never look at the longer-term effects, not just on costs but on performance, it is easier to sustain.

One thing we do know about this approach is that it weakens connections between employer and employee and makes it easier to look at employees as a commodity, coming in and out via the labor market. When we envision employees as just passing through our organizations, it is easier to think of them as a cost item and not to worry about longer-term effects. The further we move in that direction, the more difficult it is to get commitment from employees or ideas or discretionary effort, pitching in when no one is looking. It is possible to operate that way, but it is also contrary to the decades of evidence we have as to what works.

5

How Work Gets Done

Identifying the specific tasks or independent actions that employees must perform, establishing how they should be done and by whom, are the essential tasks of management. Chapter 4 described the push to shift work to nonemployees. Here, we are thinking about how work actually gets done, and recent developments to shift control and decision-making away from employees reflects the optimization trend described in Chapter 2, itself pushed along by the influence of financial accounting.

Engineers brought sophistication and rigor to these questions in the 1920s through scientific management where the goal was to optimize, to figure out the "one best way" in the language of its founder, Frederick Winslow Taylor, to perform any task. The assumption was that experts could best figure that out, and once that was done, management was about getting employees to comply, either by rewarding them with incentives for good performance or punishing them if they did not. Standards were set for how fast the work was done, followed by monitoring and measuring performance, with the goal being to adapt human performance to the work systems and machines.

There is no doubt that the initial scientific management system was wildly more effective than the relative chaos that had come before it in the workshops of the 1920s. It is an easy approach to understand, especially for the engineers who designed the machines and ran the companies during the last century.

There is also no doubt that people hated working in it, as parodied by the famous Charlie Chaplin movie *Modern Times*, where workers literally become part of the machines to which their work was tied. Psychologists provided evidence that structuring individual tasks efficiently while ignoring the human needs and feelings of workers would lead to problems. Even on assembly lines, employees have enough discretion that how they feel about their work becomes hugely important to performance and outcomes, and as work becomes less routine, the importance of that discretion increased. The Human Relations School starting in the 1930s built on Western Electric's experiments that played with team structures and rewards in assembly tasks to make the basic point that human behavior mattered.[1] The under-lying conflict between the two was described as Theory X (the rational, ec-onomic view of employees) and Theory Y (the more realistic view informed by psychology) by Douglas McGregor and then later on as "the low road" for the former, because it was hard on employees, and "the high road" for the latter, because it appeared both more productive and better for employees.[2] "Scientific management," the term Justice Louis Brandeis gave it, is the no-tion that jobs can be broken down into tasks, that there was a one best way to perform any task, and following that one best way is what we should do.

The McDonald Brothers famously laid out the organization of their epon-ymous burger restaurant and its "Speedee Service System" with exactly the same principles of scientific management used in assembly lines. They broke the process down into separate tasks in each station and then put them together so that food flowed efficiently from one station to an-other and out to the customer. The movie *The Founder*, about Ray Kroc and the rise of McDonald's, offers a slightly fictionalized version of how they developed and laid out that system. See clip at https://youtu.be/jTag euhPfAM.

To summarize a generations-long response after the Human Relations School, early efforts to engage employees in problem solving with the equiv-alent of quality circles during World War II were successful but then were pushed back by scientific management arguments when the war ended. The decline of quality in manufacturing not just in the United States but around the Western world in the 1970s had a lot to do with ever more aggressive sci-entific management, especially in the auto industry. It also had to do with a new baby boomer workforce around the industrialized world less tolerant of numbingly boring jobs their parents had accepted in return for higher wages.

The arrival of products from Japan—fuel-efficient, higher-quality cars and then a slew of other products manufactured using a very different approach—made the decline hard to miss. It led to change, first in the unionized auto in-dustry with "quality of work life" programs that engaged workers in solving safety problems; then "quality circles" borrowed from Japan (but originally from the United States) where workers identified the causes of quality problems; and then lastly lean production, where workers took over some of the tasks of the in-dustrial engineers, redesigning their own jobs to improve quality.

These practices clearly worked better, improving both quality and produc-tivity, but their adoption had to overcome sometimes protracted resistance from executives and the engineers advising them. Their initial response was to automate as many jobs as possible. Starting in the early 1980s, first General Motors and then Fiat and Volkswagen made massive investments in robotics to automate assembly plants. The idea was that if workers would not adapt to the jobs as engineers designed them, then they would be replaced by more machines. As my colleagues John Paul MacDuffie and Frits Pils described it, this approach was a massive failure. Toyota demonstrated in its US plants that regular workers with fewer machines outperformed GM and other manufacturers both in quality and productivity simply by managing them differently.[3] The evidence that it worked was simply too overwhelming to ignore.

By 1985, these alternative approaches had generated such a body of positive evidence that Harvard Business School professor Richard Walton asserted that the basic Theory Y view and empowerment in particular had now won the day.[4] They got a further push from public policy in 1990 by the Carnegie-funded report *America's Choice: High Skills or Low Wages?*[5] At a time when the United States appeared to be losing the competitive battle with Japan in manufacturing, the report argued that employers needed to transform the way they operated. To compete against low-wage, foreign competition required greater productivity and effectiveness. That required more empowered employees executing higher-skilled tasks, and the workforce needed higher skills to do so. This approach was embraced by the George H. W. Bush administration, then especially so by the Clinton administration, but abandoned by the George W. Bush administration, which returned to a more traditional view that competitiveness was best advanced by giving employers more control.[6]

A similar argument for managing employees differently was already underway in an unexpected area, the field of marketing. Leonard Schlesinger, James Heskett, and colleagues at the Harvard Business School described the service-driven approach: "The basic premise is simple: the old model puts the people who deliver service to customers last; the new model puts frontline workers first and designs the business system around them."[7] In other words, customer service pays off, and taking care of employees was the way to get better customer service. The older engineering model, they argued, was obsolete, citing examples like Taco Bell, which both increased service quality and lowered costs with this approach.

This story drew support from the older human relations community but also an intense pushback from employers defending their traditional approach, including the argument that it was not possible financially to put employees first in many business environments. The only way to compete, they argued, was to drive employees harder—Theory X.[8] One of the examples used to critique the service-driven approach was Sears Roebuck in the 1990s. The assertion was that despite still being the dominant retailer, the rise of big-box low-wage stores and price competition meant Sears could never survive without squeezing their employees to keep costs down.

The irony, which was unfortunately not captured in the public debate, is that just a few years later, Sears Roebuck became the most prominent example of succeeding with the newer approach of focusing on frontline employees. Sears restructured itself in the mid-1990s around the insight that employees who care about the business create a better customer experience and that increases profits. Sears demonstrated in a rigorous way that educating employees about the business as well as paying attention to their needs led to higher profitability and drove the turnaround of that business.[9] As we saw in Chapter 3, this did not last as the investors who took over Sears next shifted it sharply back to a cost-focused direction and are now left with just a handful of stores.

I know of no studies refuting the findings about the service-driven approach, or indeed of the high-performance work systems before it, but the idea that taking care of frontline employees could be crucial to company success faded by the time of the dot-com boom. In an exception that proves the rule, Vineet Nayar, the CEO of Indian IT company HCL Technologies, put forward exactly the same idea in his company: making frontline consultants dealing with customers in the field the first priority because it paid off. When he wrote about the idea of "employee first, customer second" a decade later in 2010, its apparent novelty created a minor sensation.[10] But interest in it did not catch on.

Yet another push for the employee empowerment idea came from a different, unlikely direction: software engineers. Its best-known source was the Agile Manifesto articulated first at Adobe, although like many good ideas, a thousand fathers claim it. One could be forgiven for thinking that agile was really just an absence of structure and empowering teams instead, as startups tried to figure out how to create software cheaply without the financial control systems that large corporations had developed. The essence of the approach was reasonably close to that, pulling back the formal models of financial control and project management created by finance departments and engineers, giving the teams doing the work complete control over everything and whatever resources they needed to make it happen.[11] The consequence was a radical empowering of employees and their teams, not only giving them control over quality, as the quality of worklife movement had done, and production decisions, as lean production had done, but giving them control even of design decisions involving what they were creating.

Management's mission was to support those agile teams with resources and patience along the way, which requires giving up the cost control and predictability that came with tight control systems and close oversight. As with lean production, the evidence that agile approaches and its cousins like fast prototyping work were effective, especially for generating innovations faster and cheaper, was overwhelming. By 2010, it was cemented as *the* approach for creating software, and its benefits—faster, cheaper, better—had been documented extensively.[12] It was easy to see why. It would save a lot of time and energy if we could skip the time spent laying out a plan about exactly what we would do months from now before we started a project, exactly how much we would spend in each month and on which categories or expenses, and what the item we were producing would do and just get on with it. The bigger savings, as everyone who has run a project knows, is to have to manage to that formula (or to pretend to manage from it) and deal with all the inevitable problems that we could not predict before we started.

Agile spread across IT companies, including giants like IBM, and manufacturing companies like GE. By 2017, the vast majority of US companies across industries surveyed reported they either had already or were planning to implement it as a way of managing employees, especially performance appraisals.[13]

The Tale of Two Brothers

A popular teaching case discusses the story of brothers Anuj and Rajat Khurana, who each started successful IT solutions companies but ran them with opposing Theory X and Theory Y practices. Anuj's ARK company focused heavily on performance-based measures, analytics, and traditional control systems to run the business, while Rajat's WCC company put employee needs front and center and invested time and energy in meeting their behavioral needs. The different approaches were suited best to different challenges, but overall the higher turnover at ARK attributed to these optimizing approaches was a decisive detriment to ARK's future. Source: "Two Brothers, Two Methods: Happiness Index vs. Data and Analytics," Los Angeles, CA: USC Marshall School of Business, 2019.

Rewriting Theory Y

Those empowerment pushes didn't last either, as optimization thinking slowly made a comeback. In 1995, Google Scholar showed only 1,390 articles talking about optimization in the context of people management issues. By 2018, there were 21,600. By contrast, there was no growth in the number of articles referring to employee empowerment, only 5,510 in 2018, just about where it was in 1995.

Another indication of the move back toward optimization thinking is to see what has been happening to the most recent Theory Y innovations, lean production and agile. Both are now being radically redefined in ways such that—remarkably—they sound like they fit the optimization approach that most top executives favored.

Consider lean production, which had the empowerment of frontline workers as its core. Surveys of how practitioners thought about and used lean indicated a root cause analysis of problems and management practices that involve employees in solving those problems.[14] Yet a quick internet search on the term "lean" now will find definitions and descriptions of lean with no reference to empowered teams at all. As one CFO business magazine put it, "By its actual definition, 'lean' commonly refers to *any* operations [emphasis mine] system that can minimize waste without compromising productivity or quality."[15] That definition is actually that of Pareto efficiency. The idea that lean is based on the Toyota system, let alone has empowered teams at its core, has been completely forgotten. As a consulting group now defined it, "More simply, lean involves doing more with less," working optimization into the definition, "through perfect processes that create zero waste."[16] Lean as it is now used in the business press and consulting world just means finding ways to drive productivity, preferably through optimization efforts.

An example of the change in that direction can be seen in retail operations like Target and Walmart, which sound like empowerment programs. Walmart's new "Great Workplace" initiative creates smaller workgroups called "teams," and some jobs—especially those of greeters—are broader; they now include additional tasks to be performed when there is downtime.[17] But the initiative does not give workers any authority to identify and solve problems or to coordinate with others around them. Its objective appears to be to keep everyone busy, not to empower and engage people. Target's "modernization" program broadens the jobs of regular shift workers and in the process eliminates night-shift jobs such as inventory support and shelf-stocking. Rather than reducing part-time jobs and create more full-time jobs, which was part of its goal, it expanded part-time work to make it easier to get that optimal match with workloads.[18]

Perhaps the best example of the walking back of lean comes in manufacturing where lean production began. Companies like auto supplier Denso now use software and cameras to make the productivity adjustments in tasks that workers used to figure out and implement on their own.[19] Data science innovations have driven this development with an approach called "machine vision" as opposed to machine learning, which is based on existing data. It captures what employees are doing now with cameras exactly as Frederick Taylor's engineers did by watching. Some of the new software ends there, monitoring assembly line workers constantly—a "perfect foreman," as some people put it—to make sure that they perform the tasks exactly as designed. Some of this might be perfectly sensible, watching for safety violations, for example. Of course, it also turns them into Charlie Chaplin's characters from *Modern Times*, perhaps even more so because the electronic foreman is always there.

Other software called Robotic Process Automation now goes further by taking those video images and figuring out that one best way to perform the tasks. One of the vendors in this field describes what their software does: "deconstructing jobs into tasks, evaluating ways to optimize work—across technology, employees and nontraditional talent—and reconfiguring the work into new, more optimal jobs."[20] This is close to the classic optimizing known as deskilling introduced by scientific management: strip the simpler tasks away from higher-skilled jobs, and bundle them up into new jobs that are lower-skilled and lower-paid. The creation of lower-paid nurse assistants to take over tasks from more expensive registered nurses is a classic illustration of this process.

This might look like an unmitigated good thing, making the best use of the time of higher-skilled specialists. It has the downside of creating narrow jobs that are extremely dull because they lack variety, which has a negative effect on work quality. The big difference is that with lean production, employees were deciding the best way to perform their jobs, even if doing so meant doing their tasks repetitively. That control is what made the boring jobs tolerable. The other downside is that this optimization approach disconnects tasks in work systems, requiring more proscribed handoffs and communication between workers because they otherwise no longer see the connection between tasks. In a healthcare context, for example, the new hierarchy of jobs means that the nursing assistant has to notice something about a patient and pass it along to the licensed practical nurse, who then has to remember to notify the registered nurse on the next shift, who is in a position to bring it to the attention of the attending physician to act on it. In short, the new optimization approach takes the tasks of designing work back from the lean production teams and gives them over to Frederick Taylor's engineers, who are now data scientists.

Agile is experiencing an even bigger rewrite. Its definition has changed from being a noun—an approach to project management—back to an adjective—being flexible. Steve Denning is one of the leaders popularizing agile management as an approach to managing projects with constant feedback and empowered teams that came out of Adobe and other software companies. He notes the new term "strategic agility," which is entirely different from operational agility and describes the ability of an organization to innovate by being flexible.[21] A contemporary search of business publications will find that agile is now defined by phrases like "adapting and evolving to external forces and trends." The heart of agile approaches, empowered and supported teams, has gone completely missing. Planning even makes a comeback in advice on how to achieve this definition of agile, a practice that was the antithesis of the agile approach.

McKinsey brings optimization thinking explicitly into this redefinition of agile, asserting that a liquid workforce of contractors can be necessary to achieve agility.[22] When CEOs were asked about how best to create resiliency, which they defined the same way as agility, 68 percent said by purchasing new technology while only 31 percent said investing in the workforce.[23] One explanation for this redefinition of the term is that it allows leaders to say they are doing "agile" without turning control over to teams that are the heart of the agile revolution.

A final, and likely fatal, problem that agile project management faced is that the structures and planning that they pull back from management to give teams more freedom are largely financial control systems. As described in Chapter 1, a typical project in a typical corporation requires that the proposer lay out a proposal to be approved by the CFO: a timeline with what will be spent when and for what, when the project will be completed, what the intermediate outcomes will be, what it will look like when it is done, and what financial revenue it will create. Agile approaches pull all that back, which means taking the control and authority away from CFOs. The rollout of agile approaches in traditional corporations and financial institutions often involved the CEOs overruling resistance from the CFOs, who were not keen on losing control. The redefinition of agile is a comeback victory for them and for financial control systems.

More Pushback from AI

Artificial intelligence promises to take control a step further, not just moving decisions away from employees but away from their supervisors as well. Frederick Taylor would be pleased.

Data science facilitates optimization and undercuts the human dimension by making it much easier to monitor performance. To see that, look at a job that had been a bastion of individualism and autonomy: over-the-road trucking. Once upon a time, truckers could drive how and when they wanted as long as they got their delivery to its destination on time. They were paid by miles driven and, if employees, by hours spent in driving.

Now AI systems monitor everything the drivers are doing along the way and match it up against what prior evidence has shown are the lowest-cost practices. The truck cab is like an automated Skinner box in the way it monitors the drivers and collects information both to enforce the algorithm's requirements and to improve it. Cameras watch to see if drivers take their hands off the wheel, docking their pay if they do; speed and driving time are closely monitored minute-by-minute; drivers are given turn-by-turn instructions that determine when and how they get to each destination, eliminating left-hand turns, for example, because they account for more accidents and take more time.[24]

An example of where this can lead comes from Amazon and its 300,000 warehouse employees. They are given targets created by algorithms defining how long it should take to find and bring back each item in their order, with a clock counting down to that target time. Failure to meet the target leads to a warning, also issued by the algorithm, and three warnings are grounds for dismissal. The supervisor still has the final call on firing the employee, but how long that will last is not clear.[25]

The Amazon example has gotten so much attention in part because it has been done in what had been the reasonably unstructured world of warehouse work. Amazon standardizes tasks in the same way that assembly lines did: estimate how much time it takes on average for a good performer to retrieve the items, set hard performance targets for achieving that task, monitor employee performance on a minute-by-minute basis, and create motivation with serious consequences: the threat of being fired for poor performance turns out to be cheaper than the promise of higher pay for good performance. That is a very credible threat, because the jobs are made to be simple so that workers can easily be replaced.

As with other AI interventions, when we take away decisions from employees and they are not accountable for them, their interest in contributing extra effort falls. With AI-based algorithms making decisions, it isn't even clear how employees could help if they were inclined. Suppose an employee truck driver learns from someone in a rest stop that they are shutting down a road on the route mapped out for him by the company's AI system. A delay won't be their fault, and drivers are paid largely by the hour. Will they try to do something to avoid it—if so, how do they go around the mapping algorithm without getting in trouble—or just sit out the delay and get paid for it?

Scheduling Work

Transferring decision-making from line managers and workers to experts and software also undermines supervisors and line managers whose authority had been a source of their power. A common example is software to determine worker schedules. It is not a new idea, but its use has expanded considerably to a wide range of jobs. Forty-two percent of US companies now use it.[26]

The algorithms that underpin it are mathematical rather than empirical, but the optimization goal is even more explicit. For historical reasons associated with the first applications, it is referred to as "the nurse roster problem."[27] Here that one goal being optimized is to minimize the total amount of labor needed to cover assignments. This contrasts with flextime and other approaches where employees themselves work out schedules through a process of negotiations and social exchange: I'll cover for you this weekend if you take my shift next week, for example. Scheduling algorithms cut both employees and supervisors out of the process.[28]

The evidence that the flexible approach works is, by the standards of rigorous research, about as good as it gets. It improves a range of outcomes for employees, such as better job attitudes[29] and better accommodation of life challenges outside of work; there is evidence that it is worth extra salary to employees.[30] For employers, it leads to better productivity.[31] It even got a public policy endorsement from the White House.[32]

Scheduling software's appeal is that it can ensure that there is no excess capacity in the workplace, or put differently, that no one is paid when there is not much for them to do. It assumes that the workers are interchangeable, of course; it imposes schedules without any consideration as to the varying needs of individual employees; and it is not at all flexible when last-minute problems pop up. As with many of these new practices, the question is, what problem is it really solving, and is the solution worse than the original problem?

It might well save management time initially to use that software, because getting a team to the point where it can negotiate schedules and flex requires some effort. But think about how it affects supervision and management: What does the supervisor say to a complaining employee who has been slotted by algorithmic scheduling software to work three Saturdays in a row? How can that supervisor go back to the employee later and ask her for extra help when the supervisor can't do anything for her? The exchange of favors that builds relationships and creates the sense for employees that the organization supports them disappears in this environment.

A survey of employers in 2020 found 28 percent reporting that they were already using data science tools to "replace line manager duties in assigning tasks and managing performance," in other words, taking over the work of supervisors. Thirty-nine percent would start doing so the next year.[33] My exposure to the vendors who are developing these tools suggests that how they might affect the employees has not been considered. As described in Chapter 2, the main reason is that the engineers designing these tools have had little if any exposure to what we know about managing employees.

Monitoring Regular Employees

Now we come to monitoring the performance of white-collar workers, something that had been extremely difficult to do and was arguably the reason employers have been especially concerned about maintaining employee commitment in those roles. Now it is much easier. More than 50 percent of employers say they monitor employee emails, and IT employees, whose departments manage the monitoring, say the number is far higher.[34] Even if they are not reading them word for word, natural language processing software allows us to tell what they are about at a reasonably granular level—are they about business, or something else?

New performance-management software that counts keystrokes and captures and analyzes screen shots to track goof-offs are just the tip of the data collection iceberg for anyone working on a computer, as virtually all white-collar workers are. Vendors such as Teramind and InterGuard sell off-the-shelf systems that provide all these functions and more to tell employers what their workers are doing. Software we already use, such as Microsoft Outlook Calendar and project management software such as Slack, identifies who we have been meeting with and how much time we have spent with them, and then helps build models of how long it should take to get given projects done.

Most companies monitor emails, and many monitor conversations in meetings. Smart office software can already tell us who is spending how much time in their office just by measuring how long the motion detector lights stay on. The old time clock is back in the form of badges that swipe us in and out of the office, tracking when we arrive and leave as well as which offices we swipe into in order to see other people. Indoor mapping software goes much further, identifying where individual employees are in our facilities in real time. Vendors now offer software that claims to identify individuals in the office by how they walk—gait analysis—even when their faces can't be observed. Companies such as Google are monitoring conversations in team meetings to try to understand what types of interaction lead to better outcomes. Sensors measure who is meeting with whom, how long we sit at our desks, and so forth.

Innovations in monitoring are not simply an office work development, of course. Programmers are now measured on the code they produce via keystrokes entered;[35] gloves with embedded RFID technology have made it possible to count the hand movements of employees performing sorting tasks and reward them per task performed;[36] and Amazon has patented a wristband that signals to employees with vibrations when they have made a mistake in, say, sorting, or presumably when their work pace has slowed.[37] More than half of large US companies report that they already use nontraditional forms of monitoring employees, including wearable technologies like these to track employee performance.[38]

Amazon is not unique in pushing the optimization-through-algorithm lever hard. Earlier in its history, Instacart moved away from contract workers to employees because it felt it needed more influence over how its shoppers worked and interacted with customers. But then it pushed those part-time employees hard with various metrics on their performance that they had to hit, with leader boards in the break rooms showing everyone's performance compared to peers, and many people were fired for not hitting those performance targets. Instacart also used the scheduling approach of cutting back hours when performance lagged.[39]

Letting people know how they are doing in a job is not a bad thing per se, even when that information is constant. The problems begin with what we do with that data. Interesting research reveals that showing our performance in individual tasks within our control can make it possible to turn the tasks into something like a game, seeing how much we can get done with different approaches. As soon as we attach incentives to the outcomes, however, the game aspect disappears. Not surprisingly, if we use that data to drive standards higher and harder, it can take away our autonomy and make the work miserable.[40]

More recent research describes new efforts to quantify performance in a wide range of jobs where few measures existed before, such as education. Quantification like this changes not only how jobs are performed but how we think about the outcomes.[41]

The notion that we manage what we measure leads employers to determine employees' salary, career, and employment almost solely on these quantified measurers. Aruna Ranganathan and Alan Benson describe how for very simple tasks having simple and clear performance measures can turn the work into something of a game for workers, although that does not work for more complex tasks.[42] Jodi Kantor and Arya Sundaram describe how employers like United Healthcare use simple measures tracking their time on computers to generate productivity scores, which in turn are used to dock their pay if they fall below a given norm.[43] Except for simply tracking time away from the office, these tools appear to manifest the worst kind of suboptimization for office jobs as they are measuring crude inputs (such as whether someone's mouse is moving) rather than tangible outcomes.

One of the many accounts of what hourly jobs are like where optimization thinking and the close monitoring of performance with IT systems meets management willingness to push employees harder with software to enforce it is Emily Guendelsberger's account of working in a call center, a McDonald's restaurant, and an Amazon warehouse—archetypal service jobs. What she describes are physically exhausting workplaces—she walked fifteen miles each day as part of her warehouse job. Guendelsberger had little opportunity to talk with other workers in call centers or control anything about how she did her job, enforced by constant reminders from monitoring systems of how close she was to being fired.[44]

In white-collar work, monitoring is less precise, as are performance targets, because tasks are less predictable and more open-ended. That open-ended aspect can make jobs worse, as Erin Kelly and Phyllis Moen assert, because it allows performance standards to simply ratchet up; we can never be sure that we are finished working. Even for employers widely described as "good ones," they describe widespread intensification of work among office jobs: too much to do, and high expectations for always being available, especially in the office.[45]

> The WaterSaver Faucet Company installed card readers on bathrooms to monitor use outside of scheduled break times and rewarded employees with gift cards if they avoided using the bathroom during work time. They also punished employees whose average bathroom use outside those time exceeded six minutes per day. Source: Patrick M. Sheridan, "Company Limits Bathroom Breaks to 6 Minutes Per Day," CNN Business, July 15, 2014, https://money.cnn.com/2014/07/15/smallbusiness/bathroom-time-penalty/index.html.

All this information from monitoring could also be used to design better office layouts or fix schedules for meeting rooms. But it could also identify which employees duck out of the building for extended periods of time, and who seems to be organizing March Madness betting pools. Ethan Bernstein and Ben Waber note that top-down efforts to design workplaces to produce desired outcomes often backfire, for instance by reducing collaboration rather than increasing it. They recommend a decentralized approach, where we experiment to see what practices work in each situation to get the outcomes that matter.[46]

Monitoring rarely works as intended, because employees find ways to get around it. Employees admit to covering the webcam on their work computer, switch to their cellphone rather than the company phone to talk to coworkers to prevent their employers from listening to them, and so forth.[47] They also find ways to game performance measures after they figure out what they are. Once employees learn that the smart office system is monitoring when they leave work by clocking how long the motion detector lights stay on in their office, for example, some will surely keep one of those perpetual motion toys going on their desk. They will send numerous emails to each other to make them appear central to network analyses, or maybe put their Fitbit from the wellness program in the dryer to make it seem as though they are climbing the stairs. Creativity is endless in this arena.

Monitoring employees, imposing costs on them for disobeying, and the range of practices that limit the rights of employees raise more questions than simply their efficacy for management. Philosopher Elizabeth Anderson has summarized these concerns around this question: Why do we allow private organizations to restrict rights in ways that we would never tolerate if governments did so?[48]

Moving toward AI-based optimization isn't free in terms of actual costs, either. Just as the adopters of Frederick Taylor's scientific management required an influx of experts from the emerging field of industrial engineering, today's optimization efforts are feeding demand for data scientists. Jobs for data scientists who build the algorithms grew 56 percent in 2019, and they aren't cheap. Their average pay is $130,000.[49] (If it is outsourced, it does not show up as an employment cost, of course.) Nor does the work stop once the algorithms are in place. They need to be updated continuously.

But given the focus on reducing employment costs, the promise of replacing employees with algorithms is extremely enticing to CFOs. Amazon's push to develop a hiring algorithm was apparently driven by the goal of getting rid of recruiters and turning the process over to faster, cheaper algorithms and software that could offer a "one best way" solution for picking candidates and ultimately making promotion decisions, scheduling work, and the range of actions that central staff, supervisors, and even the employees themselves used to do.

The new approaches pull control back to the center, away from employees and also from their supervisors. The tasks that supervisors need to perform now, such as assigning work, creating schedules, monitoring performance, and motivating employees, can now be done by algorithms. Is it cheaper? We do not know. We know almost nothing about how well these models actually work, perhaps because the vendors who create them find that unnecessary as a selling point.

Monitoring employees does not stop at the workplace. Seventy percent of employers screen the social media profiles of candidates before hiring them, 30 percent of companies have a staff role whose job it is to monitor social media, and half report that what they find is sufficient not to hire candidates they would otherwise have offered jobs. More surprisingly, almost half also say that they would not hire a candidate if they cannot find any online profile for that candidate, apparently because of the assumption that they were hiding their online behavior.[50] How much monitoring of social media goes on for current employees is difficult to say. David Egger's novel *The Circle* describes the intrusiveness of the "radical transparency" approach of trying to be open about everything work-related in a loosely camouflaged Silicon Valley company where the employer digs into their personal lives via social media to find out who is truly committed to the company.

Employers also try to shape social media, an effort that began in earnest with the understandable interest in what employees and others were saying about them on social media. It became common, and arguably necessary, for employers to monitor the comments about them on sites such as Glass Door, where potential recruits go to get the inside story from anonymous employees and former employees as to what jobs are like. Employers would counter assertions that were false, and some went further and encouraged employees to post positive comments.

This led to an embarrassing cat-and-mouse game at Amazon, which had created a group called Amazon Fulfillment Center Ambassadors (read: warehouse workers) to post positive comments about the company and their jobs. Among other things, the Ambassadors asserted that they were not compensated for their postings. The online investigative community Bellingcat.com, famous for identifying Russian online trolls and Putin critic Alexei Nalavny's poisoners, revealed the stage-managed nature of the postings of the Ambassadors, who it turns out among other things were compensated for posting comments. The company quietly abandoned the program.[51]

Are these developments—transferring tasks from supervisors to software, using monitoring technology to pull back the control that workers have over their jobs—undermining the relationship with employees? A set of employee surveys sponsored by the American Psychological Association asked about participation in decision-making and found the perceived lack of it increased sharply in the last few years, 48 percent reporting that it was a significant factor increasing their stress in 2021 as compared to 39 percent in 2019. They also reported a sharp increase in stress in their relationship with their supervisor, up from 35 percent to 44 percent over the same period.[52]

This kind of optimization could be described simply as short-sighted: we are trying to achieve efficiency by making optimal decisions, but by disempowering employees, we are actually creating more problems than we solve.

Part-Time Work

Another example of optimization thinking has to do with scheduling the work of the 21 percent of employees in part-time jobs with regular schedules (less than thirty-five hours per week).[53] It is the regular schedules of part-time work that differentiates them from on-call jobs where employees are only called in when there is work to do. After the Great Recession, employers started to wait until the last minute, when needs are clearer, to schedule part-time workers. This essentially turns them into on-call workers, or as they are described in the United Kingdom and elsewhere, working on a "zero-hour" contract:[54] they are only called to work when there is demand for them.

It may sound as though this is necessary to meet fluctuations in demand, but schedule requirements can be predicted quite accurately far in advance. Most of the short-term variation in demand in retail operations is highly predictable: evenings are busier than midday, Saturdays are busier than Mondays, some seasons and holidays are busier than others depending on the stores. Predicting sales for a given store, especially over short periods of time, is one of the simpler forecasting challenges. Even the most basic inventory software that any retail chain can access does well predicting virtually all the variance in demand within a few months.[55] I attended a meeting at the White House during the Obama administration about the topic of scheduling work shifts, and my sense from the discussion was that the vendors were convinced that scheduling to meet demand in advance was pretty easily done, and also that at least some large employers were not trying to do so. When there are unpredicted variations, it typically requires adjustments of only a few employees to meet the changes.

This practice of last-minute scheduling is not actually about efficiency. Julia Henly and Susan Lambert at the University of Chicago have conducted a series of studies of scheduling practices for part-time work, and the explanation began with the fact that the stores maintained a stable of part-time workers who virtually all wanted more hours than the store was giving them. In other words, they have created more part-time jobs offering fewer hours. Supervisors then assigned more hours to the better performing and more cooperative workers, rewarding them and essentially punishing those who were not by cutting their schedules.[56]

The question is whether it is so much worse for employees that it ends up hurting their performance and that of their organizations. The uncertainty of their schedules makes it impossible to hold another job, go to school, provide childcare, and carry out other tasks that require some predictability—all common reasons for working part-time in the first place. If they are unavailable when the supervisor schedules them, then their hours are cut further. An interesting experiment changed this approach and returned to more predictable schedules, engaging employees in the process along the lines of flextime. Doing so caused business performance to improve.[57] No doubt the contingent approach sounded smart, but giving employees more control and predictability is what paid off. A different study found that the general approach of imposing schedules from the top down inevitably needed adjusting, something like last-minute patches to deal with some uncertainties in demand and in workers such as illness.[58] A flexible system where employees are involved works much better for making those adjustments than does a top-down one.

The high level of quitting and employer complaints about a very tight labor market for frontline service workers as the economy recovered in 2021 and 2022 provided a useful test to see if real business needs lead to a change in practice. The complaints are that retail employers, in particular, cannot find enough workers to fill jobs and often lose business as a result. Estimates suggest that roughly 30 percent of all workers in retail are part-time,[59] although at the customer service level in stores it is common for it to be a majority. Data from employees in these jobs collected by the Shift Project at Harvard find it is still the case that roughly one-third to one-quarter of those workers want more hours than they can get.[60] If it is so difficult to find workers and retail employers already have ones willing to work more, why doesn't this happen? Why did they not give them more hours? It would seem to be the simplest and most efficient way to deal with the apparent staffing shortage.

It was not necessary to turn the part-time jobs into full-time jobs to expand hours and trigger requirements to pay employee benefits.[61] An explanation begins with Shift Project data showing that two-thirds of these part-time workers do not know their work schedule more than two weeks in advance, suggesting that employers were still using the uncertainty of short hours as a discipline tool even though it led to gaps in staffing. If this uncertainty is difficult for workers, and employers are desperate to attract new hires and keep the ones they have, why does this continue to happen?

Once again, the answer from employers was the need for flexibility. But that does not seem plausible, for the reasons noted above. The simpler explanation is that even in that extremely tight labor market, employers wanted to hold out work as a reward and discipline device.

A further problem with this suboptimal approach emerged in early 2022, when employees on shorter hours started quitting to move to other jobs that offered more hours. The irony of not having enough labor because employers will not give their current staff more hours has gotten worse. Interviews with employers and vendors who manage schedules for them suggests that the larger—and one would have thought more sophisticated—employers have not changed their practices. Rather than increasing hours for these workers, they seek to bring in new ones.[62] Local ordinances have pushed back on this practice with predictive schedule laws limiting the employer's right to make changes unilaterally and, among other things, requiring that current employees have the right of first refusal for additional hours before new hires are added.[63]

Optimization Undermines the Relationship with Employees

The practices outlined above have a collective effect that undermines the most basic aspects of how employees are managed. The explanation begins with studies first done in anthropology on the functions of gift-giving and the norm of reciprocity it generates. As opposed to the explicit trading of one thing for another—buying and selling—these are implicit exchanges often in the form of favors that creates obligations to reciprocate: a customer slips the maître d' in a restaurant a tip and later asks for a better table; welcome the new neighbors with a cake, and they feel obligated not to report your dog when it is off the leash. This social exchange has been at the heart of the modern employment relationship since the 1920s, when the welfare capitalism movement urged employers to be good to their employees so that the employees, in turn, would not support unions. The general idea was that taking care of your employees would make them feel like looking after your interests, which was especially important when you weren't watching them and when they had discretion over how to behave. In a more contemporary sense, if you feel an employer was not treating you fairly, it is easier to justify stealing from them or at least withholding your best ideas and not warning them of trouble you may see coming.

The idea of social exchange plays out in several contemporary psychological concepts, all of which have been documented to show how it helps employees drive better performance:

- **Perception of organizational support (POS):** The idea here is that when employees feel the organization both supports them and recognizes that they are contributing, they feel the need to reciprocate.[64]
- **Psychological contract:** The definition is the expectations the employee has of what the employer will do for them and what is expected of them in return. The central issue here is arguably what happens when those expectations are not met. More modest violations and more severe contract breaches lead to negative responses from employees, from withdrawal of discretionary effort all the way to sabotage.[65]
- **Leader-member exchange:** The notion here is that the more important relationship in organizations is an interpersonal one between supervisors and their subordinates and that the relationship is established over time, in part through an exchange of information and favors flowing from the supervisor to the subordinate. The better those relationships are, the better job performance will be.[66]

To what extent do business leaders think this way? The evidence from previous chapters suggests that they think quite differently, based at least in part on their backgrounds. At least for many and especially those in the finance and accounting area, business leaders tend to consider employment as a transaction that should be optimized with as few employees as possible, spending as little on them as possible; dealing with the issue of employee discretion by taking it away; and defining as clearly as can be what workers should do and how they should do it, and then measuring the outcomes to ensure compliance.

Generations of Wharton MBA students have learned about the downsides of this optimization approach in investment banking with a case about the "the bull pen," where junior analysts are held together, separate from management, and seen as a collective resource like the old-fashioned typing pool from scientific management days available on a just-in-time basis. The pool is kept small enough that everyone is always busy: when a new task comes in, it's given to the person who has just become available. Tasks come down to the manager of the bull pen, who passes them out, sometimes breaking them up so the workload is evened out. The manager may know who is good at what tasks and where possible matches them up. So far, so good.

The problems start because the junior analysts only work on a piece of a puzzle that came to them that day, and they have no idea what they are working on or why: What is this valuation for? Because it's the same thing over and over—doing what they know how to do already—they get bored. Given that their only connection to the work is the intermediary of the bull pen manager, they get no feedback as to what happened with the piece of work they did, unless they made mistakes, and the person above them typically fixes them and moves on. Turnover is high, there are a lot of mistakes in work quality, and morale is low. Yet on paper, this approach optimizes the use of associates.

A common response to this situation, especially from former investment bankers, was simply, "So what?" We just have to live with those problems. But of course that is only true if you don't think that quality and turnover problems are costs as well, that optimizing or minimizing the number of associates is not the only goal, and that turnover and work quality could be improved with simple interventions, mainly about how workers are supervised: put the associates in touch with the directors who have assigned the work so that they can learn what it is about; give them bigger, longer tasks to work on and let them see what happens with the project afterward; and vary their tasks.

The irony of this case is that it is about a bank fifty years ago, but most of the current MBA students who come from banking say it could be the bank they just left.

The Postpandemic Response

A revealing moment in employee relations came with the COVID-19 shutdowns, when by some measures up to 70 percent of office workers were sent home to work. Many and arguably most employers had resisted pressures to allow employees to expand working from home before, but now they had no choice. At first virtually all employers trusted them, perhaps because they had no choice. The consensus was that the performance of those workers was good, much better than most any business leaders expected. The limited evidence we have suggested that employee levels of commitment and engagement improved during the pandemic. Although it is difficult to know with any certainty, at least part of the explanation is the sense from employees that they were all "in it together" with their leaders and that they felt trusted by their organizations, particularly to use their time wisely to get the work done.[67]

Then things shifted. Drew Harwell of the *Washington Post* reports a sharp rise in the use of tattleware software that watches everything that employees working at home do via their computer use. One vendor quoted in Harwell's article said its clients feel "completely entitled to know what employees are doing" at home. Amazon AWS was an early entrant into the pandemic monitoring arena, offering employers a tool to monitor compliance with mask mandates using existing security and desktop cameras.[68] Konrad Putzier and Chip Cutter of the *Wall Street Journal* report that the use of employee monitoring software like this doubled during the pandemic.[69] A 2021 survey during the pandemic finds 69 percent of HR managers saying that their organization has or is installing productivity monitoring software on devices employees use remotely.[70]

The irony of the push toward monitoring at-home workers is that it is difficult not to think of it as motivated by the assumption, rooted in ideology, that they will goof off if we don't watch them closely—despite recent evidence to the contrary.

In 2021, Amazon's new CEO Andy Jassy took over that company with something of a mandate to pay more attention to the health of employees, give them more opportunities to grow, and so forth. The question is how that could be done without changing in a fundamental way the management-by-algorithm and monitoring approach. It would be an extremely difficult needle to thread. Some believe the way around that will be to automate those predictable jobs where algorithms rule, in the process getting rid of those employees, so that the more Theory Y approaches can be applied to office workers whose jobs are at least not yet manageable by algorithm.[71] The lessons of lean production should be recalled here, of course, where hourly employees managed in an empowered manner beat the robots handily.

The consequences of disempowering employees extend well beyond reducing their productivity and even making their jobs less psychologically meaningful, however. Adina Schwartz kicked off a discussion in philosophy in 1982 that continues today about the appropriateness of allowing work that denies employees autonomy over what employees do and how they do it if societies want to be considered just.[72] One of the attributes of just societies, she argues, is that the individuals in them should have control over their lives in important ways; in other words, they should have as much autonomy as possible, and autonomy should be a goal. The more that work denies them autonomy—control over what they do and how they do it, especially when that denial is not justified on reasonable criteria—the more difficult it is to see the management of employees by that practice as acceptable.

How work actually gets done takes us perhaps the deepest into the nitty-gritty details of management. Here we see the century-old fight between two quite different ways of managing, each centered in two quite different assumptions about human nature. There is no doubt that Theory Y is a much more accurate view of how employees think and behave, and there is also no doubt that it is more complicated and harder to understand. Theory X rests on the same set of assumptions as engineering and traditional economics and finance that most executives already know. As those ideas rose in importance, so did the Theory X approach, even though it is worse in terms of outcomes for the performance of organizations. To be fair, it takes reasonably sophisticated thinkers and operators to move back and forth between the two, but that is what operating the most effective organizations requires.

6

The Impact on Employees

It is not surprising that the push to minimize employment costs has not been good for employees. It is perhaps more surprising to see the various ways in which that push plays out—shifting work to nonemployees, using optimization approaches to simplify and monitor jobs, and so forth—and how it created unforeseen problems for management and the organization.

Many people now describe the period after World War II at least until the mid-1970s as a relative golden age for employees. Jobs were secure and wage growth was strong, especially in the 1960s, and workers had power through unions but also through tight labor markets. It might be accurate to describe the period since then as almost the reverse: the entry of the huge and more educated baby boom cohort into the labor market, dramatically weakened unions, and a political context more sympathetic to employers. This shift made it easy to hire, easy to shift the consequences of restructuring onto employees with layoffs and other cuts, possible to have employees pay for acquiring their own skills, and simply to push employees to do more without pay going up.

Wages illustrate this trend well. They are only one part of the relationship with employees, but they are probably the most important part: few of us would work if we were not getting paid to do it. There are many different ways to look at wages, but the overall story and the attention-getting one is what has happened to hourly paid wages discounting for inflation (see Figure 6.1).

Just before the pandemic, average real wage earnings adjusted for inflation had just gotten back to the level of the late 1960s. If we look at real wage growth from 1979, close to the nadir of postwar wages, to 2019, just before the pandemic, they rose on average by 8.8 percent. It is quite a different story for managers and executives. Wages rose by 41 percent for those in the top ninetieth percentile,[1] which is part of the well-known story of growing income inequality.

One politically sensitive way to think about the experience of employees is whether they are now likely to earn more than their parents. As we can see in Figure 6.2, the answer is decidedly no. Some of the decline in that ability

Average hourly wages in the United States, seasonally adjusted

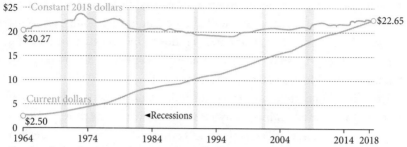

Note: Date of wages of production and non-supervisory employees on private non-farm payrolls. "Constant 2018 dollars" describes wages adjusted for inflation. "Current dollars" describes wages reported in the value of the currency when received. "Purchasing power" refers to the amount of goods of services that can be bought per unit of currency.

Figure 6.1 Americans' Paychecks Are Bigger than Forty Years Ago, but Their Purchasing Power Has Hardly Budged

Source: PEW Research

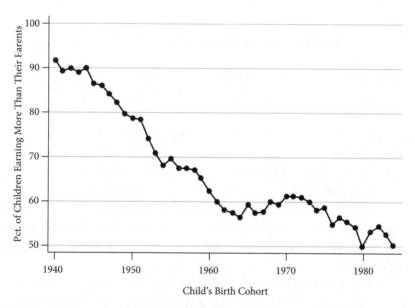

Figure 6.2 The Decline in Upward Mobility

Source: Raj Chetty, David Grusky, Maximilian Hell, Nathaniel Hendren, Robert Manduca, and Jimmy Narang, "The Fading American Dream: Trends in Absolute Income Mobility since 1950," *Science* 356, no. 6336 (2017): 398–406

is reflected in the fact that many parents of older baby boomers suffered through the Great Depression where they earned little, so it was easier for their children to beat that. Some of the decline in the ability of younger cohorts to earn more than their parents is due to the fact that the parent cohort in the 1960s did so well: real income for men grew by almost 60 percent in that decade. But other factors are afoot as well.

There is a huge literature trying to understand these trends. Arguably, more of it is focused on inequality rather than the decline of real wages for lower-paid workers. Until recently almost none of it considered the decisions of individual employers and the choices they make, pushed along by financial accounting's priorities and optimization norms, to squeeze all employment costs.[2] There are also a few studies looking at other manifestations of power, such as the ability to bargain with employers over pay as explanations.[3] The practices examined in this chapter have more straightforward relationships with the squeeze on pay and get much less attention.

Compensation: How We Are Paid (or Not)

For our purposes, executive pay is especially important as it shapes the behavior of executives and, in turn, how they manage everyone else. As noted by Robert Baylis, former chairman of Credit Suisse First Boston, "There is nothing as riveting in corporate life as a meeting of the compensation committee." The huge increase in the pay for executives in recent decades is well-known. What is less well-known is that executives are managed as if they were contractors. That, in turn, affects how they run their organizations. We use psychological mechanisms like employee commitment and engagement to get employees to act in the interests of the employer, but when it comes to executives, we rely almost completely on rewards and contracts to address that problem.

When professional managers began to take over from owners in running the new corporations in the 1920s, the power they had to manage them in their own interests as opposed to those of the owners became a new and important problem, at least for the owners. The total pay of executives in the early years actually fell in real terms during World War II, then rose modestly through the 1970s. The structure of pay changed after the introduction of restricted stock options and bonuses following the 1950 Revenue Act, with slow increases in the use of equity-based compensation until the mid-1990s.

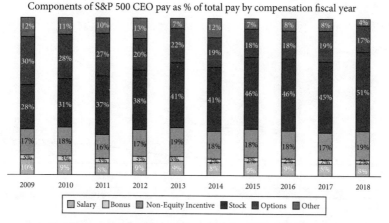

Figure 6.3 Stock Comprises the Majority of CEO Pay in 2018 Fiscal Year

Source: John Roe and Kosmas Papadopoulos, "2019 US Executive Compensation Trends," Harvard Law School Forum on Corporate Governance, 2019

Arguably the important change in the way executives are paid began in 1993 with section 162(m) of the Internal Revenue Code, which was designed to restrict excessive executive pay by preventing companies from deducting salary costs greater than $1 million paid to the company's top five executives. (That amount sounds quaint today.) An exemption was for performance-based pay based on objective performance outcomes, which had a formula-like aspect to them. The effect of the change was to shift pay toward stock-based compensation, where it rose with share prices, and away from salary and bonuses, over which the board would have more discretion and control.[4]

Stock-based pay was roughly 20 percent of total compensation by 1990, then almost half by 2000, reflecting the rise of stock prices. Long-term bonuses rose from 1 percent of total compensation in the 1940s to 5 percent in 1960 and then 25 percent in 2003.[5] Since then, it has continued to rocket up, growing five times faster than the increase for the median worker over the 2010s. Salary is now only a trivial component of CEO pay, down to roughly 4 percent, as shown in Figure 6.3. The gap between their pay and that of median workers, as seen in Figure 6.4, has grown enormously.

The pay increases for CFOs—the best-paid functional role—are not far behind, as about half their pay comes from long-term incentives of various kinds.[6]

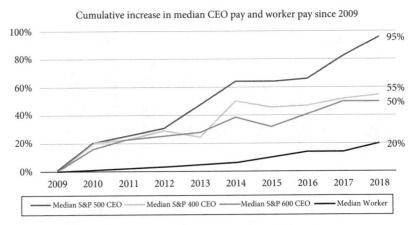

Figure 6.4 CEO Pay Increases at a Faster Pace than Worker Pay

Source: John Roe and Kosmas Papadopoulos, "2019 US Executive Compensation Trends," Harvard Law School Forum on Corporate Governance, 2019

The financial accounting hook is that stock-based pay does not raise the amount of compensation in a company's financial accounting. This is also true for stock options. Their current value in accounting is booked as business expenses rather than employee compensation. For example, stock or options issued to scientists would be recorded as business expenses for research and development.[7]

One can see more generally why stock options are so attractive from the perspective of financial accounting because their value comes from stock appreciation—in other words, from the stock market itself, when buyers are willing to pay more for the shares than when the employee got them. It does not come from operating expenses and therefore the gain does not show up as part of compensation costs. It is essentially free from the perspective of financial accounting. Employers could rightly argue that stock options and broad-based stock ownership plans (for nonexecutives) make it possible to set wages that show up in financial accounts lower.

Because the big rewards for executives—and they are big—come from formula-based pay tied to stock appreciation, CEOs focus on that along with the attributes from financial accounting that are seen as driving investor perceptions of a stock's value. Chapter 1 outlined the many and often quirky management practices that make financial accounts look better.

As described in Chapter 2, executives including CEOs are now largely governed by contracts, and that includes their pay. Eighty-three percent of large companies set executive pay based on formulas that outline in advance how much they get paid for what outcomes.[8] Compared to earlier periods, the board of directors may be more involved than in the past, but they have less discretion in managing CEOs because so much is now specified in the text of these contracts. It is not surprising that they might want their own employees to be paid in the same way.

What has gotten much less attention is the great difficulty all this creates for leaders in defining a purpose for the organization and for the employees in it. Trying to rally the troops around a mission of making money for face-less shareholders, many of whom we might imagine are quite wealthy given the distribution of ownership, is extremely difficult. When I have seen them try—the shareholders have given us their money, we have to make more money for them—it falls flat with employees. It is probably not surprising that employees express a desire for social purpose when employers articulate that the purpose of the organization is to make money for other people. Further, trying to make a pitch that we in the company are all in this together becomes impossible when the rewards for the leaders are so much more generous than for everyone else.

Paying Regular Employees

Before the 1980s, and still included in most business textbooks used today, is the notion that compensation was a practice designed to knit the organization together and keep people for the long term.[9] The fundamental principle guiding the design of pay systems was fairness in the form of providing a common criterion for pay in every job, and in turn every employee within that job, paying attention to the comparisons that employees are likely to make. That common criterion was the value a job contributed to the organization, a process known as job evaluation.

To make that happen required that pay be based largely on the job one held, and pay grades or bands were designed to make sure things worked that way. Getting more pay typically required getting a promotion, something that became more difficult when organizations flattened starting in the 1990s.

Pay structures adjusted first with "broadbanding," which simply extended the range of pay within grades. Along with broadbanding came an increase in complaints about fairness and inconsistencies as many more jobs were lumped in together.[10] Jobs at the top of pay grade 4, for example, might pay more than those at the bottom of the higher pay grade 5. Efforts to address those concerns gradually evaporated.

Worry about compensation equity meant having on occasion to pay more for some jobs than the market rate. When outside hiring moved from the exception to the rule, the end was near for traditional compensation systems and their concern with internal equity. By 2003, a survey by WorldatWork, the rebranded successor to the American Compensation Association, found that only 2 percent of companies relied on their job evaluations to set base pay for jobs, 21 percent relied on market pricing or benchmarking the market for all jobs, and 38 percent used job evaluations only to modify the market pricing.[11]

Companies like salary.com and payscale.com bypassed the traditional process of surveying employers to learn about the market pay to going directly to employees with a brilliant and tempting proposition: tell us what you are paid now—information that builds our database—and we will tell you what the market price is for jobs like yours in companies like yours, even in communities like yours. Their databases now have information on tens of millions of individuals and the pay of their job that is updated constantly. Armed with that information, employees are initiating discussions with their current bosses and with potential employers about why they should be paid more than they are. That information leads to negotiations, which are another area where pay practices are now quite different.

Moving to negotiated pay does not make employees better off, of course. That depends on their skill at negotiating, their opportunities elsewhere, and their information. Employers do far more negotiating over pay than does any individual employee, and employers have embraced negotiating, as well as individualized pay, in an effort to pay as little as necessary for each employee. Employers typically initiate salary discussions with job candidates now by asking employees what they were paid before, which tends to anchor the negotiations at a lower rate than otherwise: all they need to do is beat that figure, and the deal is often done.

Fifty-two percent of employers report that their initial offers in salaries are lower than the standard salary they plan to pay, providing room to negotiate up if necessary. But the hope is that candidates will not try or be unable to negotiate them up, so that the employer can price-discriminate against those employees who are willing to work for less. In fact, most employees do not try to negotiate.[12] Employers are then price discriminating: some employees get paid more to do the same job than others based on how well they negotiate. The employer saves money, as compared to paying everyone what they think the market rate is.[13] The downside is that they end up with inequities in pay: identical people paid different amounts for identical work, which generates problems in the workplace. Signing bonuses are one way to pay differently without obviously altering base pay. The "doing good while doing well" programs to help employees pay off their student loans was also a way to pay new hires in the tight labor market more without rubbing it in the noses of existing employees.

An extreme version of this approach was related to me by a colleague whose business used a trucking company that had been struggling to keep up with demand because of a shortfall in drivers. What they suggested was that my colleague's company hire drivers themselves, pay higher wages to get them, and then let the trucking company use those drivers for my colleague's routes. This is much like the travel nurses example from Chapter 4.

Examples of this kind of price discrimination in paying employees became more obvious during the pandemic, when the need for some workers surged even as it collapsed for others. During the holiday season in 2020, for example, Amazon offered hiring bonuses of up to $3,000 to new warehouse workers while giving current employees coupons and vouchers worth about $20, depending on the warehouse.[14] Whether this was a reasonable or necessary practice is certainly up for debate, but it illustrates the market decline in the interest of fairness norms in the form of comparisons in setting compensation. The travel nurse example in Chapter 4 shows not only an extreme version of inequity in pay for the same job, but also how such arrangements can unravel what remains of the employment relationship. These practices reflect a simple-minded view of optimization that ignores the likely effects that follow from creating those inequities.

One place where fairness questions still rule in compensation, however, is with top executives. A survey of company directors finds 77 percent saying that they wanted to pay their CEO more than they did, and of those, 42 percent reported that the CEO was less motivated as a result, apparently because they did not perceive their pay as fair.[15]

Another erosion in pay practices stems from the fact that larger firms traditionally paid more. Because they were more profitable, the argument went, they could afford to pay more to hire better quality workers, and more broadly to "share the rent" they were making in the labor market to ensure greater loyalty and commitment, another aspect of the social exchange approach.[16] In recent years that practice reversed as the large-company wage premium disappeared—another example of cutting wage costs at the expense of other outcomes.[17]

Merit Pay and Performance Appraisals

The notion of paying employees doing the same job differently based on their performance came quite late to the party, given how common the practice is now. The first systematic assessments of individual employee performance were derived from the military in World War I where the purpose was to assess the capabilities of soldiers, not their performance per se, to determine where they should be assigned. After the war, US companies adopted the military practice.[18] Corporations used them to figure out who should be promoted and what they needed to do next to get there. In a famous 1957 *Harvard Business Review* article, Douglas McGregor argued for engaging subordinates in setting performance goals and having them assess themselves, a process that would engage them in learning and improvement. He assumed that employees wanted to perform well and would do so if supported properly. He noted one drawback: doing it right required more time from management.[19]

The use of appraising job performance to set pay did not really arrive until the 1970s when oil price shocks sent inflation rocketing, up to 10 percent or more per year. In that context where the budgeted increases to offset inflation might be 10 percent, it was possible to differentiate increases in a huge way: giving one employee zero meant another could get a 20 percent increase, and that was enough to get anyone's attention. With anti-discrimination laws now on the books, there was also pressure to award pay increases more objectively. By the 1980s, supervisors were expected to assess subordinates on competencies, behaviors, and their overall performance against their goals agreed on in advance. This would be three assessments on three very different criteria for each employee in addition to an overall assessment of their performance. At the same time, restructuring meant that spans of control—the number of direct reports per supervisor—were increasing. The new ideal was fifteen to twenty-five direct reports (up from six before the 1960s).[20] In addition to the appraisals being much more involved than before, the number that supervisors had to do could easily double. There was just not enough time to do it, especially when the supervisors were no longer held accountable for doing so.

The solution was to do them badly. A review of the state of practice at the end of the 1980s described the performance management process as notable for the absence of any assessment as to whether it was working or, indeed, what it was doing.[21] A Towers Watson survey found 45 percent of managers saying they did not see value in their appraisal systems; a Deloitte survey reported 58 percent of human resource managers saying they were not an effective use of the HR manager's time.

In a moment we might think of as the business equivalent of a revolution in the mid-2010s, company after company dropped their formal performance appraisal system and moved toward something that looked like continuous conversations between supervisor and subordinate, addressing problems in the moment. These included the biggest names in business: GE, IBM, Deloitte, PwC, P&G, and financial companies like ING.[22]

There is no doubt that serious conversations in real time are far more important for improving performance than an annual wrap-up. In companies that eliminated that end-of-the-year exercise, there was almost always rejoicing. Although many employers gave up that annual performance appraisal—by some estimates a third or more in the United States—a survey found that employees actually got less feedback when their employers dropped the annual review, apparently because they did nothing new in response.[23] The experience of Deloitte is revealing. They went from a traditional approach to a very public move to continuous conversations, and then back to the use of a short version of the old model, with a score and a traditional form, conducted four times a year. The explanation for the rollback is that partners were comfortable with numbers, and as a partnership, the firm yielded to the partners. What is not said in many organizations is that supervisors simply found it difficult to talk to employees about their performance, and the organizations did not expend the resources to change that. Pushback also came from the executive ranks, where many still thought the purpose of the appraisal process was to hold people accountable. What we appear to have now in most organizations is another stripped-down practice: dropping the goal setting and the competency and behaviors assessments, and sometimes even the annual review, but replacing it with nothing. Even though the practice of continuous discussion is widely recognized as better, it takes resources to make that change, and few organizations want to do that.

Performance-Based Pay

Aside from the dominant position that the market plays in setting corporate pay, the other new development is performance-based pay, a more up-front version of incentives than merit pay. One type is a "share-the-wealth" idea, usually based on company or organization-wide performance. Employee ownership, including stock options and employee stock ownership where shares are accrued (ESOP), may be the most commonly used. Part of the idea here is to make regular employees think and act like shareholders. Almost a quarter of employees in companies that issue stock receive at least some in one form or another.[24] There is little evidence that stock options improve the performance of employees. Especially in larger companies, most employees have no ability to influence share prices. It is also the case that unless employees have the ability to make changes in how work is done, they have little ability to improve performance. Leaders believe it works because they believe so strongly in the basic idea of incentives. My colleague Martin Conyon and I found that holding more options did not cause employees to perform better.[25] But oddly enough, when share prices did rise and employees exercised those options, their job performance did go up afterward, in the manner of a social exchange: I got a benefit from the company, and now I feel the need to reciprocate.

As with executive compensation, what stock appreciation plans do for regular employees is take a significant amount of pay off the financial accounts and allow employers to appear to pay less by cutting the amount of employee compensation.

An aspect of compensation that has moved us further in the contract mode is the use of bonuses to reward specific behavior: do this, get that. (See Figure 6.5 for the trend.) The intellectual justification for bonuses, as with

Please select the bonus program(s) that your organization currently uses.

	2001	2005	2008	2010	2014	2016	2021
N =	133	477	240	1,023	713	673	957
Sign-on	62%	54%	58%	54%	74%	76%	79%
Referral	70%	56%	66%	60%	63%	65%	75%
Spot	53%	47%	49%	43%	60%	61%	61%
Retention	34%	26%	30%	25%	51%	55%	57%
We do not use any of these bonus programs	New option in 2010			15%	9%	10%	7%

Figure 6.5 Use of Incentive Pay Over Time

Source: 2021 Bonus Programs and Practices Survey, WorldatWork

stock-based compensation, also rests on the idea of incentives: perform certain tasks or achieve goals we want, and we will reward you for that. But it is not clear that these bonuses do much to improve performance. Gallup data find, for example, that only 21 percent of employees strongly agree that their pay and incentive programs motivate them. Perhaps that is because only 20 percent also believe that the means used to assess them are within their control.[26] Although they do not move pay out of the employment column in financial accounting the way stock-based pay does, they do have the advantage of making it less fixed and more variable, especially if it goes down when the business is down, something that investors like.

As the use of performance-based pay increased we began to learn more about its drawbacks, or at least see more persuasive examples of them in research. Some of the problems are well known, and often described as agency problems or incomplete contracts. If you reward me for one thing—say, finding new clients—I ignore other things that might be important, such as maintaining existing clients. If you pay me for something that I already thought was the right thing to do, I change my opinion of it—it becomes something I am doing for money—and I may actually do less of it. For example, I may have spent time helping out our new hires because I remember what it was like to feel lost when I arrived, and I feel good doing so. But if the employer gives me a $50 bonus for showing new hires around, I may well decide that it's now just another part of the job and something I don't have to do if I don't want to.

The most prominent of the many recent examples of performance-based pay gone awry is the Wells Fargo incentives for branch employees to get customers to open more accounts. The pressure on those frontline employees to meet those targets led them to open 2.6 million new accounts for existing customers, without the customers' permission. When these practices were uncovered, Wells Fargo went from one of the most admired US companies, with Banker of the Year awards for their leaders in part for their cross-selling success, to a pariah institution that paid $3 billion to settle criminal charges while its CEO and other top executives resigned.[27] One estimate put the cost of the scandal to shareholders just in 2017 at $100 billion.[28]

To make the obvious point, there is no way that the benefits of the aggressive performance targets for employees would offset those costs. Law professor Laura Stout provides an encyclopedic overview of the growing use of incentives as the means to motivate employees to the detriment of overall behavior. She reports strong evidence that financial incentives crowd out unselfish, helping behaviors, and that high-powered incentives contribute to misconduct and even criminality in order to get those rewards.[29]

Pandemic-Related Pay as an Illustration

One could argue that the 2020–2021 pandemic that sent, by one measure, 70 percent of all those whose jobs could be done remotely to work from home was the greatest workplace experiment of modern times. It is still not clear what we should have learned from it, but it did advance at least two CFO-led conversations about compensation and how to cut it.

The first is a continuation of efforts to cut the costs of employment by shrinking office space. Getting people to work remotely and do so on a permanent basis allows the employer to cut back on offices and their real estate expenses. It is no surprise that the companies pushing or allowing this are all in locations where office real estate is extremely expensive, mainly tech companies in Silicon Valley. In the first month of the pandemic, March 2020, 74 percent of CFOs surveyed said that they expected an increase in permanent work from home to cut office space and costs.[30] By the summer of 2020, a majority of CFOs reported that their company was already planning to make remote work permanent after required work from home ended.[31]

The second approach, which is much more controversial, is to actually cut the pay of employees who want to work remotely. One argument by the companies asking for cuts in pay is that employees will no doubt be moving to places that are cheaper to live, so it is fair to pay them less. The Silicon Valley company Stripe is the most up-front and transparent about their policy. They offer to give employees $20,000 to move from its offices in New York City, Seattle, and Silicon Valley to a cheaper location, with a corresponding cut to their salary of 20 percent.[32] The tell here is that it does not matter where one moves, even if it is to a location that is more expensive. There is no reason why it should it matter to employers what the cost of living is where you live if it is your choice rather than the company's. If an employee decides to live further away to get a cheaper house and endure the commute, why would we cut their pay?

The other justification put forward by these companies is that pay should be based on the labor market, working on the assumption that every other place will pay less than they do. Most companies with policies like this are more indirect. Facebook told employees that if they relocate to a new location, their pay will be cut to the level of pay at those locations.[33] Google's policy applies even to employees who do not move but commute some distance. If they work from home remotely, their pay will be cut to the wage level Google says prevails in the location where they live. The company's "work location tool" will tell employees what they will be paid based on where they decide to work.[34]

No doubt these companies are not paying their executives less when they are commuting in from their second homes in resort locations, nor do they pay consultants less based on where the consultant's house is located. There is no labor market or normative justification for these policies. As with price discrimination in starting salaries, it is simply an opportunity to extract a price for something that employees might be willing to pay to get.

At the same time, some employers who have pay differences based on geographic locations are rethinking that practice, which were based in part on the fact that some lower-level jobs do have different market wages by location and for managers when the company required them to relocate. Forty-four percent of employers who use the practice consider dropping it if employees can choose where they work.[35] Some smaller IT companies are moving in this direction as a competitive advantage. The online real estate company Zillow, for example, has made clear that it will not adjust pay to location for remote workers in part because it gives them a recruiting advantage against the Silicon Valley competitors who are doing so.[36]

Finally, there is another work-from-home issue where employees and employers see eye to eye on what they want but are 180 degrees apart on what it implies for pay. A fascinating survey that compared employer and employee responses found that both groups felt the model of paying people based on time spent working did not make sense. But employees thought that when there was nothing to do or if they got their work done early, they should be able to do other things—thus the appeal of remote work. The employers, by contrast, felt that when there was nothing to do, we should not have to pay the employees.[37] This is the idea of a liquid workforce—no prizes for guessing which view is more likely to prevail.

Careers and Advancement

One of the key issues in management, perhaps the most important issue, is how the employer gets employees to act in their interests. In an earlier period of corporate history, the answer was closely tied to relationships: we take care of you, the employees, and so you take care of us—the notion of social exchange and reciprocity. A big part of that quid pro quo was possibilities for advancement, which were nonexistent elsewhere because competitors also promoted from within. Restrictions on preexisting conditions in healthcare locked employees in because any conditions they had that required care would not be covered if they moved to a new employer and insurance policy. Pensions with vesting requirements kept them in place as well.

Once companies began to restructure with layoffs and then filling vacancies from outside, opportunities for advancement declined. As we have noted throughout, paternalistic practices that took care of employees over the long term gave way to the short-term cost minimization focus. How do we keep employees in place?

Restrictive Covenants

The biggest development in this area has been the rise of restrictive covenants, legal contracts that employees are required to sign if they want to take a job and that restrict their ability to leave. The most straightforward of these are noncompete agreements that limit where employees can work if they decide to leave. Noncompete agreements rule out precisely those direct competitors most interested in hiring you because they need very similar skills and experience. The US evidence suggested that one in four workers have signed noncompete agreements at some point in their career, a figure that has risen sharply from 12 percent in the early 2010s to 22 percent by the end of the decade.[38] This includes almost 40 percent of franchise employees—typically in fast food—who are affected by noncompetes. Alan Krueger and Orley Ashenfelter found that 58 percent of fast-food franchise agreements prohibit the franchisee from hiring employees away from other franchises in the same chain where they might be most useful. Noncompete agreements are also used in states where they are not enforceable, as they are seen as intimidating employees into not leaving.[39] Their use remains essentially unchanged at the state level even after legal changes render them unenforceable.[40]

Because noncompete agreements lower the demand for workers, they lower their market wage as well. Simply working in a state where such agreements are legal leads to a 10 percent lower salary for the average fifty-year-old employee.[41] When Oregon banned noncompete agreements, the estimate is that it raised the wages of workers that had been bound by them by 14 percent or more.[42] A similar ban in Hawaii increased the mobility of tech workers across employers by 11 percent.[43]

Nondisclosure agreements are another type of restrictive covenant that limit the spread of employer trade secrets more directly, but they also keep employees from moving. A recent survey finds 48 percent of employees covered by them (another 9 percent thought they were covered), while a whopping 71 percent of firms reported that their employees were covered by them (and another 17 percent reporting that some of their employees were covered).[44] The bite with nondisclosure agreements is the inevitable disclosure doctrine, which asserts that it is almost impossible for an employee to not transfer some proprietary knowledge when they are doing similar work elsewhere because it is embedded in how they perform their tasks and what they know. Therefore, to protect that original intellectual property, employees should not be allowed to work anywhere that such information could be harmful to the original employer. They also keep employees from quitting. These restrictions reduce the spread of knowledge and innovation across competitive markets, and removing them is associated with a greater spread of knowledge.[45]

Nondisclosure agreements also prevent employees from revealing information about their employer that are not trade secrets. A novel study using changes in state laws that loosened nondisclosure requirements found that doing so led to state-wide increases in critical comments about employers on the Glassdoor website, supporting the idea that these requirements restrict criticism of employers, even when given anonymously.[46]

The final category of restrictive covenants is nonsolicitation agreements. The original idea behind these was to prevent employees who leave from taking clients or customers of their employer with them. They have been extended to prevent employees who leave from recruiting their former colleagues to leave with them. A national survey found that 18 percent of individuals were covered by them (another 8 percent thought they probably were), while 33 percent of employers reported that their employees were covered by them (a further 24 percent said that some of their employees were).[47]

There is a trade-off between the career interests of employees and the employer's interest in keeping their knowledge from getting to competitors. The rise and expansion of these practices indicate which interest has been winning that trade-off. All told, 62 percent of US employees are covered by some combination of restrictive covenants, and they collectively have a greater effect on suppressing wages than when used individually.[48]

A justification for these requirements is that employees do not have to sign them if they do not want to; they could work elsewhere. The response is that these practices have expanded so quickly and they are now so ubiquitous that employees have little choice but to work someplace that has them. It is not surprising that the use of restrictive covenants exploded right after the Great Recession, when the slack job market gave employees few options but to sign them.

Training and Development

We often hear that training is the key to career advancement and higher pay. Employers do not want trained employees to leave and take those investments with them, and restrictive covenants are one way to keep them. Are they actually making those investments, especially as restrictive covenants have increased?

The data we have on training are extremely limited and imperfect. Even defining what constitutes training is difficult. Although different surveys report a very wide range of estimates as to how many employees receive any formal training in a given year—from about 14 percent to 90 percent—a reasonable estimate might be half.[49] Put differently, about half of employees say they get no training in a year. For those who do receive training it is difficult to measure how much they get, but it appears to have declined. Typical estimates are a day or two of training per year, and if we say that half of employees get that, then a good guess is that the average employee gets roughly a day of training in total over the course of a year.

Perhaps the more interesting question is the extent to which that number is going up or down over time. Here the evidence is even more limited, because few surveys are available that ask the question over time. One that does shows that the incidence of training declined substantially—down by 28 percent—between 2001 and the spring of 2009, just before the Great Recession.[50] There is no credible argument to suggest that it increased after that cost-cutting period.

Is one or two days of training a lot or a little? There are many surveys of job seekers and employees reporting that they want more training. One of the most interesting is a PwC survey of roughly ten thousand respondents, which found that about a third of employees would take a pay cut of about 12 percent to get more training. They also said that opportunities to upskill themselves were the most important factor next to compensation in deciding whether to accept a job.[51]

Employers seem to understand the shortfall in training. For example, a Conference Board survey of employers and their experience with hiring school leavers found that these new hires had substantial gaps in their abilities, especially in areas like critical thinking. But the employers reported that they were not providing training to address them.[52] A survey of employers conducted by Deloitte found 74 percent saying that their current workforce would need new skills within the year, but only 10 percent were ready to help them do so.[53] When we look around the globe, CEOs from North America, primarily the United States, are the least likely of those in any region to see training as a response to skill needs. Hiring is their preferred response.[54]

It is certainly true that legal restrictions on dismissals and layoffs in many countries make employees more of a fixed cost, and that may both require and make it easier to train employees. But the United States seems to be the outlier even among countries where this is not the case. Compare the IT industry in India, where job hopping is at least as big an issue. Virtually all the big IT companies in India have extensive training for new hires: onsite, full-time training that goes on for weeks, often at dedicated training facilities. They create IT workers from recent college graduates who graduated with degrees in other fields. Nothing like this exists among the major IT companies in the United States, which rely on colleges to supply graduates with IT degrees or immigration.

An exception in the United States that proves the rule is the recent experience at IBM of creating an apprenticeship program to convert experienced workers from other backgrounds into IT workers. The program requires that candidates first complete a pre-apprenticeship program of 160 hours or so of instruction on their own time. It has rightly been seen as a progressive and innovative program unique among its competitors, and it gets a lot of attention. There are about 300 of these apprentices, however, and IBM employs about 300,000 people, roughly a third of them now in the United States. Infosys in India, with roughly the same number of employees, has a dedicated residential training center that takes in 13,500 new employee trainees at a time, typically with few IT skills, for six weeks or more of paid training.[55]

Why aren't we training? US employers often say that if they train, employees will simply leave and take the training with them. But the widespread use of restrictive covenants is typically attributed to the need to train, although of course they lower wages as well. In fact, there are many ways for employers to recoup training costs, basically by finding clever ways for employees to pay for it. The best known might be apprenticeships, where the apprentices earn less while being trained but also contribute as they learn. Accounting firms and consulting firms use modern versions of this approach by taking fresh college grads and putting them to work under the supervision of slightly more experienced employees—learning by doing. Sending employees to college is another cheap option, because the employees are doing all the learning on their own time. These programs attract better-quality employees and keep them longer.[56] Another option is explicit contracts, where employees have to pay back training costs if they leave. These appear to be used widely, and the payback costs are a factor restraining mobility.[57]

Once again, it is difficult not to believe that the better explanation as to why employers are not training is that training adds to employment costs, which we are trying to whittle down. Because training is treated as discretionary spending, it is easy to cut, such as whenever it appears that companies are not going to hit their forecast numbers in a given quarter.

Rotational Assignments and Relocations

A related aspect of development that had been seen as fundamental to management careers and that appears to have taken a hit is assignments requiring relocation within the company. In large corporations, it was common for management employees to be relocated every three years or so for new roles, typically development assignments where one was rotated on a planned basis into other functional areas to get to understand them. Picking up and moving was a requirement, paid for by the employer.

In the 1950s and early 1960s, just under 20 percent of the US population moved each year. In the most recent data, however, only about 8 percent move each year.[58] How much of that decline was because employer relocations fell is hard to say, but about two-thirds of employers now report using alternative approaches, such as shorter assignments or commuting, to achieve the same end as the rotational assignments. Employers with more than 5,000 employees in the long-running Atlas Movers Relocation survey now relocate just 2 percent of their workforce each year.[59] To put that in some perspective, about 36 percent of employees leave their employer in typical years, most often for other jobs.[60] Even the few employees who have the opportunity to relocate don't always say yes; about a quarter said no in 2018.[61] A common explanation for not moving is that employees cannot trust that there will be a next step, and they don't want to relocate themselves and their families and then find themselves out of a job.

Internal Advancement

The points above raise the question as to whether there is much promotion from within by contemporary organizations. The answer appears to be no. Only 28 percent of talent acquisition leaders in companies today report that internal candidates are an important source to fill their vacancies. Whether that is because their organizations do not develop their employees or because the employees were not capable of being developed in the first place is not clear, but either way it is a remarkable finding. A survey of employers in 2020 found that the workplace priority with the biggest reduction in importance since 2017 was developing internal talent, just as the labor market was getting very tight on the hiring front.[62]

As noted earlier, US corporate employers fill only about 30 percent of their vacancies from within, which means that they are looking outside and hiring to fill 70 percent, a remarkable turnaround from the days when virtually all advancement was from within. A Pew Foundation survey in 2022 found that the top reason employees quit (as opposed to threatening to quit), tied with pay, is that they saw no opportunities to advance their careers where they were.[63]

In addition to the time and effort of hiring from outside to fill positions, which is typically all that gets counted in turnover costs, my colleague Matthew Bidwell found that outside hires take three years to perform as well as internal candidates in the same job, while internal hires take seven years to earn as much money as those outside hires are paid.[64] As he points out, we pay more and get less by going outside. Outside hiring also drives turnover, because current employees see the lack of internal advancement as a reason to leave. In a different study looking at career moves within organizations and across them, Bidwell and my colleague Ethan Mollick find that one could get as big a pay increase just by moving to do the same job elsewhere as by taking on a promotion in one's current employer.[65]

Why don't we promote from within more often? It would seem to come back again to employment costs, and some planning costs that employers have been trying to drive down. Subordinates do not learn how to do their bosses' jobs simply by doing their own job well, although when we do promote from within we often do that: promote the best subordinate as assessed by their own individual contributions. An interesting study looked to see what happens when we do, and it turns out that we get worse supervisors whose teams perform badly.[66] Being an excellent individual contributor does not make one a good supervisor, just as being a good player does not make one a good coach. The skill sets are quite different.

An important and novel response to job hopping in the 1990s was the development of bidding and posting systems—what are now called internal recruitment—where employees decide themselves to apply for different jobs in their current company. These internal job boards were a smart way to deal with the problem that it was often easier to get a new job with another employer than to get a different job with your current employer—even if it was not a promotion—because so many approvals were required for the latter. An important attribute of the internal job boards was that they prevented one's own manager from knowing that you were trying to move in the company for fear they would try to block it, and then you would leave the company altogether.

Those programs appeared to be quite effective at stemming turnover. Dow Chemical, for example, reported that its annual turnover fell by half when it put in place a global bidding and posting system. For companies that no longer have planned internal development programs, they at least offer candidates the opportunity to see what jobs are available and have a chance to apply. Virtually all large companies put these programs in place.

JR Keller at Cornell University examined the effectiveness of bidding and posting programs in a context where hiring managers had the choice of filling a vacancy with someone they already had in mind for the position versus throwing it open so that anyone could apply. When the manager went with their hand-picked candidate, they got someone whose performance turned out to be worse and less diverse than when they were able to pick from the broader pool of applicants.[67] An additional conclusion here is that enterprises don't really know the talent and capabilities they have inside their own organizations.

Where has this sensible bidding and posting process gone? Backward. Only 40 percent of large employers now have a formal process in place for filling vacancies internally. An astonishing one in four employers say that they do not do internal recruiting at all. Fifty-one percent reported that internal candidates had no advantage over external candidates in filling an opening.[68] A different survey found that only 30 percent of employers report that they have internal candidates for half or more of their open positions.[69] Most discouraging, almost 60 percent of employers now require that one's current manager must give permission for you to even apply for positions elsewhere in the company,[70] up from about 10 percent twenty years ago. A local manager responsible for their own unit's performance has no interest in having a good employee leave to go elsewhere. It is the same for them if that employee leaves your operation for another unit in the company or leaves the company altogether. Commenting on this requirement to get permission from one's manager first, an observer noted how the likelihood of irritating one's manager by doing so essentially shuts down internal mobility: "It's effectively career suicide; for most logical people, the risk/reward ratio of this deceptively simple step in 3 out of 5 internal recruiting processes just isn't worth it."[71]

Why have we seen the rollback in this otherwise very sensible policy? It ran counter to the short-term interests of the individual units with profit and loss responsibility and the problem raised by vacancy chains: when an opening in one unit is filled by a candidate from a second unit, it creates a vacancy there, and so forth. Why should a vacancy in your department cause a headache in mine and cost me money to fix it? Therefore, the pushback to prevent my employees from leaving to fix your problem. For the company as a whole, internal mobility through these processes has huge advantages, but from the perspective of individual units, it is a bother. In other words, this is another example of suboptimization: making individual units focus on holding their own costs down causes them to keep promising employees from transferring inside the company, which ultimately causes them to leave altogether. The rollback seems to have started in the slack labor markets after the Great Recession, when the company-wide concern about quitting to leave for other employers was minimized.

The problem of managing individual units as if they were their own little company with their own profit and loss has obvious advantages in keeping costs down, but it also comes with obvious drawbacks when the goal is to help the company succeed overall. My colleagues working in divisions describe a process that most of us find familiar. The goal is to always meet but not greatly exceed the expectations for performance from headquarters for fear that exceeding them will make the targets go up next time, and it will get increasingly difficult to keep hitting them. Further, the costs of missing targets are vastly worse than the benefits of exceeding them, because falling short may cause the overall company to miss its overall financial targets for industry analysts. Division heads deal with these perverse incentives first by trying to pad their budgets, knowing that headquarters will squeeze them down, especially for headcount. Clever managers can allocate the budget for headcount in areas that are safer from cutting, in some cases research and development, where tax breaks might be bigger. They also know to hold back some achievements, what are sometimes called "cookie jar reserves," in case next quarter's performance is weaker, and to prevent exceeding target by too much.[72]

Are We at Least Developing Top Leaders?

The management task with perhaps the biggest disconnect between rhetoric and reality is succession planning. One can think of succession planning as workforce planning brought down to the individual level: Who will fill which job when it becomes vacant?

Trying to anticipate what a job will require years into the future and who will fill it can obviously be a fool's errand, and few companies bother doing so, even at the CEO level. A survey from the University of South Carolina found that 44 percent of companies had no successor to the CEO at present, and 51 percent said it would take six months to get an internal successor (see Figure 6.6).[73] More important is that they are not developing people who could become leaders: 51 percent of public companies report that they have no pipeline or regular flow of candidates who could be CEO. In private companies, that figure is 70 percent (see Figure 6.7)—when the owner is the CEO, they may have little interest in identifying who could replace them, and there is no board pressure to make that happen.[74]

One new development—especially in Europe but also now in the United States—is interim CEOs and other executives, where typically someone internal holds the job while a thorough search goes on, and also true temporary executives who step in with a contract to take over an executive role, including the CEO job, and then exit the company altogether.[75] In other words, the liquid workforce has come to the executive suite.

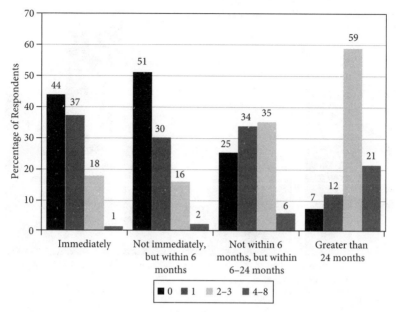

Figure 6.6 Number of Internal Successor Candidates and Their Timeframe Readiness

Source: Patrick M. Wright, Anthony J. Nyberg, Donald J. Schepker, Ormonde R. Cragun, and Michael D. Ulrich, "Current Practices in CEO Succession," Center for Executive Succession, Darla Moore School of Business, University of South Carolina, 2016

The conclusion about investments in employees is that we are not making many of them. This is consistent with the general squeeze on employment costs, and the complaint that "we will just lose them if we train them" seems inconsistent with the widespread use of restrictive covenants and other means of retaining training investments, such as contracts and the rolling back of internal job boards that reduced quitting. The immediate consequence means more outside hiring of candidates who are not as prepared as those developed internally, which in turn drives more turnover, and overall inefficiency.

Retirement Plans

Roughly 71 percent of US employees still have access to some retirement plan provided by their employer. Those plans virtually all require contributions

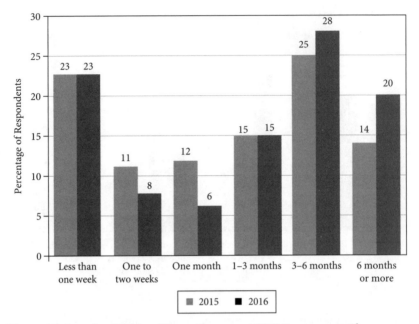

Figure 6.7 Length of Time to Have a Permanent CEO Successor in Place

Source: Patrick M. Wright, Anthony J. Nyberg, Donald J. Schepker, Ormonde R. Cragun, and Michael D. Ulrich, "Current Practices in CEO Succession." Center for Executive Succession, Darla Moore School of Business, University of South Carolina, 2016

from the employee, which helps explain why only 78 percent of employees participate in them: we are unlikely to participate in them if we think we are moving on. Together, that means that about 55 percent of employees are covered by these plans.[76]

Employer support for employee retirement began as pension plans, which guaranteed retired employees so much per month. The logic behind these defined benefit plans was clear. For individuals, it made planning for retirement easier because you knew what you would be receiving each month. It was also cheaper for the employer, because of their greater ability to manage risk than their individual employees. Think of them as insurance: individuals are risk-averse and therefore willing to pay a price to get certainty, or put differently, are happier with a smaller, predictable income than they would be with a greater, uncertain income. That is why people pay considerable amounts of money to swap their retirement investments for annuities that guarantee a fixed rate of return.

Once again, we see something changing sharply in the 1980s: the now well-known and dramatic shift away from these defined benefit plans (Figure 6.8). The number of people covered by defined benefit plans has not declined as much as the number of plans, because so many smaller plans have ended, but the percentage of employees covered by them still fell sharply, from 38 to 20 percent from 1980 to 2008, then further to 12 percent in 2018.[77] The drop is even larger than these data suggest, because many of the pension plans are now "frozen" in that no new employees can participate in them. They will eventually disappear.

Given the clear evidence that companies are much better at managing financial risk than employees, why did they move retirement programs from pensions and defined benefit arrangements where benefits were constant to defined contributions where benefits varied with the stock market? There are many explanations offered. Pensions are administratively complex to run, for example, and especially difficult for small employers because that burden is similar no matter how many employees one has. The Revenue Act of 1978 created the 401(k) defined contribution plan. We can see this in the sharp expansion of defined contribution plans before 1980. As employees began to move more often from employer to employer, the vesting requirements of

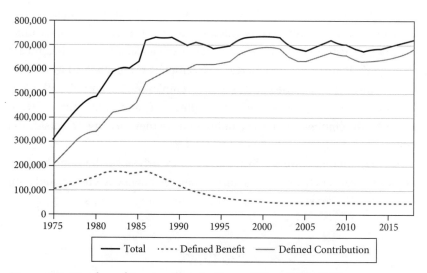

Figure 6.8 Number of Pension Plans by Type of Plan, 1975–2018
Source: US Department of Labor

pensions became burdensome, although the rout of pensions was well underway by then.

The common view that pension plans actually cost employers more money and that it was cheaper to operate defined benefit plans does not seem to hold up. A series of studies from the National Institute on Retirement Security found that pension plans actually have a considerable cost advantage over 401(k) and defined contribution plans.[78] The booming stock market the United States has experienced in the last few decades also means that employers would have had that benefit if they operated pension plans.

Nevertheless, it is hard to escape the obvious downsides of pensions from the perspective of financial accounting: they represent very large liabilities on the company's books. As the importance of financial accounting grew in the 1980s, the downsides of pensions increased. Pressure from more aggressive shareholders with a shorter-term orientation also played a role. The presence of shareholders taking a longer-term perspective, by contrast, was associated with retaining defined benefit plans with their more relational approach to employees.[79]

The Boundary between Work and Life Weakens

Employer practices and the efforts to cut employment costs no longer stop at the workplace, however. That is especially true in the United States. Unlike all other industrialized countries, most US employees get their healthcare through their employer, and increasingly, employers are involved in shaping the health-related lifestyle choices of their employees. Also unlike all major industrial countries, US sick leave, vacation time, and even hours of work are set by the employer, as is the amount of work they do at home outside the workplace.

The developments we see in these areas are driven by the same policies as those in earlier chapters: the effort to squeeze down costs associated with employees. We consider some of the more surprising practices below.

Healthcare

Healthcare and the insurance supporting it are extremely expensive endeavors in the United States, which have grown more expensive over time.

The quality of care and the conditions we can treat have increased, which those cured of something see as worthwhile. It is a real burden for employers who pay for most of it, especially compared to foreign competitors. US businesses must build employee health insurance costs in their prices. Their competitors in every other industrialized country where healthcare is provided by the government do not. The United States spends just under 17 percent of its gross domestic product on healthcare, and the country in second place, Germany, spends about 12 percent.[80] It is completely understandable that employers should be trying to slow these costs down.

Just under 160 million people are covered by employer plans, including employee family members, and the average employer contribution is around $15,000 per year.[81] The cost of employer healthcare has outpaced wage growth and inflation for decades, and the employee contribution of those costs has risen faster than the employer share, suggesting the employer interest in cutting their side of the costs.[82] The percentage of Americans who received their healthcare through an employer—theirs or a family member's—declined over the last twenty years from 67 percent in 1998 to 58 percent in 2018,[83] which is especially surprising given that the Affordable Care Act ("Obamacare") starting in 2010 considerably increased the requirements on employers to provide healthcare to its employees. Yet coverage still declined.

One of the stranger developments in employer-provided healthcare was the rapid rise and then rapid fall of HMOs. They were driven by the novel idea that they would have a financial incentive to keep the costs of healthcare down by being responsible for it now and in the future. To do so, they would head off problems using preventative care and then avoid more expensive treatments in the future.

It was an appealing proposition, and legislation allowing for this novel arrangement was introduced in 1973. It took some time for them to get started—in 1983 they covered only 3 percent of individuals with health insurance—but by 2000, they were up to one-third of employees covered by their employer's health insurance plans. That percentage fell to 16 percent by 2021.[84] HMOs had many challenges, some of them technical, such as anticipating what their costs would be now and in the future. One challenge, however, relates directly to employer practices. The main benefit of HMOs for employers was considerably lower healthcare costs in the future, because more preventative care early on cuts those costs. But if you do not retain your employees, that benefit evaporates. From the perspective of the HMO, the financial benefits of keeping patients healthy also disappears if those patients do not stay with you.

Employers began to focus on the initial premium costs of insuring their employees and shopping around to get the lowest cost, changing providers in the process. HMOs responded by cutting back on the care they offered, especially preventative care,[85] thereby undermining the model that made HMOs so appealing.

Arguably the more significant recent development has been the rapid rise of employee wellness programs designed to get employees to adopt healthier life practices. For those who like them, these programs pursue the interest of employees and of employers in having healthier employees. If you don't like these programs, they represent a hard push by employers into the private lives of employees. Either way, they represent a big change.

It is hard to be sure when these programs first started. Paternalistic employers in the 1920s had a lot of ideas about having healthier employees and had no qualms about pushing them hard. Henry Ford, for example, prohibited employees who were drinkers from receiving his famous $5-per-day wage and sent monitors into their homes to check. The Kellogg's cereal company began as a sanitarium and pushed on employees numerous ideas about healthy living and eating.

Active efforts to shape the health of employees largely disappeared after World War II until around 1970, when Johnson & Johnson CEO James Burke articulated what was then the novel goal of having a healthy workforce, in part to cut healthcare costs. By the 1980s, there was evidence that healthier employees were more productive, or at least that sicker ones were less so, and by that time rising healthcare costs were hard to miss. At the end of that decade, 80 percent of corporations had some health awareness program for their employees. These programs basically explained how to be healthier, if you were so inclined to use them. Following that, we saw the rise of exercise facilities and health centers at places of work and programs like smoking cessation and other help to support those who wanted it.

The push from voluntary to more compulsory programs started in the 2000s, driven by dramatically higher costs and the failure of other approaches to do much to slow them down. An estimate of employer healthcare expenses suggested that they were rising by almost 12 percent per year in 2007, vastly outrunning general inflation and wage increases.[86] Another factor was the growing awareness that those costs were driven by chronic illnesses rooted in lifestyle choices. Smoking, obesity, lack of exercise, and failure to keep up with medicine drove chronic diseases like diabetes and hypertension, which accounted for the largest share of healthcare expenses.

The shift from offering help to making employees take it was subtle but inexorable. I recall hosting a meeting of human resource executives and wellness experts where there were assurances on all sides that incentives to participate would never turn into penalties. But that happened quite quickly. The prizes for participating soon transitioned to discounts on the employee's health insurance premiums. There are good reasons for making that link, because it makes the tie to wellness and health costs more salient for employees, but it didn't take long for employee advocates to recognize that those "incentives" were equally penalties: your charges are higher if you don't comply. The Affordable Care Act supported the use of wellness programs by employers, and while the EEOC issued a ruling limiting the size of the incentives (or penalties) to 30 percent of an employee's insurance contributions, that limit was overturned by the courts.[87]

Overall, half of US employers now have something that looks like a wellness program, and the percentage of employers with truly comprehensive wellness programs doubled between 2004 and 2017.[88] Sixty percent of all large firms offer health risk assessments, which require gathering information on one's health history, current situation, and lifestyle choices—such as whether you smoke, and so on. Fifty percent of those use biometric screening, which means measures of one's body, typically body mass index, blood pressure, cholesterol levels, and so on. Sixty-five percent who have such screening also use financial incentives to encourage employees to participate, and 18 percent have rewards and penalties for improving one's biometric outcomes.[89] A majority of employers that offered any incentives tie them to reduced health insurance premiums, as we see in Figure 6.9.[90]

Eleven percent of the broader group of employers that offer healthcare benefits now collect data on employees through mobile devices such as Fitbits, a number that has increased quite rapidly.[91]

The push into the private lives of employees through wellness programs represents a big change from previous approaches. Is it reasonable for your employer to penalize you for lifestyle decisions you are making outside of work or for attributes that in part you might be born with? On the one hand, employers are paying the price for those decisions, so why shouldn't we share the cost of them? But not all health outcomes are completely within our control, such as our blood pressure, cholesterol levels, or weight. Some people

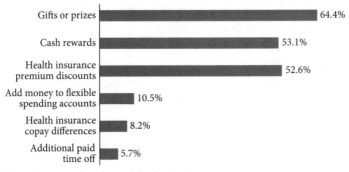

Note: Percentages based on weighted estimates.

Figure 6.9 Types of Incentives Offered by US Workplaces
Source: Centers for Disease Control and Prevention

need much more aggressive treatment to hit targets on those outcomes than others, and even then, they may be hard to achieve.

These are tricky ethical questions, but here is the most important fact about these wellness programs: they don't seem to work. Despite the enormous difficulty in the world of research in getting reports of no effect published, there is a stunning list of carefully designed, randomized trial studies showing that wellness programs have no measurable effect on employee health outcomes.[92] There is some modest evidence that incentives can encourage employees to participate in the programs—but they are not producing better health outcomes for the employees.

To be clear how these programs and the incentives work, say you are a smoker. Your insurance costs go up. Say your body mass index is high. Your insurance costs go up. Ditto for high cholesterol levels. Those costs go down if your BMI and cholesterol scores decline or if you stop smoking.

My colleague Iwan Barankay, who has done many of these studies on incentives, explained these otherwise puzzling results in a conversation with me in January 2022 as follows. The incentives to stop smoking or get your blood pressure under control are already about as big as we can imagine, because they reduce your risk of dying. If that doesn't change your behavior, why should a few dollars more in pretax income? The use of programs like gym memberships go mainly to people who would have used the gym anyway.

These studies are not a secret, so why are wellness programs expanding? One reason seems to be the power of optimization thinking: incentives are the right thing to do, so if they aren't working, we just need to push incentives harder. As it stands, we have increasingly intrusive programs that have broken through the traditional boundary between work and our private lives in a serious way. They aren't working as intended, yet they continue to be advanced. It is a triumph of hope—in this case, theory—over experience.

A fundamental challenge to employers taking an overweening interest in the health of their employees is the strong evidence that management practices, especially those that increase stress and working time for exempt employees, adversely affect employee health.[93] Employer wellness programs could push to change the practices that cause stress or help employees learn to live with it through stress management programs, but so far, there is little progress in that direction.

The most obvious intrusion into life outside work are employer drug tests. Employee drug testing is a relatively recent phenomenon, pushed forward initially by the federal government as part of a general war-on-drugs effort: President Reagan's executive order in 1986 mandating drug testing of federal employees, followed by the 1988 Drug Free Workplace Act for federal contractors. These were mainly punitive programs to catch and discipline—principally dismiss—drug users. From there, drug testing shifted from a posthire exercise focused on catching impaired employees who posed safety risks to a pre-employment screen of applicants that checks for use of drugs rather than impairment. Drug testing has been pushed along by an industry of vendors and organizations that advocate its use, like the Drug and Alcohol Industry Testing Association.

As noted in Chapter 2, these are used more in hiring job candidates than are any tests of skill, knowledge, or abilities. For those who have not experienced them, these are not tests of impairment, as we might see with blood alcohol tests for drivers where there is reason to believe someone might be drunk. Instead, they check for the use of drugs no matter when they were taken, even if the amounts present in our body are below levels that affect our work. Some of these tests are mandated by law (for truck drivers, for example), but most are not.

The more troubling tests are those that continue after people are employed and hired. They are not limited to situations where there is evidence about impairment. Random drug tests and comprehensive tests (e.g., as part of annual physicals) are common. By the mid-2010s, 71 percent of employers reported that they screened current employees for drug use.[94] Of particular interest is testing for marijuana, which continues despite the fact that it is now legal for recreational use in fifteen states and for medical use in seven-teen more. According to a least one 2021 survey, only 5 percent of employers had dropped or considered dropping marijuana testing even after these changes in state laws.[95]

As work-from-home arrangements proliferate, many employers have ar-ranged for drug tests at home.[96] One wonders why employers are concerned about monitoring drug use by office workers who are doing their jobs from home. These are not wellness-related tests. With few exceptions, the goal of drug tests is deterrence associated with punishment if one is caught, rather than rehabilitation. Drug use remains a federal crime (even medical marijuana allowed under state laws), but few employers spend time trying to ascertain other illegal behavior outside of working hours. We don't spend anywhere as much effort checking on other illegal practices employees might commit outside of work. Nor do we do random alcohol tests to assess impairment at work—which makes one wonder why so much effort is spent to catch drug use.

Time Off from Work

It is not a surprise to discover that US employees work longer and get less time off than their peers in other countries.[97] Some of this is simply because the United States is the only industrial country that has no requirements for employees to have paid leave. We only have national holidays (see Figure 6.10).

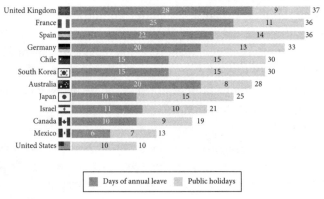

Figure 6.10 Statutory Minimum Paid Leave and Public Holidays in 2016 (Selected Countries)

Source: Statista

Some employers offer no paid time off—mainly small ones with hourly employees who turn over frequently—and many offer no vacation time in the first year of work. Seventy-nine percent of private sector employers have some kind of paid vacation leave, and 75 percent of all employees have some kind of paid sick leave.[98] The average employee who receives vacation time gets ten days in their first year but only twenty after their twentieth year, which puts them below the mandatory minimum for entry-level workers in the European Union.

An important difference with respect to paid leave in the United States returns us to the topic of financial accounting. Because paid leave is a business expense, it has to be captured somewhere in our accounting system. It is—as a liability. Traditionally, and still the case in most organizations, employees accrue or earn vacation and other paid leave through working time and length of service: so many quarters of work equal so many sick days and vacation days that employees have a right to use. As long as employees can roll over unused vacation or cash it out if they leave, the cost of those days count as financial liabilities that have to be offset by assets. Financial Accounting Standards Board procedures require that companies account for all existing obligations to employees in the form of paid time off as liabilities that count against assets.[99]

A surprising finding is that US employees tend not to take vacation time even when we have it. The US Travel Association, another business group with an interest in employer practices, has been tracking time off and how it is used for decades. They report that US employees fail to use 27 percent of all the paid time off (the combination of vacation, sick leave, and personal days) to which they are entitled. Interestingly, higher-paid employees tend to use a greater percentage of their earned paid time off, using all but 14 percent.[100] Presumably the informal pressure from supervisors to not take it is less of an issue with them.

The trend in Figure 6.11 shows that the decline in days actually used has grown since 2000. The uptick after 2014 has been offset by sharp declines during the pandemic. A Glassdoor survey reported that 54 percent felt guilty about taking vacation time, and 19 percent reported pressure from their managers not to take it. Even when they do take it, about half of respondents say they check in with their office while away.[101] During the COVID-19 pandemic when many office employees were working from home, the use of sick leave fell dramatically. Perhaps people were simply less sick this year, in part because the quarantine cut down on colds and flu, or because slightly

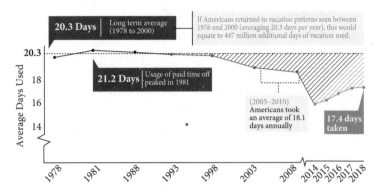

Figure 6.11 America's Vacation Trend
Source: US Travel Association

sick people could still work from home. Anecdotal evidence indicates that vacations fell off as well, no doubt because there was no place to go.

What is new now are efforts to persuade employees to use their paid time off, to take sick days and vacation time. These involve incentive plans where employers actually give money to employees if they take time off, or sometimes actually mandate that employees must do so. One reason was due to the concern that too many employees would wait and take it at the same time, over the holidays.[102] Another reason is that the value of that accrued time off—the equivalent of the compensation per day times the number of paid days off for each employee—otherwise sits as a liability on the company's balance sheet, and grows where employees can carry it over. An investigation of the balance sheets of US companies concluded that these liabilities totaled more than $224 billion.[103] When employees take their paid time off, it discharges that obligation and reduces the liability on the employer's financial accounts.

The strange dilemma here is that the pressures on employees that lead them to skip time off, keep working, and hit higher performance goals are at the same time biting the employer financially because the more time off employees skip, the greater are the liabilities their company carries, and the less valuable the company becomes. We might imagine fights between line managers, who are pushing employees harder to hit performance targets, and CFOs, who complain that doing so actually hurts the company's financial viability. This also explains more easily the logic behind the move toward unlimited vacation days described in Chapter 1. Because it is unlimited, that time off is not accrued, and therefore vacation cost are no longer liabilities that count against assets in a company's financial accounts. With a stroke of the pen, the financial picture of the company improves dramatically.

To summarize, the pressures of financial accounting to squeeze compensation costs and benefits make life difficult for employees in ways beyond simply leaving vacancies open longer, which ups the workload; reducing training that could make the employee more valuable; and reducing the investments that could help their career advancement. Employers have intervened in new areas to keep the costs of remaining employees down with legal contracts that limit their ability to move and into their private lives with wellness programs and testing. Some of these, such as making pay more contractual, will likely change how employees behave, undermining their discretionary effort. Practices that seem to undermine existing rights, like privacy or the right to quit, may lead to resentment. Whether on balance these practices will help employers is an open question.

Final Thoughts

Many authors and perhaps most find that the book they end up writing is not the one they anticipated. What began here as an effort to describe how employers actually manage their employees ended up revealing some important patterns not just about the workplace, but about what drives business decisions.

An important conclusion is to reinforce the notion that ideas matter a lot, especially ideas about what we are supposed to be doing when running companies. The microeconomic assumption that entire generations in college were taught—that operating efficiency was not only the goal of firms but something that is required in competitive markets—is not close to being true. Setting aside the fact that determining what is efficient is a limitless and never-ending task (what is, e.g., the efficient amount to spend on being efficient?), an array of other factors disconnect any simple relationship between efficiency and profitability, which is the more accurate goal. Better marketing, deal-making, and financing can make inefficient organizations very valuable, and efficient organizations can be highly unprofitable because of those factors. There are many issues that business leaders have to manage, and the efficiency of their internal operations is only one. Yet the assumption that firms simply must be choosing the best management practices has prevented us from asking whether they are actually doing so and what might be preventing that.

A big reason why companies do not operate efficiently has to do with financial accounting, the necessary medium for translating operations into judgments about profitability. Profit turns out not to be a simple thing to measure, in contrast to our simple notions of firms. Just answering the different ways in which an expense can be treated makes for a long evening. Financial accounting's quirks in dealing with human capital create incentives to operate in ways that seem to objective outsiders strange, at best.

Then we come to the issue of what we mean by maximizing shareholder value, which has become the explicit goal of public companies. If maximizing current profits was the measure of a company's share price, then we cannot explain why companies like Tesla and Amazon, which went decades without making any profit, had such sky-high share prices.

A company's current profitability is in the rearview mirror of investors, whose buying and selling determine share prices. Their buying is based on expectations about the future. How companies manage their operations does matter there, and financial accounting determines what those investors see about internal operations. It also determines what are "good" expenses (buying capital, including buying back one's own shares) and "bad" expenses (employees).

One of the biggest ways in which financial accounting distorts decision-making has to do with how a company meets its forecasted financial performance as measured by financial accounting. Woe unto a management team that fails to do so. In order to meet quarterly forecasts and expectations about a company's financial performance, the companies manage their earnings, making short-term adjustments—typically cost cutting—to change their reported performance.[1] Despite the fact that accounting treats employment costs as fixed costs, layoffs are the instrument of choice for managing earnings because, despite that fixed-cost label, they can be done quickly and relatively easily. They also cut a good deal of expense and the "worst" expense—employment—from an accounting point of view. Yet nothing is more disruptive to the efficient operations of an organization than to cut a lot of workers on short notice, typically the most experienced ones, as they are the most expensive. Those negative effects are long-term, and they are clearly driven by these financial demands.

As this book was being written, we are watching the unwinding of the most important model for managing companies around the financial accounting outcomes most important to investors: the General Electric company, as put together by Jack Welch. Although it was arguably good at many things, its distinctive competency was clearly financial control systems, which is another way of saying that financial accounting ruled. In 2022, the complexity of the problems associated with running a company that way led to its splitting up into three separate businesses. The great exception in its approach was that GE was also famous for making long-term and extensive investments in employees. Now it is selling its famous Crotonville leadership center and dropping its internal financial management program for developing financial control leaders.[2] My bet is that the influence of those cuts and the continued decline of leadership development will have more influence than any rethinking about the management of companies around share-holder measures.

The second factor associated with the mismanagement of employees relates even more strongly to ideas, and that has to do with the return to optimization thinking associated with the different experiences of contemporary leaders, most prominently the decline in management training that had been associated with places like Crotonville. Some of this thinking is pushed along by the tremendously influential vendor industry, created when companies began to outsource so many HR tasks. Vendors rarely sell advice on how to manage employees better. They sell software and other optimization solutions that substitute for employees and management of them.

There is one more reason why we see less effort to invest in and manage employees carefully now. Managing employees well is a lot of work. Engaging employees in their efforts, making use of their insights, and managing organizational culture so that they feel willing to contribute requires the active and continuous efforts of the leadership team. They have to show up, interact with employees, and pay attention to shopfloor issues, including boring tasks like making sure performance appraisals are taken seriously. It is not the kind of work that easily suits introverted people and those whose expertise is rooted in technical areas. It is also not the kind of work that draws accolades from the business and investor community the way fancy financial deals or mergers and acquisitions with immediate outcomes do. Investing in and managing employees is very important, of course, and as we saw in the later chapters, it contributes not just to less efficient operations but to negative effects on employees, particularly unnecessary instability in jobs and careers and a lack of investment in training and skills.

A Way Forward

There are many other arguments about how business executives should manage differently, why they should have different priorities that pay less attention to shareholders, and so forth. I appreciate those arguments. The difference here is that these ideas already align with the way our economic and business systems work. They do not require adopting any different value systems, and so are the easiest to change.

Except for vendors pushing optimizing solutions, the status quo does not have a big fan club. If we take financial accounting, which is arguably the most important issue here, the most important constituency of the Securities and Exchange Commission and of the Financial Accounting Standards Board to which it delegates decision-making is investors. They do not like the current arrangements and have been pressing for change that allows them to have a better view as to what is going on inside the companies they own. It is a little surprising for many employee advocates that at least on this one issue, important investors are aligned with them. There has been some change in response to investor pressure, albeit so far symbolic, but it does suggest that movement is possible.

What would be the way forward to make the management of employees more sensible, employers more effective, and employee outcomes better? Here is where having such a clear and powerful set of institutions already in place is helpful, because seeing how they drive current behavior shows how they could change future behavior.

The simplest changes that are likely to have the biggest effects are modest additions in financial reporting requirements. There have been many recommendations here, but I think four reasonably objective measures, most of which are straightforward to collect and report, would go a long way to end the distorting effects we saw through the chapters.

The first two simply break out costs that are already reported in aggregate measures:

- How much are companies spending on labor other than their own employees? We have no sense of how efficient operations are when these other labor costs such as leased workers are hidden. The accounting advantages associated with shifting work from one's own employees to someone else's go away with this change.
- How much is spent on training and other employee development efforts? This task requires some accounting guidance as to what counts as an expense here (e.g., do we include the costs of the buildings used for training?), but it is no more difficult than what is required for other expenses.

The next two are simple to collect, and any sensible employer already using applicant tracking systems has them at their fingertips:

- What is the employee turnover rate, which measures the human capital going out the door? How much of that is due to quitting? That information, along with the total number of employees, which companies already report, will allow us to estimate the number of dismissals—an additional and even more important sign of management problems than quitting.

- What percentage of vacancies are filled from within? That reveals the extent to which a company is growing its own talent or having to buy it from outside.

These are modest changes to a very powerful set of practices that could improve effectiveness and outcomes on all sides.

Notes

Introduction

1. David Weil, *The Fissured Workplace: How Work Got So Bad for So Many and What Can be Done About It* (Cambridge, MA: Harvard University Press, 2017).
2. Louis R. Hyman, *Temp: How American Work, American Business, and the American Dream Became Temporary* (New York: Viking Books, 2018).
3. Ben Schneider, "People Management in Work Organizations: Fifty Years of Learning," *Organization Dynamics* 50, no. 4 (2020): 1–10.
4. Marshall Fisher, Santiago Gallino, and Serguei Netessine, "Setting Retail Staffing Levels: A Methodology Validated with Implementation," (Wharton Working Paper, August 1, 2018, http://dx.doi.org/10.2139/ssrn.2977812). It paid off to increase staffing levels.
5. I describe this in some detail in "Stop Overengineering People Management," *Harvard Business Review*, September–October 2020, 2–9.
6. For evidence, see Shigeru Fujita and Giuseppe Moscarini, "Recall and Unemployment," *American Economic Review* 107, no. 12 (2017): 3875–3916. For a general discussion of temporary layoffs, see Robert E. Hall and Marianna Kudlyak, "Unemployed with Jobs and without Jobs" (NBER Working Paper 27886, National Bureau of Economic Research, 2021).
7. "Employment Recovery in the Wake of the COVID-19 Pandemic," *Monthly Labor Review*, December 2020.
8. Peter Coy, "I Got to the Bottom of All Those Flight Cancellations," *New York Times*, December 30, 2021. It is certainly true that COVID surges contributed to flight cancellations, although the surges were not completely unpredictable, either.

Chapter 1

1. Self-reported data from the US Current Employee Survey shows a decline over the last twenty years to 6.3 percent of the US workforce. Administrative data, such as those filing IRS 1099 forms for nonemployee compensation, have risen over this period, to 11.3 percent in 2012, the most recent reported data, but a majority of those filings are for transient experiences, such as selling on eBay (see Katharine G. Abraham, John C. Haltiwanger, Kristin Sandusky, and James R. Spletzer, "Measuring the Gig Economy: Current Knowledge and Open Issues" [NBER Working Paper No. 24950,

National Bureau of Economic Research, 2018] for a summary). Outside the United States, the numbers are greater: more than 15 percent of workers are self-employed independent contractors in industrialized countries ("Self-Employment Rate," OECD Data, https://data.oecd.org/emp/self-employment-rate.htm).

2. Jonathan Shaw, "Who Built the Pyramids?," *Harvard Magazine*, July–August 2003.

3. For descriptions, see D. Q. Mills, *The IBM Lesson: The Profitable Art of Full Employment* (New York: Times Books, 1988).

4. This change is described in Peter Cappelli, *The New Deal at Work: Managing the Market-Driven Workforce* (Boston: Harvard Business School Press, 1999).

5. Sloan Wilson, *The Man in the Gray Flannel Suit* (New York: Simon & Schuster, 1955); Walter Kirn, *Up in the Air* (New York: Doubleday, 2001); Mike Freedman, *King of the Mississippi* (New York: Random House, 2019); Ed Park, *Personal Days* (New York: Random House, 2009); Joshua Ferris, *Then We Came to the End* (Boston: Little, Brown, 2007); Donald Westlake, *The Ax* (New York: Grand Central Publishing, 2001).

6. For examples and a rebuttal, see Ben Casselman, "Enough Already about the Job-Hopping Millennials," Fivethirtyeight.com, May 15, 2015, https://fivethirtyeight.com/features/enough-already-about-the-job-hopping-millennials/.

7. Among the many rigorous treatments of this topic are Gerald F. Davis, *Managed by the Markets: How Finance Re-Shaped America* (New York: Oxford University Press, 2009). A critique of the notion that shareholder value is somehow required is Lynn Stout, *The Shareholder Value Myth: How Putting Shareholders First Harms Investors, Corporations, and the Public* (New York: Random House, 2012). Critiques of US practice with respect to the role of finance include Mary O'Sullivan, *Contests for Corporate Control: Corporate Governance and Economic Performance in the United States and Germany* (Oxford: Oxford University Press, 2000).

8. The most famous and arguably influential of these statements was Michael C. Jensen and Kevin J. Murphy, "CEO Incentives: It's Not How Much You Pay but How," *Harvard Business Review* 68, no. 3 (1990): 138–149.

9. *Statement of Corporate Governance* (New York: The Business Roundtable, 1997).

10. For an account, see Owen Walker, *Barbarians in the Boardroom: Activist Investors and the Battle for Control of the World's Most Powerful Companies* (London: Pearson/FT Publishing, 2015).

11. See, e.g., Michael Useem, *Investor Capitalism: How Money Managers Are Changing the Face of Corporate America* (New York: Basic Books, 1996).

12. B. J. Bushee, "Do Institutional Investors Prefer Near-Term Earnings over Long-Run Value?," *Contemporary Accounting Research* 18, no. 2 (2001): 207–246.

13. "Business Roundtable Redefines the Purpose of a Corporation to Promote 'An Economy That Serves All Americans,'" Business Roundtable, August 19, 2019.

14. It would also be difficult to draw comparisons across companies from internal accounting data because companies can vary as to how they do it. Company leaders may well use information from their internal accounting to support their view of the company's future that it presents in analyst calls, "investor days," and in their "reason to believe" statements about the future.

15. See, for example, Caitlin Rosenthal, *Accounting for Slavery: Masters and Management* (Cambridge, MA: Harvard University Press, 2018).
16. Bureau of Labor Statistics, "Employee Tenure in 2020," News Release, September 22, 2020.
17. Kathy Adams McIntosh, "Accounting for Prepaid Maintenance Contracts," BizFluent, September 26, 2017, https://bizfluent.com/info-7737222-accounting-prepaid-main tenance-contracts.html.
18. The starting point appears to be Walter Y. Oi, "Labor as a Quasi-Fixed Factor," *Journal of Political Economy* 70, no. 6 (1962): 538–555.
19. Data on layoffs is presented every month in the Bureau of Labor Statistics' "Job Openings and Labor Turnover" website: www.bls.gov/jlt/.
20. To be precise, 3.8 years. See News Release Bureau of Labor Statistics, "Employee Tenure in 2018," US Department of Labor, September 20, 2018.
21. Who actually "pays" payroll taxes—are they offset by lower wages, for example—is an empirical question, but no sensible estimates suggest that they are zero for employers.
22. M. J. Bidwell, "Politics and Firm Boundaries: How Organizational Structure, Group Interests, and Resources Affect Outsourcing," *Organization Science* 23, no. 6 (2012): 1622–1642.
23. The 1980 estimate comes from Steve Langer, "Personnel/Industrial Relations Report: An Overview of Current Staffing and Budgeting Ratios," *Personnel Journal* (1980): 59: 95–98. It was based on a survey of 724 companies. There are several sources for contemporary staffing ratios. The *SHRM Customized Benchmarking Report* (Alexandria, VA: Society for Human Resource Management, 2017) reports a ratio of one HR employee to every 158 employees.
24. Peter J. Kuhn and Lizi Yu, "How Costly Is Turnover? Evidence from Retail?" (NBER Working Paper No. 26179, National Bureau of Economic Research, 2019).
25. S. Kesavan and C. M. Kuhnen, "Demand Fluctuations, Precarious Incomes, and Employee Turnover" (Working Paper, Kenan-Flagler Business School, Chapel Hill, NC, 2017).
26. Robert J. Gordon and Hassan Sayed, "A New Interpretation of Productivity Growth Dynamics in the Pre-Pandemic and Pandemic Era US Economy, 1950–2022" (NBER Working Paper 30267, National Bureau of Economic Research, 2022).
27. The annual contribution may be a current liability for that year, but unlike a pension, the 401(k) per se is not a continuing liability.
28. See, e.g., William B. Fornia and Dan Doonan, "A Better Bang for the Buck 3.0: Post-Retirement Experience Drives Pension Cost Advantage" (National Institute on Retirement Security, 2022).
29. The seminal work in this area is arguably Eric Flamholtz, *Human Resource Accounting* (Encino, CA: Dickenson Publishing, 1974). For an illustrative application of asset-based accounting incorporating human capital that was applied to European football, a situation where human capital is the real value of a team, see Steven Morrow, "Football Players as Human Assets. Measurement as the Critical Factor in Asset Recognition: A Case Study Investigation," *Journal of Human Resource Costing & Accounting* 1, no. 1 (1996): 75–97.

30. Ganesh M. Pandit, "First Look at the Human Capital Disclosures on Form 10-K: Analyzing the SEC Mandate and Comparing It to SASB and EU Standards," *The CPA Journal* August/September, 2021.

31. *SASB Human Capital Bulletin* (San Francisco: Sustainability Accounting Standards Board, November 2020).

32. Among them are the Workforce Disclosure Initiative of the Coalition for Inclusive Capitalism and the Sustainable Accounting Standards Board.

33. Elizabeth Howcroft and Simon Jessop, "Most Companies Silent as Pressure Mounts for Workforce Data," Reuters, March 30, 2021, https://www.reuters.com/article/uk-companies-workers-investors/most-companies-silent-as-pressure-mounts-for-workforce-data-idUSKBN2BM3DZ.

34. Matt Wirz and Paul Kiernan, "Investors Seek More Information about Companies' Struggles to Hire, Retain Staff," *Wall Street Journal*, February 17, 2022, https://www.wsj.com/articles/investors-seek-more-information-about-companies-struggles-to-hire-retain-staff-11645045610?mod=hp_featst_pos4.

35. Wirz, "Investors Seek More Information."

36. Accounting works the same way in private companies, but even less reporting is required. More of their funding may come from banks that may require much more information from companies than investors can get from public companies. They may require an audit of a company's operations, although typically just to test the accuracy of the company's financial reporting. Banks may also require covenants with the clients that stipulate dimensions on how the company will operate until the debt to the bank is repaid. Here again, the concerns rarely get into anything to do with employment other than headcount. When buying "errors and omissions" insurance, which protects companies from claims of poor work or negligent actions, the underwriters may well nose around to look at how work is performed, but their interest in employees and employment is secondary to concerns about overall business execution.

37. For a very detailed description of how different player transactions can be deal with under IFRS rules, see "Accounting for Typical Transactions in the Football Industry Issues and Solutions under IFRS," PWC.com, 2018, https://www.pwc.com/gx/en/audit-services/ifrs/publications/ifrs-9/accounting-for-typical-transactions-in-the-football-industry.pdf.

38. Optimal staffing models, sometimes also known as capacity management, have a long history in operations research using queuing theory and increasingly complex forms of mathematics. See, for example, S. David Wu, Murat Erkoc, and Suleyman Karabuk, "Managing Capacity in the High-Tech Industry: A Review of Literature," *The Engineering Economist* 50, no. 2 (2005): 125–158. In practice, though, most of the models in use appear to be simple linear abstractions.

39. "Twitter CFO Ned Segal on the Workforce of the Future," Bloomberg, December 1, 2020, video, https://www.bloomberg.com/news/videos/2020-12-02/twitter-cfo-ned-segal-on-the-workforce-of-the-future-video.

40. Kory Wagner, "The Importance of Workforce Planning," FEI Daily, June 11, 2020, https://www.financialexecutives.org/FEI-Daily/June-2020/The-Importance-of-Workforce-Planning.aspx.

41. See, e.g., Mahlon Apgar IV, "Uncovering Your Hidden Occupancy Costs," *Harvard Business Review*, May–June 1993.

42. June Langhoff, "Does Place Still Matter? The Role of the Workplace in a Distributed World," New Ways of Working Network summary, May 1, 2007, http://www.westernc ontract.com/wp-content/uploads/Does-Place-Still-Matter.pdf; Nikil Saval, *Cubed: A Secret History of the Workplace* (New York: Doubleday, 2014).

43. C. C. Sullivan, "Earn as You Churn: Minimizing Outlays for Corporate Layouts," *Buildings*, September 1, 1993, https://www.thefreelibrary.com/Earn as you churn: minimizing outlays for corporate layouts.-a014436365.

44. Heather Ogilvie, "This Old Office," *Journal of Business Strategy* 15, no. 5 (September/October 1994): 26–34..

45. Thomas Wailgum, "What Happened to That Whole Hoteling Concept?," *CIO Magazine*, February 15, 2007, https://www.cio.com/article/290580/what-happened-to-that-whole-hoteling-concept.html.

46. Kimberly D. Elsbach, "Relating Physical Environment to Self-Categorizations: Identity Threat and Affirmation in a Non-Territorial Office Space," *Administrative Science Quarterly* 48, no. 4 (2003): 622–654.

47. John Tierney, "From Cubicles, Cry for Quiet Pierces Office Buzz," *New York Times*, May 19, 2012.

48. Ethan Bernstein and Ben Weber, "The Truth about Open Offices," *Harvard Business Review*, November/December 2019.

49. David Brooks, "The Immortal Awfulness of Open Plan Workplaces," *New York Times*, September 8, 2022.

50. "Gartner CFO Survey Reveals 74% Intend to Shift Some Employees to Remote Work Permanently," Gartner Newsroom Press Release, April 3, 2020, https://www.gartner.com/en/newsroom/press-releases/2020-04-03-gartner-cfo-surey-reveals-74-perc ent-of-organizations-to-shift-some-employees-to-remote-work-permanently2

51. A review of the issues on postpandemic hybrid work is Peter Cappelli, *The Future of the Office* (Philadelphia: Wharton Press, 2021).

52. Katherine Bindley and Eliot Brown, "Silicon Valley Pay Cuts Ignite Tech Industry Covid-19 Tensions," *Wall Street Journal*, October 11, 2020.

53. These accounting problems are not new, and fifty years ago they were prominent enough to generate a subfield of inquiry called "human resource accounting." Unfortunately, the goal was not to change accounting practices but to create alternative or we might say parallel sets of internal accounting within human resources. These efforts have almost completely disappeared.

54. "About the PEO Industry," NAPEO, https://www.napeo.org/what-is-a-peo/about-the-peo-industry/industry-statistics#:~:text=PEOs%20provide%20services%20 to%20175%2C000,is%20estimated%20at%20%24270%20billion (accessed January 29, 2023).

55. The best of these studies is arguably A. Edmans, "Does the Stock Market Fully Value Intangibles? Employee Satisfaction and Equity Prices," *Journal of Financial Economics* 101 (2011): 621–640, which finds that companies making the "best places to work" ranking have higher than anticipated share prices in future years. In other words, not only do those companies perform better but they do so in ways that investors don't

get, so one could beat the market simply by betting on them. A different study finds the same market-beating performance for companies that have greater managerial integrity and ethics: Luigi Guiso, Paola Sapienza, and Luigi Zingales, "The Value of Corporate Culture," *Journal of Financial Economics* 117 (2015): 60–76. In a global study, companies that have better management, including more sophisticated human resource practices, perform better on a wide range of dimensions. Nicholas Bloom and John Van Reenen, "Why Do Management Practices Differ across Firms and Countries?," *Journal of Economic Perspectives* 24, no. 1 (2010): 203–224.

Chapter 2

1. Harry Rubey, "The Engineer Becomes a Professional Manager," *Journal of Engineering Education* 43 (January 1953): 338–341.
2. Edwin C. Nevis, "The Personal Side of Engineering," *Machine Design*, July 25, 1957, 103–104.
3. "How to Become a CEO: What Makes a Great Chief Executive?," Robert Half, September 18, 2019, https://www.roberthalf.com.au/blog/jobseekers/how-become-ceo-what-makes-great-chief-executive.
4. Gary Burnison, "CFO to CEO: The Right-Brain Leadership Gap," Korn Ferry, https://www.kornferry.com/insights/articles/cfo-ceo-right-brain-leadership-gap (accessed January 18, 2023).
5. Burak Güner, Ulrike Malmendier, and Geoffrey Tate, "Financial Expertise of Directors," *Journal of Financial Economics* 88, no. 2 (2008): 323–354.
6. Nelson Flighstein, *The Transformation of Corporate Control* (Cambridge, MA: Harvard University Press, 1990).
7. Dirk Zorn, "Here a Chief, There a Chief: The Rise of the CFO in the American Firm," *American Sociological Review* 69, no. 3 (2004).
8. See, e.g., Jeffrey S. Sanders, "The Path to Becoming a Fortune 500 CEO," *Forbes*, December 5, 2011.
9. Ralph Mortenson and Alan Mead, "CFO to CEO: Inspiration or Lunacy?," *The Psychologist-Manager Journal* 21, no. 3 (2018): 151–162.
10. In particular, see my book *The New Deal at Work: Managing the Market-Driven Workforce* (Boston: Harvard Business School Press, 1999).
11. How much of this was actually true is another matter. See, e.g., Bert Spector, "Flawed from the 'Get-Go': Lee Iacocca and the Origins of Transformational Leadership," *Leadership* 10, no. 30 (2014): 361–379.
12. Thomas A. Kochan and Lee Dyer, *Shaping the Future: A Handbook for Action and a New Social Contract* (New York: Routledge, 2021), 202.
13. Julie Wulf, "The Flattened Firm—Not as Advertised" (Harvard Business School Working Paper 12-087, April 9, 2012).
14. David Geddes, *The Man Who Broke Capitalism: How Jack Welch Gutted the Heartland and Crushed the Soul of Corporate America—and How to Undo His Legacy* (New York: Simon and Schuster, 2022).

15. Peter Cappelli, "Why Bosses Should Stop Thinking of A Players, B Players, and C Players," *Wall Street Journal*, February 17, 2017.

16. See Edward E. Jones and Victor A. Harris, "The Attribution of Attitudes," *Journal of Experimental Social Psychology* 3, no. 1 (1967): 1–24.

17. See, e.g., D. C. Hambrick, "Upper Echelons Theory: An Update," *Academy of Management Review* 32, no. 2 (2007): 334–343.

18. Abigail Johnson Hess, "Here's Where 10 of the Most Powerful Fortune 500 CEOs Went to Business School," CNBC, July 12, 2018, https://www.cnbc.com/2018/07/09/ where-10-powerful-fortune-500-ceos-went-to-business-school.html.

19. Mu-Jeung Yang, Michael Christensen, Nicholas Bloom, Raffaella Sadun, and Jan Rivkin, "How Do CEOs Make Strategy?" (NBER Working Paper 27952, National Bureau of Economic Research, 2020). Other studies have found relationships between academic courses and business outcomes. See, e.g., E. P. Lazear, "Entrepreneurship," *Journal of Labor Economics* 23, no. 4 (2005): 649–680, where he finds that a broader curriculum leads to graduates with a higher probability of becoming entrepreneurs.

20. Judith Aquino, "33% of CEOs Majored in Engineering—and Other Surprising Facts about Your Boss," Business Insider, March 23, 2011, https://www.businessinsider. com/ceos-majored-in-engineering-2011-3?op=1#33-of-the-sp-500-ceos-underg raduate-degrees-are-in-engineering-and-only-11-are-in-business-administration-1.

21. Kimberly A. Whitler, "New Study on CEOs: Is Marketing, Finance, Operations, or Engineering the Best?," *Forbes*, October 12, 2019, https://www.forbes.com/sites/kimb erlywhitler/2019/10/12/new-study-on-ceos-is-marketing-finance-operations-or- engineering-the-best-path-to-the-c-suite/#1e982b3f5e07.

22. David Egan, "Here Is What It Takes to Become a CEO, According to 12,000 LinkedIn Profiles," LinkedIn, June 11, 2018, https://business.linkedin.com/talent-solutions/ blog/trends-and-research/2018/what-12000-ceos-have-in-common.

23. The Lou Harris poll is reported in "More Than One Quarter of Managers Said They Weren't Ready to Lead," CareerBuilder, March 28, 2011, https://press.careerbuilder. com/2011-03-28-More-Than-One-Quarter-of-Managers-Said-They-Werent-Ready- to-Lead-When-They-Began-Managing-Others-Finds-New-CareerBuilder-Survey.

24. For the rise of management training, see Peter Cappelli, *Talent on Demand: Managing Talent in an Age of Uncertainty* (Boston: Harvard Business Press, 2008), Chapter 2.For the 2007 evidence on supervisory training, see Institute for Corporate Productivity, *New Supervisor Training Program Practitioner Consensus Survey* (Seattle: Institute for Corporate Productivity, August 2007). The 1955 Conference Board study is re- ported in J. Dennis O'Brien, "Finding Future Executives," *American Business*, September 1955, 22–23. The contemporary data is from AMA Enterprise, *Developing Successful Global Leaders: The Third Annual Study of Challenges and Opportunities* (New York: AMA Enterprise, 2019).

25. The classic discussion of these differences is Anna Lee Saxenian, *Regional Advantage: Culture and Competition in Silicon Valley and Route 128* (Cambridge, MA: Harvard University Press, 1994).

26. Dan Lyons, *Disrupted: My Misadventure in the Start-Up Bubble* (New York: Hachette Books, 2016).

27. Dan Lyons, *Lab Rats: Why Modern Work Makes People Miserable* (New York: Atlantic Books, 2019).

28. Catherine Turco, *The Conversational Firm: Rethinking Bureaucracy in the Age of Social Media* (New York: Columbia University Press, 2016).

29. Adolf A. Berle and Gardner C. Means, *The Modern Corporation and Private Property* (New York: Harcourt, Brace, 1932).

30. Stuart L. Gillan, Jay C. Hartzell, and Robert Parrino, "Explicit versus Implicit Contracts: Evidence from CEO Employment Agreements," *Journal of Finance* 64, no. 4 (2009): 1629–1655.

31. "What 2019 Proxy Statements Reveal about Executive Perquisites," *Compensation and Benefits Digest* 27, no. 6 (2019), https://www.ayco.com/content/dam/ayco/pdfs/us/en/compensation-benefits-digest/2019/digest_1906.pdf?sa=n&rd=n.

32. L. A. Stout, "Killing Conscience: The Unintended Behavioral Consequences of 'Pay for Performance,'" *Journal of Corporation Law* 39 (Spring 2014): 525–561.

33. John Roe and Kosmas Papadopoulos, "2019 U.S. Executive Compensation Trends," Harvard Law School Forum on Corporate Governance, April 16, 2019, https://corpgov.law.harvard.edu/2019/04/16/2019-u-s-executive-compensation-trends.

34. For a template, see Board Source, "Elements to Include in a Chief Executive Employment Contract," February 17, 2017, https://boardsource.org/resources/chief-executive-employment-contract/.

35. John B. Donaldson, Natalia Gershun, and Marc P. Giannoni, "Some Unpleasant General Equilibrium Implications of Executive Contracts" (NBER Working Paper 15165, National Bureau of Economic Research, 2009); Henry L. Tosi, Steve Werner, Jeffrey P. Katz, and Luis R. Gomez-Mejia, "How Much Does Performance Matter? A Meta-Analysis of CEO Pay Studies," *Journal of Management* 26, no. 2 (2016): 301–339.

36. Stewart J. Schwab and Randall S. Thomas, "An Empirical Analysis of CEO Employment Contracts: What Do Top Executives Bargain For?," *Washington and Lee Law Review* 63 (Winter 2006): 231–267.

37. Chartered Institute for Personnel Development and the High Pay Centre, "CEO Pay and the Workforce," December 2020, https://www.cipd.co.uk/Images/ceo-pay-workforce-report_tcm18-87761.pdf.

38. Patrick Thomas, "Elon Musk Decries 'M.B.A.-ization' of America," *Wall Street Journal*, December 9, 2020.

39. See, e.g., Mina Kimes, "At Sears, Eddie Lampert's Warring Divisions Model Adds to the Troubles," *Bloomberg*, July 13, 2013, for a description of the business model. Adam Hartung, in "The 5 Ways Ed Lampert Destroyed Sears," *Forbes*, February 11, 2016, assesses his leadership approach. Suzanne Kapner, Rachael Levy, and Juliet Ching, in "Edward Lampert, the Hedge-Fund Star Who Bet on Sears, Is Unrepentant," *Wall Street Journal*, October 17, 2018, describe more recent developments.

40. The low point is arguably Brian Sozzi from Yahoo Finance's claim that Lambert was the worst CEO of the past fifty years. See discussion thread on TheLayoff, https://www.thelayoff.com/t/12FYZ50V (accessed January 18, 2023).

41. My colleagues and I outlined a great many of the important issues when data science intersects human resource issues in Prasana Tambe, Peter Cappelli, and Valery Yakubovich, "Artificial Intelligence in Human Resources Management: Challenges and a Path Forward," *California Management Review* 6, no. 4 (2019): 15–42.

42. A popular debunking of many of these claims is Avrind Navayaran, "How to Recognize AI Snake Oil," Center for Information and Technology Policy, Princeton University, https://www.cs.princeton.edu/~arvindn/talks/MIT-STS-AI-snakeoil.pdf (accessed January 18, 2023).

43. Josh Bersin, "HR Technology Market 2020: Report Now Available," JoshBersin.com, December 19, 2019, https://joshbersin.com/2019/12/hr-technology-market-2020-report-now-available/.

44. PwC, "The Future of Recruiting," https://www.pwc.com/us/en/services/consulting/workforce-of-the-future/library/hr-recruiting.html (accessed January 18, 2023).

45. Mary Baker, "AI Shows Value and Gains Traction in Human Resources," Gartner, March 2020, https://www.gartner.com/smarterwithgartner/ai-shows-value-and-gains-traction-in-hr.

46. Alec MacGillis, "The Case against Boeing," *The New Yorker*, November 11, 2019.

47. Douglas McGregor, *The Human Side of Enterprise* (New York: McGraw Hill, 1960).

48. W. Ocasio, "Towards an Attention-Based View of the Firm," *Strategic Management Journal* 18 (Summer Special Issue): 187–206.

Chapter 3

1. *SHRM Customized Talent Acquisition Benchmarking Report* (Alexandria, VA: Society for Human Resource Management, 2017). Also see "Quantifying Quality of Hire," *HR Today*, http://www.hrotoday.com/news/talent-acquisition/quantifying-quality-of-hire/ (accessed January 30, 2023).

2. "Recruiting Metrics Cheat Sheet," LinkedIn, https://business.linkedin.com/content/dam/me/business/en-us/talent-solutions/resources/pdfs/cheatsheet-recruiting-metrics-for-smbs_v2.pdf (accessed January 30, 2023).

3. Andrew R. McIlvain, "Unlocking the Quality of Hire Conundrum," *HR Executive*, June 3, 2019.

4. In this survey, three-quarters of those reporting that they did not measure quality of hires say that the reason was that they did not have time to do so. See Jim Davis, "2017 Annual Recruiting Survey," HR Daily Advisor, Mar 7, 2017, https://hrdailyadvisor.blr.com/2017/03/07/2017-annual-recruiting-survey/, and "A How-to Guide for Improving Your Quality of Hire," Ideal, https://ideal.com/quality-of-hire/ (accessed January 30, 2023).

5. "Recruiting Metrics: A How-to Guide for Showing the Business Value of Your Recruiting," Ideal.com, https://ideal.com/recruiting-metrics (accessed January 30, 2023).

6. "The 4 Recruiting Trends You Need to Know for 2021," XOR, https://app.hubspot.com/documents/4317413/view/96395513?accessId=10ee1e (accessed January 30, 2023).

7. "The C-Suite Outlook," The Conference Board, https://www.conference-board.org/press/pressdetail.cfm?pressid=7295 (accessed January 30, 2023).

8. "The Talent Challenge: Harnessing the Power of Human Skills in the Machine Age," PwC, https://www.pwc.com/gx/en/ceo-survey/2017/deep-dives/ceo-survey-global-talent.pdf (accessed January 30, 2023).

9. The Vacancy Duration Survey, now discontinued, was published by DHI.com through 2018.

10. Roy Maurer, "Why Is Hiring Taking So Long—and What HR Can Do about It?," Society for Human Resource Management, June 2016, https://www.shrm.org/hr-today/news/hr-magazine/0616/pages/why-hiring-is-taking-so-long-and-what-hr-can-do-about-it.aspx.

11. "Managing Your Brand throughout the Recruitment Process," Robert Walters Group, 2012, https://www.robertwaltersgroup.com/content/dam/robert-walters/country/united-kingdom/files/whitepapers/robert-walters-insight-series-managing-your-brand-throughout-the-recruitment-process.pdf.

12. "2016 Human Capital Benchmarking Report," Society for Human Resource Management, November 2016, https://www.shrm.org/hr-today/trends-and-forecasting/research-and-surveys/Documents/2016-Human-Capital-Report.pdf.

13. "Job Openings and Labor Turnover Summary," US Bureau of Labor Statistics, https://www.bls.gov/news.release/jolts.nr0.htm (accessed January 30, 2023).

14. Forty-five percent of all spending is on talent acquisition. Matt Norton, "Workforce Solutions Ecosystem Defining the Staffing Industry and Other Workforce Solutions," *Staffing Industry Analysts*, November 30, 2020.

15. Lauren Helper, "Tech Boom to Bust: Recruiters among Hardest Hit by Coronavirus Layoffs. Protocol," Protocol, April 2, 2020, https://www.protocol.com/coronavirus-cuts-recruiting-and-recruiters. The shutdowns ended up lasting a year and a half, but there was no anticipation of that in March 2020 when these layoffs took place. About half those jobs did come back within a month or so of the initial shutdown.

16. *SHRM Customized Talent Acquisition Benchmarking Report.*

17. Seventy-six million people left jobs, for a net loss of 5.7 million positions. "Job Openings and Labor Turnover Summary," Economic News Release, US Bureau of Labor Statistics, December 9, 2020, https://www.bls.gov/news.release/jolts.nr0.htm.

18. "Source of Hire Report," CareerXRoads, Presentation slide deck, 2015.

19. "Hiring and Practices Survey," ERC, 2015.

20. Matthew Bidwell, "Paying More to Get Less: Specific Skills, Matching, and the Effects of External Hiring versus Internal Promotion," *Administrative Science Quarterly* 56, no. 3 (2011): 369–407.

21. "Talent Trends," LinkedIn, 2014, https://business.linkedin.com/talent-solutions/c/14/3/talent-trends/2014?trk=s-bl.

22. These figures are reported at Bart Turczynsky, "Hiring Statistics: Job Search, Hiring, Recruiting, & Interviews," Zety.com, 2020.

23. "Inside the Recruiting Funnel: Essential Metrics for Startups and SBUs," Lever.com, 2017, https://www.lever.co/resources/recruiting-metrics-for-startups-and-smbs-rep

ort/. (Lever.com is a company that provides workforce analytic support to twelve hundred smaller companies.)

24. For the early experience with electronic hiring, see Peter Cappelli, "Making the Most of Online Hiring," *Harvard Business Review*, March 2001.

25. This reaction apparently took some time to abate. See Kashmir Hill, "Did Joining LinkedIn Cost This Guy His Job?," *Forbes*, January 5, 2012, https://www.forbes.com/sites/kashmirhill/2012/01/05/did-joining-linkedin-cost-this-guy-his-job/?sh=4d64d4084cb7.

26. "2021 Sources of Hire Report," Breezy.com, https://assets-global.website-files.com/6127d83f257132e4fe0bddc6/622b514c331dc92089300cd2_breezyhr-2021-sourceofhire.pdf. This statistic on sources of hire and others like it comes from applicant tracking systems. Even candidates who are identified via personal contacts, such as friends of the CEO, have to be entered into the ATS process, because it is the record-keeping system for hiring. It systematically counts all the channels through which applicants, interviewed applicants, and hires take place. The major applicant tracking systems account for millions of jobs, but it is fair to note that each one is reporting on its client's results, and those clients are not a random draw of the population.

27. For evidence on the cost savings of ATS systems, see S. Laumer, C. Maier, and A. Eckhardt, "The Impact of Business Process Management and Applicant Tracking Systems on Recruiting Process Performance: An Empirical Study," *Zeitschrift Für Betriebswirtschaft* 85, no. 4 (2015): 421–453.

28. The median number of requisitions per recruiter was half that, however, which likely means that considerable variance exists across organizations, perhaps because of differences in their use of help from vendors. See "How Do I Determine an Appropriate Recruiter Workload?," Society for Human Resource Management, https://www.shrm.org/resourcesandtools/tools-and-samples/hr-qa/pages/how-do-i-determine-an-appropriate-recruiter-workload.aspx (accessed January 30, 2023).

29. "Recruiter Nation Report: Agility: The Essential Ingredient for Recruiting Success," Jobvite, https://www.jobvite.com/wp-content/uploads/2021/09/Jobvite-RecruiterNation-Report-WEB-2.pdf (accessed January 30, 2023).

30. "2020 Recruiter Nation Survey," Jobvite, https://www.jobvite.com/wp-content/uploads/2020/10/Jobvite-RecruiterNation-Report-Final.pdf (accessed January 30, 2023). The "campaigns" and "search" items in the rows represent types of active searches.

31. Among the differences with this data are that employee referrals account for far fewer applications than in other surveys, although the ratio of applicants to hires for referred candidates is about the same as in the other surveys.

32. Bo Cowgill and Patryk Perkowski, "Agency and Workplace Diversity: Evidence from a Two-Sided Audit" (Columbia University Business School Research Paper No. 898, December 29, 2020).

33. Kathleen de Lara, "10 Key Findings from the 2018 Recruiting Trends Report," Entelo.com, 2017, https://resources.entelo.com/download-2018-entelo-recruiting-trends-report. These results come from a survey of 1,143 "talent acquisition professionals," or professional recruiters in organizations.

34. Andrew Chamberlain, "Why Interview Sources Matter in Hiring: Exploring Glassdoor Interviews Data," 2015, https://www.glassdoor.com/research/interview-sources/#.

35. "Job Seeker Nation Survey 2020," Jobvite, May 2020, https://www.jobvite.com/wp-content/uploads/2020/05/FINAL-Jobvite-JobSeekerNation-Report1_5-11.pdf.

36. Ines Black, Sharique Hasan, and Rembrand Koning, "Hunting for Talent: Firm-Driven Labor Market Search in America" (Duke University Working Paper, April 2020).

37. Anna Cooban, "95% of Workers Are Thinking about Quitting Their Jobs, According to a New Survey—and Burnout Is the Number-One Reason," Business Insider, July 7, 2021.

38. C. Carrillo-Tudela, B. Hobijin, P. Perkowski, and L. Visschers, "Majority of Hires Never Report Looking for a Job," Federal Reserve Bank of San Francisco Economic Letter, 2015.

39. "Job Seeker Nation Survey 2020."

40. Black, Hasan, and Koning, "Hunting for Talent."

41. Gerry Crispin and Chris Hoyt, "2015 CareerXroads Source of Hire Report," CareerXroads, January 9, 2016, https://www.slideshare.net/gerrycrispin/2015-careerxroads-source-of-hire-report-56847680, slide 22. This figure is almost identical to the Jobvite results at 12 percent (below).

42. "Talent Solutions / Talent Trends," LinkedIn, 2017, https://business.linkedin.com/talent-solutions/c/14/3/talent-trends/2014?trk=s-bl.

43. "Talent Solutions / Talent Trends."

44. "LinkedIn United States Staffing Trends Survey," 2015, https://business.linkedin.com/content/dam/business/talent-solutions/global/en_US/c/pdfs/recruiting-trends-global-linkedin-2015.pdf.

45. "Staffing Industry Statistics," American Staffing Association, https://americanstaffing.net/staffing-research-data/fact-sheets-analysis-staffing-industry-trends/staffing-industry-statistics/ (accessed January 30, 2023).

46. Simeon McGee, "Recruitment Fees," HR Encyclopedia, Eddy, https://eddy.com/hr-encyclopedia/recruitment-fees/ (accessed January 30, 2023).

47. Their research is described in Brad J. Hershbein and Claudia Macaluso, "The Economics of Job Search: New Insights from an Upjohn Institute–Federal Reserve Bank of Chicago Conference," Employment Research Newsletter 23, no. 3 (2018).

48. Carol Leaman, "How to Prevent Potential Employees from Ghosting You," Fast Company, May 25, 2019, https://www.fastcompany.com/90354794/how-to-prevent-potential-employees-from-ghosting-you.

49. "Job Seeker Nation Survey 2020."

50. A set of histories of the field of industrial and organizational psychology can be found at "The General History Virtual Wing," Science for a Smarter Workplace, https://www.siop.org/About-SIOP/SIOP-Museum/General-History (accessed January 30, 2022). A more detailed perspective on the European literature can be found at Helio Carpinetro, "History of Organizational Psychology," Oxford Research Encyclopedia (Oxford: Oxford University Press, 2017).

51. S. L. Rynes, "The Research–Practice Gap in Industrial/Organizational Psychology and Related Fields: Challenges and Potential Solutions," in The Oxford Handbook

of Industrial/Organizational Psychology, ed. S. W. J. Kozlowski, 409–452 (New York: Oxford University Press, 2012).

52. John C. Roach, "Would Standardized Job Testing Assist Employers in Hiring the Right Employee?," *Monthly Labor Review*, May 2016.

53. "Hiring Trends and Practices Survey," ERC, 2015.

54. Mitchell Hoffman, Lisa B. Kahn, and Danielle Li, "Discretion in Hiring," *Quarterly Journal of Economics* 133, no. 2 (May 2018): 765–800.

55. Nathan R. Kuoncel, Deniz S. Ones, and David M. Klieger, "In Hiring, Algorithms Beat Instinct," *Harvard Business Review*, May 2014, https://hbr.org/2014/05/in-hiring-algorithms-beat-instinct.

56. Brian Jacob, Jonah E. Rockoff, Eric S. Taylor, Benjamin Lindy, and Rachel Rosen, "Teacher Applicant Hiring and Teacher Performance: Evidence from DC Public Schools" (NBER Working Paper 22054, National Bureau of Economic Research, March 2016).

57. Michele Pellizzari, "Employers Search and the Efficiency of Matching" (Discussion Paper No. 1862, IZA, 2005).

58. Kevin P. Nolan, Nathan T. Carter, and Dev K. Dalal, "Threat of Technological Unemployment: Are Hiring Managers Discounted for Using Standardized Employee Selection Practices?," *Personnel Assessments* 2, no. 1 (2016): 30–47.

59. S. Highhouse, "Stubborn Reliance on Intuition and Subjectivity in Employee Selection," *Industrial and Organizational Psychology* 1 (2008): 333–342.

60. The "tree" question appears to be asked first by Barbara Walters of Katharine Hepburn, who replied, sensibly, that she would want to avoid getting Dutch elm disease, so she would be an oak. Cynthia Littleton, "Barbara Walters: Probing Questions and a Tall Tale of the Tree," *Variety*, April 8, 2014.

61. "Why Is Hiring Taking Longer? New Insights from Glassdoor Data," Glassdoor.com, June 2015, https://www.glassdoor.com/research/app/uploads/sites/2/2015/06/GD_Report_3.pdf.

62. That process is speedy compared to most other countries (forty days in Brazil), but pokey compared to India's sixteen days. Andrew Chamberlain, "How Long Does It Take to Hire? Interview Duration in 25 Countries," Glassdoor.com, August 9, 2017, https://www.glassdoor.com/research/time-to-hire-in-25-countries/#.

63. The practice was based on something like crowd-sourcing: that having more opinions was better. Apparently sitting for fifteen interviews was common. Tom Popomaronis, "Here's How Many Google Interviews It Takes to Hire a Googler," Make It, CNBC, April 17, 2019, https://www.cnbc.com/2019/04/17/heres-how-many-google-job-interviews-it-takes-to-hire-a-googler.html#:~:text=The%20'Rule%20of%20Four',Google%20with%2086%25%20confidence.%E2%80%9D.

64. Adam Bryant, "Google's Quest to Build a Better Boss," *New York Times*, March 12, 2011.

65. For an explanation as to why managers prefer unstructured interviews, see K. I. van der Zee, A. B. Bakker, and P. Bakker, "Why Are Structured Interviews So Rarely Used in Personnel Selection?," *Journal of Applied Psychology* 87 (2002): 176–184.

66. For a review, see Nicolas Roulin and Adrian Bangerter, "Understanding the Academic–Practitioner Gap for Structured Interviews: 'Behavioral' Interviews

Diffuse, 'Structured' Interviews Do Not," *International Journal of Selection and Assessment* 20, no. 2 (May 2012): 149–158.

67. Lauren A. Rivera, "Hiring as Cultural Matching: The Case of Elite Professional Service Firms," *American Sociological Review* 77, no. 6 (2012), http://journals.sagepub.com/doi/10.1177/0003122412463213.

68. "Exploring Amazon's Unique Interview Process," Amazon, January 9, 2019, www.aboutamazon.com/news/workplace/how-amazon-hires.

69. David Pedulla, *Making the Cut: Hiring Decisions, Bias, and the Consequences of Nonstandard, Mismatched, and Precarious Employment* (Princeton, NJ: Princeton University Press, 2020).

70. "The State of Entry-Level Employment in the U.S.," Rockefeller Foundation, March 2017, https://www.rockefellerfoundation.org/report/impact-hiring-survey-results/.

71. "Employers Share Their Most Outrageous Resume Mistakes and Instant Deal Breakers in a New CareerBuilder Study," CareerBuilder Newsroom, 2018, https://press.careerbuilder.com/2018-08-24-Employers-Share-Their-Most-Outrageous-Resume-Mistakes-and-Instant-Deal-Breakers-in-a-New-CareerBuilder-Study.

72. "Measuring Up: A New Research Report about RPO Metrics," Korn Ferry, 2018, https://www.kornferry.com/insights/this-week-in-leadership/measuring-up-a-new-research-report-about-rpo-metrics.

73. "The Future of Recruiting," PwC, https://www.pwc.com/us/en/services/consulting/workforce-of-the-future/library/hr-recruiting.html (accessed January 30, 2023).

74. The intuition here is that low-wage workers rely on public transport and sometimes less reliable cars to commute. The farther the commute, the more problems they have getting there. John Sullivan, "You Might Be Surprised How Much Commute Issues Hurt Hiring and Retention," ERE, April 20, 2015, https://www.ere.net/you-might-be-surprised-how-much-commute-issues-hurt-hiring-and-retention/.

75. This quote, as well as a detailed description of the project, is in Jeffrey Dastin, "Amazon Scraps Secret AI Recruiting Tool That Showed Bias against Women," Reuters, October 10, 2018.

76. Roy Maurer, "Employee Referrals Remain Top Source for Hires," Society for Human Resource Management, June 23, 2017, https://www.shrm.org/ResourcesAndTools/hr-topics/talent-acquisition/pages/employee-referrals-remains-top-source-hires.aspx.

77. See, e.g., Karla L. Miller, "The Waiting Game: What to Do When a Prospective Employer Keeps You Hanging," *Washington Post*, March 11, 2021.

78. "The Science of Talent Attraction," Indeed.com, April 6, 2020, https://www.indeed.com/lead/the-science-of-talent-attraction:-what-makes-candidates-click.

Chapter 4

1. Bennett Harrison, *Lean and Mean: The Changing Landscape of Corporate Power in the Age of Flexibility* (New York: Basic Books, 1994).

2. C. K. Prahalad and G. Hamel, "The Core Competency of the Corporation," *Harvard Business Review* 68, no. 3 (1990): 79–91. Peter Drucker has some claim to the idea as well, beginning around the same time with his article "Sell the Mailroom," *Wall Street Journal*, July 25, 1989.

3. David Weil, *The Fissured Workplace: Why Work Became So Bad for So Many and What Can Be Done about It* (Cambridge, MA: Harvard University Press, 2014).

4. "Human Resources and Benefits Administration in the US, " IBISWorld, January 10, 2023, https://www.ibisworld.com/united-states/market-research-reports/human-resources-benefits-administration-industry/.

5. "Staffing and Recruiting Industry Market Size in the United States from 2012 to 2019, with a Forecast until 2021," Statista, https://www.statista.com/statistics/873648/us-staffing-industry-market-size/ (accessed January 30, 2023).

6. "HR Consulting," Consultancy.org, https://www.consultancy.org/consulting-indus try/hr-consulting (accessed January 30, 2023).

7. "Training Industry in the U.S.: Statistics & Facts," Statista, July 5, 2022, https://www. statista.com/topics/4896/training-industry-in-the-us/.

8. "Human Capital Management Market by Component," Markets and Markets, https:// www.marketsandmarkets.com/Market-Reports/human-capital-management-mar ket-193746782.html (accessed January 30, 2023).

9. "Ranking the Biggest Industries in the US Economy," Blue Water Credit, https://blue watercredit.com/ranking-biggest-industries-us-economy-surprise-1/   (accessed January 30, 2023).

10. "Marketer's Guide to the HR Industry," Advos, https://advos.io/resources/marketers-guide-to-the-hr-industry (accessed January 30, 2023).

11. "Marketer's Guide to the HR Industry."

12. See, e.g., Richard Freeman, "Is a Great Labor Shortage Coming? Replacement Demand in the Global Economy" (NBER Working Paper No. 12541, National Bureau of Economic Research, 2006).

13. "Are Generational Categories Meaningful Distinctions for Workforce Management?" (Washington, DC: National Academies Press, 2020).

14. See, e.g. Peter Cappelli, "Skill Gap, Skill Shortages, and Skill Mismatches: Evidence and Arguments for the United States," *ILR Review* 68, no. 2 (2015): 251–290.

15. As of 2020, Aon-Willis-Watson-Towers combined four of the largest human resource consulting companies into one with the new name Watson-Towers-Wyatt. The Hay Group was acquired by Korn Ferry. Mercer, a subsidiary of Marsh & McClennan, re-mains independent, although most of its business is managing outsourced insurance and retirement products for clients.

16. "Staffing Industry Statistics," American Staffing Association, https://americanstaff ing.net/staffing-research-data/fact-sheets-analysis-staffing-industry-trends/staffing-industry-statistics/ (accessed January 30, 2023).

17. Daniel Clawson, *Bureaucracy and the Labor Process: The Transformation of U.S. Industry, 1860–1920* (New York: Monthly Review Press, 1980).

18. Sanford Jacoby, *Employing Bureaucracy: Managers, Unions, and the Transformation of Work in the 20th Century* (New York: Columbia University Press, 1985).

19. Daniel Raff and Lawrence Summers, "Did Henry Ford Pay Efficiency Wages?," *Journal of Labor Economics* 5, no. 4, part 2 (October 1987): S57–S86.

20. Oliver Zunz, *Making America Corporate, 1870–1920* (Chicago: University of Chicago Press, 1990), 48.

21. "The Talent Search to Beat Executive Shortage," *Business Week*, December 10, 1949, 30.

22. "The Talent Search to Beat Executive Shortage," 424.

23. William H. Whyte, *The Organization Man* (New York: Simon and Schuster, 1956).

24. Observers differ as to the relative weights that should be given to these different motives. Irving Bernstein in particular articulated the notion that these welfare capitalist practices were just a more effective means in the relatively progressive context of the 1920s to achieve the same goal of control over workers and their pay. See Irving Bernstein, *The Lean Years: A History of the American Worker* (Boston: Houghton Mifflin, 1960). Andrea Tone, in *Industrial Paternalism in Progressive America* (Ithaca, NY: Cornell University Press, 1997), casts welfare capitalism in the broader context of political change in society. Stuart D. Brandes, in *American Welfare Capitalism* (Chicago: University of Chicago Press, 1976), provides an encyclopedic review of practices, concluding that while it was certainly conducted for company interests, it did some good for employees.

25. Jacoby, *Employing Bureaucracy*.

26. "Can Job Agencies Find Your Man?," *Business Week*, January 1, 1949, 22.

27. J. Dennis O'Brien, "Finding Future Executives," *American Business* 25 (September 1955): 22–23.

28. W. Lloyd Warner, Darab B. Unwalla, and John H. Trimm, *The Emergent American Society: Large Scale Organizations*, vol. 1 (New Haven, CT: Yale University Press, 1967).

29. Mabel Newcomer, *The Big Business Executive: The Factors That Made Him, 1900–1950* (New York: Columbia University Press, 1955).

30. An overview of these practices is in Peter Cappelli, "A Supply Chain Approach to Workforce Planning," *Organizational Dynamics* 38, no. 1 (2009): 8–15. Interestingly, the brand "manplan" now has a number of quite different meanings, including manplan.net, which provides cloud-based software for manure-spreading tasks.

31. Peter Cappelli, "Examining Management Displacement," *Academy of Management Journal* 35, no. 1 (1992): 203–217.

32. US Bureau of Labor Statistics, Mass Layoff Statistics, https://www.bls.gov/mls/mlspnf mle.htm (accessed January 30, 2023).

33. Robert J. Gordon and Hassan Sayed, "A New Interpretation of Productivity Growth Dynamics in the Prepandemic and Pandemic Era US Economy, 1950–2022" (NBER Working Paper 30267, National Bureau of Economic Research, July 2022).

34. A thorough review of the literature on both individual and organization-level outcomes is Deepak K. Datta, James P. Guthrie, Dynah Basuil, and Alankrita Pandey, "Causes and Effects of Employee Downsizing: A Review and Synthesis," *Journal of Management* 36, no. 1 (2010): 281–348. A review of the negative health effects of layoffs is in Claire Margerison-Zilke, Sidra Goldman-Mellor, April Falconi,

and Janelle Downing, "Health Impacts of the Great Recession: A Critical Review," *Social Epidemiology* 3 (2016): 81–91. For more recent evidence on firm performance, see Wayne Francis Cascio, Arjun Chatata, and Rohan A. Christie-David, "Antecedents and Consequences of Employment and Asset Restructuring," *Academy of Management Journal* 64 (2021): 587-619 https://journals.aom.org/doi/10.5465/amj.2018.1013, which suggests that the longer firms put off downsizing, the better their subsequent performance is.

35. Douglas MacMillan, Peter Whoriskey, and Jonathan O'Connell, "America's Biggest Companies Are Flourishing during the Pandemic and Putting Thousands of People out of Work," *Washington Post*, December 16, 2020.

36. "Job Openings and Labor Turnover Table 5: Layoffs and Discharges Levels and Rates by Industry and Region, Seasonally Adjusted," Bureau of Labor Statistics Economic News Release, 2023, https://www.bls.gov/news.release/jolts.t05.htm.

37. Henry W. Chesbrough, "Environmental Influences upon Firm Entry into New Sub-Markets: Evidence from the Worldwide Hard Disk Drive Industry Conditionally," *Research Policy* 32, no. 4 (2003): 659–679.

38. This material on workforce planning is reviewed in Cappelli, "Supply Chain Approach to Workforce Planning."

39. Jeffrey Cohn, Rakesh Khurana, and Laura Reeves, "Growing Talent as If Your Business Depended on It," *Harvard Business Review*, October 2005, https://hbr.org/2005/10/growing-talent-as-if-your-business-depended-on-it/. The suspect claim that workers actually like irregular schedules is found in "Do You Need On-Demand Talent? Here's How to Know," WorkMarket, March 28, 2016, https://www.workmarket.com/blog/need-on-demand-talent-heres-know#gsc.tab=0. For a description of an entire company devoted to the on-demand view, see "Field Service Delivery in an On-Demand World," WorkMarket, https://images.adpinfo.com/Web/ADPEmployerServices/%7Bc9c33afe-2d40-4ebd-baf2-a57c451aa023%7D_FieldServiceDelivery-eBook.pdf (accessed January 30, 2023). For ideas about workforce as a service, see Mark A. Huselid, Richard W. Beatty, and Brian E. Becker, " 'A Players' or 'A Positions'?: The Strategic Logic of Workforce Management," *Harvard Business Review* 83, no. 10 (2005): 62–70. The contemporary argument for using workers in the market rather than employees is flexibility, the ability to dial up a workforce when demand rises and then spin it down should demand decline. The incentive is to not have to carry and pay workers when there is nothing for them to do, although as we will see, employers did not seem to have any problem laying off employees when business fell. The idea of a liquid workforce is analogous to turning on a tap only when you need it and off when you don't.

40. The Society of Workforce Planning Professionals calculator is at https://swpp.org/swpp-calculator-required-information/. Perhaps surprisingly, academic research in operational research continues to generate new staffing models. See, e.g., Marie-Anne Guerry Komarudin, Greet Vanden Berghe, and Tim De Feyter, "Balancing Attainability, Desirability and Promotion Steadiness in Manpower Planning Systems," *Journal of Operational Research Society* 66, no. 12 (2015): 2004–2014.

41. For an illustration, see Kory Wagner, "The Importance of Workforce Planning," FEI Daily, June 11, 2020, https://www.financialexecutives.org/FEI-Daily/June-2020/The-Importance-of-Workforce-Planning.aspx. He notes that the human resource function spends "only 15 percent" of its time explicitly trying to control labor costs. The view presumably is that the goal of human resources is to spend as little as possible.

42. "Strategic Workforce Planning: Preparing for Tomorrow, Today," Oracle Human Capital Management Cloud, https://www.oracle.com/a/ocom/docs/dc/oracle-swp-v4-sa1.pdf (accessed January 30, 2023). A complication with interpreting the results is that they are presented separately for "high-performing" and "other" companies. My assumption is that high-performing companies are not the majority, in which case the responses I cite have to be a minority.

43. The vacancy data comes from "Higher Unemployment Rates, 1957–60: Structural Transformation of Inadequate Demand," US Congress, Subcommittee on Economic Statistics of the Joint Economic Committee (Washington, DC: US Government Printing Office, 1961). The percentage is calculated from individuals with jobs.

44. Katharine Abraham, "Help-Wanted Advertising, Job Vacancies, and Unemployment," Brookings Papers on Economic Activity 18, no. 1 (1987): 207–248.

45. For an overview, see Robert Valletta, "Help-Wanted Advertising and Job Vacancies" (Federal Reserve Bank of San Francisco Economic Letter, 2005).

46. Robert Hall, "The Importance of Lifetime Jobs in the U.S. Economy," American Economic Review 72, no. 4 (1982): 716–724.

47. See "Employee Tenure in the Mid-1990s," US Bureau of Labor Statistics News Release, January 30, 1997, https://www.bls.gov/news.release/history/tenure_013097.txt. The evidence on married women is from Matissa N. Hollister and Kristen E. Smith, "Unmasking the Conflicting Trends in Job Tenure by Gender in the United States, 1983–2008," American Sociological Review 79, no. 1 (2013): 371–389.

48. Henry S. Farber, "Job Loss and the Decline in Job Security in the United States" (Princeton University Industrial Relations Section Working Paper #520, 2008).

49. "Number of Jobs, Labor Market Experience, Marital Status, and Health: Results of a Recent Longitudinal Survey," Bureau of Labor Statistics Economic News Release, August 31, 2021.

50. Matthew J. Bidwell, "What Happened to Long-Term Employment? The Role of Worker Power and Environmental Turbulence in Explaining Declines in Worker Tenure," Organization Science 24, no. 2 (2013), https://doi.org/10.1287/orsc.1120.0816.

51. Peter Cappelli and Monika Hamori, "The Path to the Top: Changes in the Attributes of Corporate Careers, 1980–2001" (NBER Working Paper 10507, National Bureau of Economic Research, May 5, 2004), and Peter Cappelli, Monika Hamori, and Rocio Bonet, "Who's Got Those Top Jobs?," Harvard Business Review, March 2014.

52. Peter Cappelli and Monika Hamori, "Understanding Executive Job Search," Organizational Science 25, no. 5 (2013): 1511–1529.

53. Abha Bhattaria, "Despite Omicron Surge, Businesses Desperate to Find and Keep Workers," Washington Post, February 5, 2022.

54. What has happened to tenure is a good illustration of the different experiences of different groups in the labor force. As noted earlier, tenure for women has nudged up as more continue to work after they have children. It is also the case that the

very youngest workers under age twenty-four, who are just starting their careers, do less job hopping now (or, less positively, they do not move as quickly to better jobs). Noncompete agreements and declining competition among employers could explain these declines, but these effects are big enough to pull up overall tenure in the labor force as a whole. For evidence on the decline of a range of transitions in the labor force—from jobs into unemployment, from unemployment out of the labor force, etc.,—see Raven Molley, Christopher L. Smith, Ricardo Trezzi, and Abigail Wozniak, "Understanding Increased Fluidity in the Labor Force" (Brookings Papers on Economic Activity, Brookings Institution, March 2016), and Michael J. Pries and Richard Rogerson, "Declining Worker Turnover: The Role of Short-Duration Employment Spells" (NBER Working Paper No. 26019, National Bureau of Economic Research, 2019). Both articles reach the same conclusion: the decline of very short-term jobs is what accounted for the uptick in overall tenure. Pries and Rogerson suggest that this decline is because of better matches in what would otherwise be short-term jobs, possibly by improved screening of candidates.

55. Charles B. Handy, *Understanding Organizations* (London: Penguin, 1976).
56. John Atkinson, "Manpower Strategies for Flexible Organizations," *Personnel Management* 16 (1984): 28–31.
57. Peter Cappelli and David Neumark, "External Churning and Internal Flexibility: Evidence in the Functional Flexibility and Core-Periphery Hypothesis," *Industrial Relations* 43, no. 1 (2004): 148–182.
58. See, e.g., "TED: The Economics Daily: 3.8 Percent of Workers Were Contingent in May 2017," US Bureau of Labor Statistics, June 14, 2018, https://www.bls.gov/opub/ted/2018/3-point-8-percent-of-workers-were-contingent-in-may-2017.htm?view_full.
59. This estimate is not without some controversy, however, as other measures, especially administrative data from tax filings, show higher numbers—just under 11 percent, and a small but steady increase over time. But this data includes anyone with any income from independent contracting, such as selling something on eBay. Those whose primary income is from independent contracting represent a much smaller number, roughly 4 percent. See Katherine Lim, Alicia Miller, Max Risch, and Eleanor Wilkings, "Independent Contractors in the US: New Trends from 15 Years of Administrative Tax Data," Internal Revenue Service, July 2019, https://www.irs.gov/pub/irs-soi/19rpindcontractorinus.pdf. Interestingly, the Bureau of Labor Statistics defines "contingent" quite differently in a way that no one else does: as regular employees who expect their job to end, excluding nonemployees altogether. By that definition, contingent work was lower before the COVID-19 pandemic than in the 1990s and below 4 percent.
60. Aminda Zetlin, "Google Is at Risk for a Massive Employment Lawsuit. Your Company Might Be Too," Inc., May 31, 2019, https://www.inc.com/minda-zetlin/google-contractors-employees-legal-risks-misclassification-california-law.htmlr.
61. "Survey: CEOs See Less Globalization, More Flexible Workforces, Broadened Corporate Missions in COVID-19's Aftermath," Conference Board Press Release, July 30, 2020, https://www.conference-board.org/press/COVID_C-Suite_Challenge_Survey.

62. Uber's shares rose 11 percent, and Lyft's were up 14.9 percent in premarket trading the morning after the election. I calculated this estimate from the following sources that documented the companies' spending on the campaign: "Campaign Finance: Yes on 22," Cal-Access, http://cal-access.sos.ca.gov/Campaign/Committees/Detail.aspx?id=1422181&session=2019&view=received (accessed January 30, 2023); George Skelton, "It's No Wonder Hundreds of Millions Have Been Spent on Prop. 22. A Lot Is at Stake," *Los Angeles Times*, October 16, 2020, https://www.latimes.com/california/story/2020-10-16/skelton-proposition-22-uber-lyft-independent-contractors; Ken Jacobs and Michael Reich, "What Would Uber and Lyft Owe to the State Unemployment Insurance Fund?," UC Berkeley Labor Center, May 7, 2020, https://laborcenter.berkeley.edu/pdf/2020/What-would-Uber-and-Lyft-owe-to-the-State-Unemployment-Insurance-Fund.pdf.

63. Peter D. Sherer, Nikolai Rogovsky, and Norman Wright, "What Drives Employment Relationships in Taxicab Organizations? Linking Agency to Firm Capabilities and Strategic Opportunities," *Organization Science* 9, no. 1 (1988): 34–48.

64. Ken Armstrong, Justin Elliott, and Ariana Tobin, "Meet the Customer Service Reps for Disney and Airbnb Who Have to Pay to Talk to You," *ProPublica*, October 2, 2020, https://www.propublica.org/article/meet-the-customer-service-reps-for-disney-and-airbnb-who-have-to-pay-to-talk-to-you.

65. Henry R. Hyatt and James R. Spletzer, "The Recent Decline in Employment Dynamics," *IZA Journal of Labor Economics* 2, no. 5 (2013): 1–21.

66. Paul Osterman, "Contract Employment: Measurement and Implications for Employer-Employee Relationships, " *ILR Review*, 76 (2023): 320–356.

67. Peter Cappelli and J. R. Keller, "A Study of the Extent and Causes of Alternative Work Arrangements," *ILR Review* 66, no. 4 (2013): 874–900. The caveat here is that some of those workers could be independent contractors.

68. Ardent Partners, "The State of Contingent Workforce Management 2018–2019," 2018, https://www.guidantglobal.com/resources/workforce-management/ardent-partners-the-state-of-contingent-workforce-management-2018-2019.

69. Contributing to the confusion, Kelly refers to these workers as "free agents," but they appear to actually be nonemployees of the client. "From Workforce to Workfit" (White Paper, Kelly Services, 2017), https://www.kellyservices.us/us/siteassets/united-states---kelly-services/files/b2b-files/white-paper_new-narrative_040518_singlepgs.pdf.

70. "How the Gig Economy Is Changing the Workforce," Ernst & Young, 2017, https://www.ey.com/en_us/tax/how-the-gig-economy-is-changing-the-workforce.

71. This information comes from the company's website Aramark.com.

72. See, e.g., Tian Luo, Amar Mann, and Richard Holden, "The Expanding Role of Temporary Help Services, 1990 to 2008," *Monthly Labor Review*, August 2010, 3–16.

73. Luo, Mann, and Holden, "The Expanding Role of Temporary Help Services." See also Nik Theodore and Jamie Peck, "The Temporary Staffing Industry: Growth Imperatives and Limits to Contingency," *Economic Geography* 78, no. 4 (2002): 463–493.

74. Nothing in the law prohibits employers from paying otherwise equivalent workers doing the same work differently unless the pattern appears driven by demographic

patterns protected by nondiscrimination laws and regulations. It is the likely reaction from those paid less that stops most employers from doing so.

75. "SIA NATHCO Benchmarking Survey Provides Insights into Travel Nurse Trends," Staffing Industry Analysts, July 18, 2019, https://www2.staffingindustry.com/eng/Editorial/Healthcare-Staffing-Report/July-18-2019/SIA-NATHO-Benchmarking-Survey-provides-insights-into-travel-nurse-trends#:~:text=The%2033%20compan ies%20participating%20in,billion%20market%20size%20in%202018.

76. Susan N. Houseman, Arne L. Kalleberg, and George A. Erickcek, "The Role of Temporary Agency Employment in Tight Labor Markets," *Industrial and Labor Relations Review* 57, no. 1 (2003): 105–127.

77. "Why Travel Nursing Will Likely Outlast the Pandemic," Advisory Board, March 18, 2022, https://www.advisory.com/daily-briefing/2022/03/18/travel-nursing.

78. Brian Wallins, "Gross Margin and Bill Rate Trends," Staffing Industry Associates, December 2020.

79. Tony Gregoire, "Workforce Solutions Buyer Survey 2020," Staffing Industry Analysts, December 4, 2020.

80. "Top 10 Managed Service Providers," EM360Tech, December 13, 2019, https://em360tech.com/tech-news/top-ten/top-10-managed-service-providers.

81. Alexandra Mateescu and Julia Ticona, "Invisible Work, Visible Workers: Visibility Regimes in Online Platforms for Domestic Work," in *Beyond the Algorithm: Qualitative Insights for Regulating Gig Work*, ed. Delepa Das Acevedo, 57–81 (New York: Cambridge University Press, 2021).

82. See "Temp-to-Perm Conversion Ratio," Contingent Workforce Strategies, cwstrategies.staffingindustry.com/temp-to-perm-conversion-ratio/ (accessed January 30, 2023).

83. For an example of this claim, see "Has Workforce-as-a-Service Arrived?," WorkMarket, https://www.workmarket.com/blog/workforce-service-arrived#gsc.tab=0 (accessed January 30, 2023).

84. John Nurthen, "Introduction to Hiring Platforms," Staffing Industry Associates, December 15, 2020.

85. "About the PEO Industry," NAPEO, https://www.napeo.org/what-is-a-peo/about-the-peo-industry/industry-statistics (accessed January 30, 2023).

86. Bruce E. Katz, "What a PEO Can Do for You," *Journal of Accountancy*, July 1, 1999., https://www.journalofaccountancy.com/issues/1999/jul/katz.html.

87. For a pros and cons discussion of outsourcing vendor management, see Stephanie Overby, "Should You Outsource Vendor Management?," *CIO Magazine*, March 21, 2016.

88. Most companies have a vendor management office that oversees contracts per se, and in recent years has concentrated on the financial risk such contracts might pose. Forrester Research provides one of the few estimates of its use from a 2011 survey finding that 47 percent of companies had one: see "Building and Enhancing a VMO That Will Change Your Company," Forrester, November 9, 2011, https://www.forres ter.com/Building+And+Enhancing+A+VMO+That+Will+Change+Your+Comp any/-/E-EVE2581. No doubt the tasks these offices perform vary, but they seem focused on drafting and negotiating the contracts rather than managing them.

89. Lauren Weber, "In the $75 Billion Videogame Industry, Hiring People Is a Last Resort," *Wall Street Journal*, April 10, 2017.

90. "Sourcing and Managing Talent in a Gig Economy" (London: Economist Intelligence Unit, 2019). The term "gig" is not defined in the survey. While it includes individual contract workers, the responses indicate that staffing agencies are the most important source for finding these workers. The fact that over 58 percent of responding companies say that more than 20 percent of the workforces are made up of these workers suggests that the answers include a broad definition of nonemployee workers.

91. Paul Osterman, "How American Adults Obtain Work Skills: Results of a New National Survey," *ILR Review*, June 2021.

92. M. J. Bidwell, "Politics and Firm Boundaries: How Organizational Structure, Group Interests, and Resources Affect Outsourcing," *Organization Science* 23, no. 6 (2012): 1622–1642.

93. See, e.g., Anthony S. Boyce, Ann Marie Ryan, Anna L. Imus, and Frederick P. Morgeson, "Temporary Worker, Permanent Loser? A Model of the Stigmatization of Temporary Workers," *Journal of Management* 33, no. 1 (2007): 5–29.

94. J. P. Broschak and Davis-Blake, "Mixing Standard Work and Nonstandard Deals: The Consequences of Heterogeneity in Employment Arrangements," *Academy of Management Journal* 49 (2006): 371–393; A. Davis-Blake, J. P. Broschak, and E. George, "Happy Together? How Using Nonstandard Workers Affects Exit, Voice, and Loyalty among Standard Employees," *Academy of Management Journal* 46 (2003): 475–485.

95. Liat Eldor and Peter Cappelli, "Agency Temps Hurts Business Performance: An Integrated Indirect Model," *Academy of Management Journal* 64 (2020): 824-850., doi:10.5465/amj.2019.0392.

96. L. Cappellari, C. Dell'Aringa, and M. Leonardi, "Temporary Employment, Job Flows and Productivity: A Tale of Two Reforms," *Economic Journal* 122 (2012): F188–F215.

97. A. Kleinknecht, F. N. Van Schaik, and H. Zhou, "Is Flexible Labour Good for Innovation? Evidence from Firm-Level Data," *Cambridge Journal of Economics* 38 (2014): 1207–1219.

98. Federica De Stefano, Rocio Bonet, and Arnaldo Camuffo, "Does Losing Temporary Workers Matter? The Effects of Planned Turnover on Replacements and Unit Performance," *Academy of Management Journal* 62, no. 4 (2019), https://doi.org/10.5465/amj.2017.0291.

99. State laws govern the application of common-law-era borrowed servant doctrines as well as whether the client becomes a "dual employer." The main relevance in employment law is who can the employee sue, and who is responsible if the employee is injured on the job.

100. The one exception to this conclusion are the several studies examining employee commitment of temp workers, which has been reported to be as high as for regular employees. The complication with those studies, however, is that we cannot tell if the temps are independent contractors or leased employees of agencies.

101. See, e.g., "About," Walmart, https://corporate.walmart.com/newsroom/company-facts (accessed January 30, 2023).

102. For details, see "H-1B Specialty Occupations, DOD Cooperative Research and Development Project Workers, and Fashion Models," US Citizenship and Immigration Services, https://www.uscis.gov/working-in-the-united-states/tempor ary-workers/h-1b-specialty-occupations-dod-cooperative-research-and-developm ent-project-workers-and-fashion (accessed January 30, 2023).

103. Daniel Costa and Ron Hira, "H-1BVisas and Prevailing Wage Levels," Economic Policy Institute, May 4, 2020, https://www.epi.org/publication/h-1b-visas-and-pre vailing-wage-levels/.

Chapter 5

1. Although many researchers were involved in these studies, most of the credit went to Elton Mayo. For the original statement, see his book *The Human Problems of an Industrial Civilization* (Cambridge, MA: Harvard University Press, 1933). A para-digmatic account of Taylor and scientific management is Robert Kanigel, *The One Best Way: Frederick Winslow Taylor and the Enigma of Efficiency* (Cambridge, MA: MIT Press, 2005).

2. Eileen Appelbaum and Rosemary Batt describe the history of these developments where the pushback against scientific management was a common thread. See Eileen Appelbaum and Rosemary Batt, *The New American Workplace* (Ithaca, NY: ILR Press, 1994).

3. John Paul MacDuffie and Frits Pils, "Changes in Auto Industry Employment Practices: An International View," in *After Lean Production: Evolving Employment Practices in the World Auto Industry*, ed. Thomas A. Kochan, Russell D. Landsbury, and John Paul MacDuffie, 9–44 (Ithaca, NY: Cornell University Press, 1997).

4. Richard Walton, "From Control to Commitment," *Harvard Business Review*, March 1985.

5. *America's Choice: High Skills or Low Wages! The Report of the Commission on the Skills of the American Workforce* (Rochester, NY: National Center on Education and the Economy, 1990).

6. My colleague Bob Zemsky and I were bit players in this process. We codirected the US Department of Education's National Center on the Educational Quality of the Workforce, where these topics were central. It began during the G. H. W. Bush ad-ministration and came to an end with the G. W. Bush administration.

7. Leonard A. Schlesinger and James L. Heskett, "The Service-Driven Service Company," *Harvard Business Review* 69, no. 5 (1991): 71–81.

8. Leonard A. Schlesinger and James L. Heskett, "Leonard A. Schlesinger and James L. Heskett Respond: 'Customer Satisfaction Is Rooted in Employee Satisfaction,'" *Harvard Business Review* 69, no. 6 (1991): 148–149.

9. Anthony J. Rucci, Steven P. Kirn, and Richard T. Quinn, "The Employee-Customer Profit Chain at Sears," *Harvard Business Review* 76, no. 1 (1998): 82–97.

10. Vineet Nayar, *Employee First, Customer Second: Turning Conventional Management Upside Down* (Boston: Harvard Business Publishing, 2010).

11. Much of this material comes from Peter Cappelli and Anna Tavis, "HR Goes Agile," *Harvard Business Review*, March–April 2018.

12. For an account of the academic research on agile, see "A Decade of Agile Methodologies: Towards Explaining Agile Software Development (Special Issue)," *Journal of Systems and Software* 85 (2012): 1213–1221.

13. Seventy-nine percent of global executives surveyed by Deloitte in 2017 rate transformation of performance management toward agile format as high priority for their organizations. Deloitte, *Rewriting the Rules for the Digital Age: 2017 Deloitte Global Human Capital Trends* (New York: Deloitte University Press, 2017).

14. Rachna Shah and Peter T. Ward, "Defining and Developing Measures of Lean Production," *Journal of Operations Management* 25, no. 4 (2007): 785–805.

15. David McCann, "Want to Go 'Lean'? First, Understand What It Means," CFO, October 29, 2019, https://www.cfo.com/operations/2019/10/want-to-go-lean-first-underst and-what-it-means/.

16. "Lean Business: What Does It Mean?," Unleashed, October 2, 2017, https://www.unleashedsoftware.com/blog/lean-business-manufacturing-inventory.

17. Nathaniel Meyersohn, "Walmart Made Changes to Greeter Jobs at Stores. Workers with Disabilities Got Squeezed," CNN Business, March 1, 2019, https://www.cnn.com/2019/02/26/business/walmart-greeters/index.html; Matthew Boyle, "Walmart's New Workplace: Gold Stars, 'Attitude Cards' and Cheers," Bloomberg, May 2, 2019, https://www.bloomberg.com/news/articles/2019-05-02/walmart-s-new-workplace-gold-stars-attitude-cards-and-cheers.

18. Shoshy Ciment, "Leaked Documents Reveal Details on Target's 'Modernization' Plan That Store Workers Say Has Backfired Spectacularly," Insider, October 9, 2019, https://www.businessinsider.com/targets-modernization-plan-has-backfired-work ers-say-2019-10.

19. Tom Simonite, "When AI Can't Replace a Worker, It Watches Them Instead," *Wired*, February 27, 2020, https://www.wired.com/story/when-ai-cant-replace-worker-watc hes-them-instead/.

20. The software is WorkVue (https://www.willistowerswatson.com/en-CH/Solutions/products/work-vue).

21. Steve Denning, "What Is Strategic Agility?," *Forbes*, January 28, 2018.

22. "The Keys to Organizational Agility," interview, McKinsey, December 1, 2015, https://www.mckinsey.com/business-functions/organization/our-insights/the-keys-to-org anizational-agility. It is true that the term "agile" had previously been used in business to refer to flexibility, but that use had largely disappeared with agile project management.

23. PwC, "22nd Annual Global CEO Survey: CEOs' Curbed Confidence Spells Caution," 2019, https://www.pwc.com/gx/en/ceo-survey/2019/report/pwc-22nd-annual-glo bal-ceo-survey.pdf.

24. A detailed description of contemporary trucking and declining autonomy is in Steve Viscelli, *The Big Rig: Trucking and the Decline of the American Dream* (Berkeley: University of California Press, 2016). A description of electronic control systems on drivers may be found in Steve Viscelli, "Will Robot Trucks Be 'Sweatshops on Wheels'?" *Issues in Science and Technology* (Fall 2020): 81–89.

25. Scott Shane, "Prime Mover: How Amazon Wove Itself into the Life of an American City," *New York Times*, November 30, 2019.

26. S. Harris and A. L. Gurchensky, *Sierra-Cedar 2019–2020 HR Systems Survey* (22nd ed.; 2020), https://www.sierra-cedar.com/2019/10/02/pr-2019-hrss-white-paper-release/.

27. For a review of this literature, see Jorne Van den Bergh, Jeroen Belien, Philippe De Bruecker, Erik Demeulemeester, and Liesje De Boeck, "Personnel Scheduling: A Literature Review," *European Journal of Operational Research* 226, no. 3 (2013): 367–385.

28. Bernstein, Kesavan, and Staat note that it is possible to try to balance the recommendations of the algorithms, but for most employers, the reason for using them is to eliminate the time needed for that process. E. Bernstein, S. Kesavan, and B. Staats, "How to Manage Scheduling Software Fairly," *Harvard Business Review*, December 2014, https://hbr.org/2014/09/how-to-manage-scheduling-software-fairly. (See Harris and Gurchensky, *Sierra-Cedar 2019–2020 HR Systems Survey* for evidence.)

29. Boris B. Baltes, Thomas E. Briggs, Joseph W. Huff, Julia A. Wright, and George A. Neuman, "Flexible and Compressed Workweek Schedules: A Meta-Analysis of Their Effects on Work-Related Criteria," *Journal of Applied Psychology* 84, no. 4 (1999): 496–513.

30. Erin L. Kelly, Ellen E. Kossek, Leslie B. Hammer, Mary Durham, Jeremy Bray, Kelly Chermack, Lauren A. Murphy, and Dan Kaskubar, "Getting There from Here: Research on the Effects of Work-Family Initiatives on Work-Family Conflict and Business Outcomes," *Academy of Management Annals* 2, no. 1 (2008): 305–349.

31. See, e.g., Byron Y. Lee and Sanford DeFoe, "Flexibility and Profitability," *Industrial Relations* 51, no. 2 (2012): 298–316.

32. *Work-Life Balance and the Economics of Workplace Flexibility* (Washington, DC: Council of Economic Advisers, 2010).

33. "Win with Empathy: Global Talent Trends 2020," Mercer, https://workingnation.com/wp-content/uploads/2020/03/global-talent-trends-2020-report.pdf (accessed January 30, 2023).

34. Melissa Locker, "Yes, Your Employer Is Probably Monitoring Your Slack or Email Activity," Fast Company, June 11, 2018, https://www.fastcompany.com/40583634/yes-your-employer-is-probably-monitoring-your-slack-or-email-activity.

35. Rosemary Batt, "Electronic Monitoring and Control at Work: What Is It Good For?," *LERA for Libraries* 14, nos. 1–2 (2015): 22–25.

36. Maggie Astor, "Microchip Implants for Employees? One Company Says Yes," *New York Times*, July 25, 2017.

37. Ceylan Yeginsu, "If Workers Slack Off, the Wristband Will Know. (And Amazon Has a Patent for It.)," *New York Times*, February 1, 2018, https://www.nytimes.com/2018/02/01/technology/amazon-wristband-tracking-privacy.html.

38. Brian Kropp, "The Future of Employee Monitoring," Gartner, May 3, 2019, https://www.gartner.com/smarterwithgartner/the-future-of-employee-monitoring. For an overview, see Aleksandr Ometov et al., "A Survey on Wearable Technology: History, State-of-the-Art and Current Challenges," *Computer Networks* 193, no. 5 (2021): 3032.

39. Johana Bhuiyan, "Instacart Shoppers Say They Face Unforgiving Metrics: 'It's a Very Easy Job to Lose,'" *Los Angeles Times*, August 27, 2020.

40. Aruna Ranganathan and Alan Benson, "A Numbers Game: Quantification of Work, Accidental Gamification, and Worker Productivity," *American Sociological Review* 85, no. 4 (2020), https://doi.org/10.1177/00031224209366.

41. See, e.g., Michael Sauder and Wendy Nelson Espeland, in "The Discipline of Rankings: Tight Coupling and Organizational Change," *American Sociological Review*, 74, no. 1 (2009): 63–82, on education measures. Masmanian and Beckman show how the measures change the way we think about jobs in Melissa Mazmanian and Christine M. Beckman, "'Making' Your Numbers: Engendering Organizational Control through a Ritual of Quantification," *Organization Science* 29, no. 3 (2018): 357–379.

42. A. Ranganathan and A. Benson, "A Numbers Game: Quantification of Work, Auto-Gamification, and Worker Productivity," *American Sociological Review* 85, no. 4 (2020): 573–609.

43. Jodi Kantor and Arya Sundaram, "The Rise of the Worker Productivity Score," *New York Times*, August 14, 2022.

44. Emily Guendelsberger, *On the Clock: What Low-Wage Work Did to Me and How It Drives America Insane* (Boston: Little, Brown, 2019).

45. Erin L. Kelly and Phyllis Moen, *Overload: How Good Jobs Went Bad and What We Can Do about It* (Princeton, NJ: Princeton University Press, 2020).

46. Ethan Bernstein and Ben Waber, "The Truth about Open Offices," *Harvard Business Review*, November–December 2019.

47. Alex Christian, "Bosses Started Spying on Remote Workers. Now They're Fighting Back," *Wired*, October 8, 2020.

48. Elizabeth Anderson, *Private Government: How Employers Rule Our Lives (And Why We Don't Talk about It)* (Princeton, NJ: Princeton University Press, 2017).

49. Alison DeNisco Rayome, "Why Data Science Is the Most Promising Job of 2019," *Tech Republic*, January 10, 2019, https://www.techrepublic.com/article/why-data-scient ist-is-the-most-promising-job-of-2019/.

50. Lauren Salm, "70% of Employers Are Snooping Candidates' Social Media Profiles," CareerBuilder, June 15, 2017, https://njsa.com/resources/Documents/News/NJSA-Social_Media_Profiles.pdf.

51. Dave Lee, "Amazon Abandons Influence Campaign Designed to Attract Staff," *Financial Times*, January 26, 2022.

52. "Compounding Pressure on the American Workforce" (Washington, DC: American Psychological Association, 2021).

53. "Labor Force Statistics from the Current Population Survey," Bureau of Labor Statistics, 2019, https://www.bls.gov/cps/cpsaat08.htm.

54. CIPD, *Zero-Hour Contracts: Myth and Reality* (London: Chartered Institute for Personnel Development, 2013).

55. A review of these models and their use can be found in Robert Fildes, Shaohui Ma, and Stephan Kolassa, "Retail Forecasting: Research and Practice," *International Journal of Forecasting* 38, no. 4 (2022): 1283–1318.

56. Their work on this topic appears in a number of studies. A directory of them is on the University of Chicago website at https://crownschool.uchicago.edu/research-faculty/faculty-research?combine=&sort_by=author&sort_order=ASC&page=4.

57. Saravanan Kesavan, Susan Lambert, Joan Williams, and Pradeep Pendem, "Doing Well by Doing Good: Improving Store Performance with Responsible Scheduling Practices at the Gap, Inc.," October 29, 2021, forthcoming in *Management Science*, https://papers.ssrn.com/sol3/papers.cfm?abstract_id=3731670.

58. Ellen Ernst Kossek, Lindsay Mechem Rosokha, and Carrie Leana, "Work Schedule Patching in Health Care: Exploring Implementation Approaches," *Work and Occupations*, 47, no. 2 (2019): 228–261.

59. This estimate comes from the industry trade association: "Retail Supports 52 Million American Jobs," National Retail Federation, https://nrf.com/topics/economy/about-retail-jobs (accessed January 30, 2023).

60. Elaine Zundl, Daniel Schneider, Kristen Harknett, and Evelyn Bellew, "Still Unstable: The Persistence of Schedule Uncertainty during the Pandemic," Research Brief, Shift Project, Harvard University, https://shift.hks.harvard.edu/still-unstable/ (accessed January 30, 2023).

61. Noam Schreiber, "Despite Labor Shortages, Workers See Few Gains in Economic Security," *New York Times*, February 4, 2022.

62. Te-Ping Chen, "A Little-Noticed Reason Why Employees Quit: Too Little Work," *Wall Street Journal*, February 28, 2022.

63. Payrolling vendors maintain up-to-date lists of these laws. See, e.g., "Predictive Work Schedule Laws: A City-by-City Guide," Paycor.com, March 25, 2021, https://www.paycor.com/resource-center/articles/predictive-work-schedule-laws-a-city-by-city-guide/.

64. The seminal article here is arguably R. Eisenberger, R. Huntington, S. Hutchison, and D. Sowa, "Perceived Organizational Support," *Journal of Applied Psychology* 71 (1986): 500–507.

65. Although the notion that expectations mattered to employees has arguably been known since work began, thinking clearly about what happens when those expectations are violated was articulately most clearly by Denise Rousseau, *Psychological Contract in Organizations: Understanding Written and Unwritten Agreements* (Newbury Park, CA: Sage, 1995).

66. See G. B. Graen and M. Uhl-Bien, "The Relationship-Based Approach to Leadership: Development of LMX Theory of Leadership over 25 Years: Applying a Multi-Level, Multi-Domain Perspective," *Leadership Quarterly* 6, no. 2 (1995): 219–247.

67. I review this literature in *The Future of the Office* (Philadelphia, PA: Wharton School Publishing, 2021).

68. "Amazon's Panorama Box Lets Firms Check If Staff Follow Coronavirus Rules," BBC News, December 2, 2020, https://www.bbc.com/news/technology-55158319.

69. The reference comes from the Gartner research and advisory firm in Tatum Hunter, "Here Are All the Ways Your Boss Can Legally Monitor You," *Washington Post*, September 24, 2021.

70. "The Virtual Floorplan: New Rules for a New Era of Work," VMware.com, 2021, https://www.vmware.com/content/microsites/learn/en/1162603_REG.html.

71. Christopher Mims, "Amazon's New CEO, Andy Jassy, Can Either Help Workers and Sellers—or Automate Them Away," *Wall Street Journal*, February 6, 2021.

72. Adina Schwartz, "Meaningful Work," *Ethics* 92, no. 4 (1982): 634–646.

Chapter 6

1. A detailed overview is provided by Sarah A. Donovan and David H. Bradley, "Real Wage Trends, 1979 to 2019" (Washington, DC: Congressional Research Service R45090, 2020).

2. The most prominent excepts are studies of monopsony—market concentration among employers that reduces competition for labor—as an explanation for lower wages. For a review, see Alan Manning, "Monopsony in Labor Markets: A Review," *ILR Review* 74, no. 1 (2020): 3–26.

3. For an example, see "Does Bargaining Help Explain Wage Inequality?," On the Economy Blog, Federal Reserve Bank of St. Louis, January 28, 2021, https://www.stl ouisfed.org/on-the-economy/2021/january/bargaining-explain-wage-inequality.

4. For an overview of the change and also evidence that the policy had little effect on salary and cash compensation, see Nancy L. Rose and Catherine Wolfram, "Regulating Executive Pay: Using the Tax Code to Influence Chief Executive Officer Compensation," *Journal of Labor Economics* 20, no. 2, Part 2 (2002): S138–S175.

5. Carola Frydman and Raven E. Saks draw these conclusions from data on the fifty largest US corporations. See their "Historical Trends in Executive Compensation," *Review of Financial Studies* 23, no. 5 (2010): 2099–2138. See also "A Decade of Executive Excess: The 1990s," Institute for Policy Studies, September 1, 1999https:// ips-dc.org/wp-content/uploads/1999/09/Executive-Excess-1999.pdf.

6. David Katz, "CFO Pay: Whopping Option Gains Bulked Up Compensation," CFO, July 19, 2001, https://www.cfo.com/human-capital-careers/2001/07/2000-cfo-pay-whopping-option-gains-bulked-up-compensation/.

7. Historically, in the period where they became most popular, they were expensed based on their "intrinsic value," which was measured as the difference between the market price of the stock and its exercise or strike price at which it can be bought or sold. Because most companies set the initial exercise price equal to the market price, the expense was zero. Partly in response to the boom in using this cost-free approach, the Financial Accounting Standards Board changed the rule on expensing options in 2004 to a "fair value" approach, which means trying to assess the current value of the option. For example, a common minimum value is that it will grow until it is exercised at a rate equal to risk-free returns in the market, usually measured by the value of US Treasury bills. This is not as attractive in terms of the appearance in financial accounting for the employer, but it still allows employees to receive income in a manner that does not show up as compensation. These stock options can also be paid off over the period until the option can be exercised, much like a depreciated asset.

8. Boris Groysberg, Sarah Abbott, Michael R. Marino, and Metin Aksoy, "Compensation Packages That Actually Drive Performance," *Harvard Business Review*, January–February 2021.

9. A simple description of this approach, which in 2018 is still presented as how salary systems are created, can be found in "How to Establish Salary Ranges," Paycor.com, 2022, https://www.paycor.com/resource-center/articles/how-to-establish-salary-ranges/.

10. For an account, see Kenan S. Abosch and Janice S. Hand, "Broadbanding Design, Approaches and Practices," American Compensation Association, 1994, https://www.worldatwork.org/docs/aca-legacy-archives/publications-books-and-booklets/broadbanding-design-1-30.pdf.

11. Seventeen percent used market pricing and job evaluation evenly, and another 17 percent used market pricing to modify the job evaluation data. "Survey of Compensation Policies and Practices," Dow Scott and Hay Group, 2003, worldatwork.org.

12. Jeff Zhong, "The Consequences of Not Negotiating Your Salary," Payscale, 2017, https://www.payscale.com/salary-negotiation-guide/consequences-not-negotiating-salary/.

13. "Most People Don't Negotiate Due to Fear and Lack of Skills," Salary.com, 2012, https://www.salary.com/chronicles/most-people-don-t-negotiate-due-to-fear-lack-of-skills/. The title is puzzling because the survey results show that most people in fact do negotiate. A Glassdoor survey conducted by Harris Poll asked a slightly different question, about what the employee did in their current job. It found that 41 percent negotiated their pay in starting their current job while 10 percent negotiated for a pay increase once in their current job. See "3 in 5 Employees Did Not Negotiate Salary in Current / Most Recent Job—Fewer Women Negotiate Than Men," Glassdoor.com, 2016, https://www.glassdoor.com/about-us/glassdoor-survey-finds-3-5-employees-negotiate-pay-currentmost-job-women-negotiate-men/.

14. Spencer Soper and Jacqueline Davalos, "Amazon's $3000 Signing Bonuses Irk Workers Who Got $10 Coupons," *Bloomberg Quint*, November 24, 2020, https://www.bloombergquint.com/business/amazon-s-3-000-signing-bonuses-irk-workers-who-got-10-coupons.

15. Alex Edmans, Tom Gosling, and Dirk Jenter, "CEO Compensation: Evidence from the Field" (European Corporate Governance Institute—Finance Working Paper No. 771/2021, June 30, 2021).

16. Charles Brown and James Medoff, "The Employer Size-Wage Effect," *Journal of Political Economy* 97, no. 5 (1989): 1027–1059.

17. J. Adam Cobb and Ken-Hou Lin, "Growing Apart: The Declining Firm-Size Wage Premium and Its Inequality Consequences," *Organization Science* 28, no. 3 (2017): 429–446.

18. N. K. Nahavandi, "A Survey of Merit Rating in Industry," master's thesis, Western Michigan University, 1962.

19. D. McGregor, "An Uneasy Look at Performance Appraisal," *Harvard Business Review* 35 (1957): 89–94.

20. "Span of Control," *The Economist*, November 9, 2009, http://www.economist.com/node/14301444.

21. R. D. Bretz Jr., G. T. Milkovich, and W. Read, "Comparing the Performance Appraisal Practices in Large Firms with the Directions in Research Literature: Learning More and More about Less and Less" (CAHRS Working Paper #89-17, Cornell University, School of Industrial and Labor Relations, Center for Advanced Human Resource Studies, 1989).

22. Peter Cappelli and Anna Tavis, "The Performance Management Revolution," *Harvard Business Review*, October 2016, https://hbr.org/2016/10/the-performance-managem ent-revolution.

23. *The Real Impact of Eliminating Performance Ratings*, (Washington, D.C.: Corporate Executive Board—Corporate Leadership Council, 2016).

24. An overview of these plans and their real effects is Peter Cappelli, Martin Conyon, and David Almeda, "Social Exchange and the Effects of Stock Options," *ILR Review* 73, no. 1 (2020): 1–29.

25. Cappelli, Conyon, and Almeda, "Social Exchange and the Effects of Stock Options."

26. Ben Wigert and Jim Harter, "Reengineering Performance Management," Gallup, 2017, https://www.gallup.com/workplace/238064/re-engineering-performance-managem ent.aspx. This is different from the practice of commission-based pay for salespeople, where sales output is thought to be more under the employee's control.

27. For an account, see Emil Glazer, "Wells Fargo to Pay $185 Million Fine over Account Openings," *Wall Street Journal*, September 8, 2016. See also Bryan Tanan, "The Wells Fargo Cross Selling Scandal," Stanford Closer Look Series, 2019, https://www.gsb. stanford.edu/faculty-research/publications/wells-fargo-cross-selling-scandal.

28. John Maxfield, "Chart: The Cost of Wells Fargo's Sales Scandal," Motley Fool, September 6, 2017.

29. Lynn A. Stout, "Killing Conscience: The Unintended Behavioral Consequences of 'Pay for Performance,'" *Journal of Corporation Law* 39, no. 525 (2014), https://scho larship.law.cornell.edu/facpub/1389/.

30. Joseph F. Kovar, "Some May Work from Home Permanently after Covid-19: Gartner," CRNTV, April 13, 2020, https://www.crn.com/news/running-your-business/some- may-work-from-home-permanently-after-covid-19-gartner.

31. PwC US CFO Pulse Survey US Findings, June 15, 2020, https://www.pwc.com/us/en/ library/covid-19/pwc-covid-19-cfo-pulse-survey.html. It does not seem as though the CFOs got their way, however, as most companies in 2022 were still dithering as to how to approach remote work.

32. Avery Hartsman, "Stripe Is Reportedly Cutting Pay for Employees Who Leave Seattle, New York, or the Bay Area, but Will Also Provide a $20,000 Incentive to Move," *Business Insider*, September 16, 2020.

33. Kate Conger, "Facebook Starts Planning for Permanent Remote Workers," *New York Times*, May 21, 2020, B1.

34. Danielle Kaye, "Pay Cut: Google Employees Who Work from Home Could Lose Money," Reuters, August 10, 2021.

35. "Geographic Pay Policy Studies," WorldatWork, April 9, 2021, https://worldatwork. org/resources/research/geographic-pay-policies-study.

36. Joni Balter, "Amazon, Microsoft, and the Seattle Shake-Out of Remote Work," *Pittsburgh Post-Gazette*, July 6, 2021.

37. "Resetting Normal: Defining the New Era of Work," Adecco Group, June 2020, https://www.adeccogroup.com/future-of-work/latest-research/reset-normal/.

38. N. Balasubramanian, E. P. Starr, and S. Yamaguchi, "Bundling Postemployment Restrictive Covenants: New Evidence from Firm and Worker Surveys," *Academy of Management Annual Meeting Proceedings*, 2021.

39. M. Marx, "The Employer Strikes Back: Non-compete Agreements and the Mobility of Technical Professionals," *American Sociological Review* 76, no. 5 (2011): 695–712.

40. Balasubramanian et al., "Bundling Postemployment Restrictive Covenants."

41. S. Quinton, "Why Janitors Get Noncompete Agreements, Too," Stateline, PEW Trusts, 2017, https://www.pewtrusts.org/en/research-and-analysis/blogs/stateline/2017/05/17/why-janitors-get-noncompete-agreements-too.

42. M. Lipsitz and E. P. Starr, "Low-Wage Workers and the Enforceability of Non-compete Agreements," *Academy of Management Annual Meetings Proceedings*, 2020.

43. N. Balasubramanian, J. W. Chang, S. Mariko, S. Jagadeesh, and E. Starr, "Locked In? The Enforceability of Covenants Not to Compete and the Careers of High-Tech Workers," *Journal of Human Resources* 57(S) (2021): 349–396.

44. Balasubramanian et al., "Bundling Postemployment Restrictive Covenants."

45. D. Contigiani, D. Hsu, and I. Barankay, "Trade Secrets and Innovation: Evidence from the 'Inevitable Disclosure' Doctrine," *Strategic Management Journal* 39, no. 11 (2018): 2921–2942.

46. Jason Sockin, Aaron J. Sojourner, and Evan Starr, "Non-Disclosure Agreements and Externalities from Silence" (Upjohn Institute Working Paper 22-360, December 19, 2022), SSRN: https://ssrn.com/abstract=3900285 or http://dx.doi.org/10.2139/ssrn.3900285.

47. Balasubramanian et al., "Bundling Postemployment Restrictive Covenants."

48. Balasubramanian et al., "Bundling Postemployment Restrictive Covenants."

49. The most recent of these estimates is Paul Osterman, "How American Adults Obtain Work Skills: Results of a New National Survey," *ILR Review* 75, no. 3 (June 2021), https://doi.org/10.1177/00197939211018191. Osterman also reviews the prior literature and estimates.

50. C. Jeffrey Waddoups, "Did US Employers Back away from Skills Training in the Early 2000s?," *ILR Review* 69, no. 2 (2016), https://doi.org/10.1177/0019793915619904.

51. "The Future of Recruiting," PwC, https://www.pwc.com/us/en/services/consulting/workforce-of-the-future/library/hr-recruiting.html (accessed January 30, 2023).

52. "The Ill-Prepared US Workforce," Conference Board, 2009, https://www.conference-board.org/pdf_free/BED-09WF_KF.pdf.

53. "Beyond Reskilling: Investing in Resilience for Uncertain Futures," August 28, 2020, in *Capital H*, Deloitte US, podcast https://www2.deloitte.com/us/en/pages/human-capital/articles/beyond-reskilling.html. See also Jeff Schwartz et al., "Beyond Reskilling: Investing in Resilience for Uncertain Futures," Deloitte Insights, May 15, 2020, https://www2.deloitte.com/us/en/insights/focus/human-capital-trends/2020/reskilling-the-workforce-to-be-resilient.html.

54. "22nd Annual Global CEO Survey: CEOs' Curbed Confidence Spells Caution," PwC, 2019, https://www.pwc.com/gx/en/ceo-survey/2019/report/pwc-22nd-annual-glo bal-ceo-survey.pdf.

55. "Training at Infosys Global Education Center," Infosys, https://www.infosys.com/careers/graduates/global-education-center.html (accessed January 30, 2023).

56. See, e.g., Peter Cappelli, "Why Do Employers Pay for College?," *Journal of Econometrics* 121, no. 1–2 (2004): 213–241.

57. Devin Leonard, "'Free' Job Training Can Cost a Fortune for Employees Who Quit," Bloomberg, August 11, 2022, https://www.bloomberg.com/news/features/2022-08-11/quitting-your-job-can-cost-a-fortune-if-you-got-free-training.

58. "CPS Historical Migration / Geographic Mobility Tables," US Census Bureau, November 2021, https://www.census.gov/data/tables/time-series/demo/geographic-mobility/historic.html.

59. These data come from the "52nd Annual Atlas Corporate Relocation Survey," Atlas World Group, 2020, https://www.atlasvanlines.com/corporate-relocation/survey/2020/relocation-volumes-budgets. As is often the case with corporate surveys, the sampling frame is not described. My calculation of the average number of relocations is imputed from reports on averages across ranges of outcomes.

60. The figure during the pandemic-related Great Resignation period is over 48 percent. See Table 3, "Total Separations Levels and Rates for Total Nonfarm by State, Seasonally Adjusted," Bureau of Labor Statistics Economic News Release, January 2022, https://www.bls.gov/news.release/jltst.t03.htm.

61. "The Top Relocation Destinations for 2017," ZipRecruiter, https://www.ziprecruiter.com/blog/time-to-move-to-where-the-jobs-are/ (accessed January 30, 2023).

62. "2020 Recruiter Nation Survey," Jobvite, https://www.jobvite.com/wp-content/uploads/2020/10/Jobvite-RecruiterNation-Report-Final.pdf (accessed January 30, 2023), is a survey of eight hundred recruiters by Zogby Analytics.

63. "Majority of Workers Who Quit a Job in 2021 Cite Low Pay, No Opportunities for Advancement, Feeling Disrespected," Pew Research Center, March 9, 2021, https://www.pewresearch.org/fact-tank/2022/03/09/majority-of-workers-who-quit-a-job-in-2021-cite-low-pay-no-opportunities-for-advancement-feeling-disrespected/.

64. Matthew Bidwell, "Paying More to Get Less: Specific Skills, Matching, and the Effects of External Hiring versus Internal Promotion," *Administrative Science Quarterly* 56, no. 3 (2011): 369–407.

65. Matthew J. Bidwell and Ethan Mollick, "Shifts and Ladders: Comparing the Role of Internal and External Mobility in Executive Careers," *Organization Science* 26, no. 6 (2015): 1629–1645.

66. Alan Benson, Danielle Li, and Kelly Shue, "Promotions and the Peter Principle," *Quarterly Journal of Economics* 134, no. 4 (2019): 2085–2134

67. Joseph (J. R.) Keller, "Posting and Slotting: How Hiring Processes Shape Quality of Hire and Compensation in Internal Labor Markets," *Administrative Science Quarterly* 63, no. 4 (2017): 848–878.

68. "The State of Internal Recruiting 2021," SmartRecruiters, https://ta.smartrecruiters.com/rs/664-NIC-529/images/State-of-Internal-Recruiting-2021-SmartRecruiters.pdf (accessed January 30, 2023).

69. "2020 Recruiter Nation Survey."

70. "The State of Internal Recruiting 2021."

71. "The State of Internal Recruiting 2021."

72. For evidence on this, see Brad Badertscher, John Phillips, Morton Pincus, and Sonja Olhoft Rego, "Evidence of Motivations for Downward Earnings Management," *Social Science Research Network Electronic Journal* (2009), SSRN: https://ssrn.com/abstract=921422 or http://dx.doi.org/10.2139/ssrn.921422.

73. Patrick M. Wright, Anthony J. Nyberg, Donald J. Schepker, Ormonde R. Cragun, and Michael D. Ulrich, "Current Practices in CEO Succession: Center for Executive Succession," Darla Moore School of Business, University of South Carolina, 2016, https://sc.edu/study/colleges_schools/moore/documents/ces_research/chro_survey_2016.pdf.

74. Barton Edgerton, "New Research Spotlights CEO Succession Challenges," National Association of Corporate Directors, April 18, 2019, https://blog.nacdonline.org/posts/new-research-spotlights-ceo-succession-challenges.

75. See Tracy Anderson and Peter Cappelli, "The Outsider Advantage," *Sloan Management Review* (Fall 2021), https://sloanreview.mit.edu/article/the-outsider-edge/.

76. "Employee Benefits Survey," US Bureau of Labor Statistics, https://www.bls.gov/ncs/ebs/benefits/2020/employee-benefits-in-the-united-states-march-2020.pdf (accessed January 30, 2023).

77. "Employee Benefits Survey."

78. Dan Doonan and William Fornia, *A Better Bang for the Buck 3.0* (Washington, DC: National Institute on Retirement Security, 2022).

79. J. Adam Cobb, "Risky Business: The Decline of Defined Benefit Pensions and Firms' Shifting of Retirement Risk," *Organization Science* 26, no. 5 (2015): 1332–1350. It is true that moving away from defined benefit plans also effectively shifted financial risk from the employer to employee, but from the perspective of finance, getting pension liability off a company's books was hugely—and immediately—more important in making the company more valuable.

80. "Health Expenditure and Financing," Organisation for Economic Co-operation and Development, 2019, https://stats.oecd.org/Index.aspx?DataSetCode=SHA (accessed April 2022).

81. Kaiser Family Foundation 2020 Employer Health Benefits Survey, https://www.kff.org/health-costs/report/2020-employer-health-benefits-survey/ (accessed 1 July 2022).

82. The employee costs have risen faster than employer costs because employers have increased employee premiums. See Sara R. Collins, David C. Radley, and Jesse C. Baumgartner, "Trends in Employer Health Care Coverage, 2008–2018: Higher Costs for Workers and Their Families" Commonwealth Fund, November 2019, https://doi.org/10.26099/btqx-ed95.

83. These data come from the Kaiser Family Foundation's analysis of the National Health Interview Survey. See "Health System Tracker," Peterson KFF, April 3, 2020, https://www.healthsystemtracker.org/brief/long-term-trends-in-employer-based-coverage/US. Census data put the figure at 56.4 percent in 2019, slightly lower. See

"Figure 1: Percentage of People by Type of Health Insurance Coverage: 2019," https://www.census.gov/content/dam/Census/library/visualizations/2020/demo/p60-271/figure1.pdf (accessed January 30, 2023).

84. These data come from the Kaiser Family Foundation's Employer Health Benefits Annual Survey, various years: https://www.kff.org/health-costs/report/employer-health-benefits-annual-survey-archives/ (accessed April 2022).

85. For examples of the cost squeeze, see Joseph B. White and Rhonda L. Rundle, "Employers Demand Cost Cuts from HMs and Hospitals," Wall Street Journal, May 19, 1998.

86. "Medical Cost Trend: Behind the Numbers 2022," PwC Health Research Institute, https://www.pwc.com/us/en/industries/health-industries/library/assets/pwc-hri-behind-the-numbers-2022.pdf (accessed January 30, 2023).

87. For an overview, see Elizabeth A. Brown, "A Healthy Mistrust: Curbing Biometric Data Misuse in the Workplace," Stanford Technology Law Review 23 (2020): 252–305.

88. "Half of Workplaces Offer Health/Wellness Programs," Centers for Disease Control and Prevention, Press Release, April 22, 2019.

89. "Employer Health Benefits: 2020 Annual Survey," Kaiser Family Foundation, https://files.kff.org/attachment/Report-Employer-Health-Benefits-2020-Annual-Survey.pdf (accessed January 30, 2023).

90. "Workplace Health in America 2017," Centers for Disease Control and Prevention, https://www.cdc.gov/workplacehealthpromotion/data-surveillance/docs/2017-Workplace-Health-in-America-Summary-Report-FINAL-updated-508.pdf (accessed January 30, 2023).

91. Brown, "A Healthy Mistrust," 252–253.

92. These include Zirui Song and Katherine Baicker, "Effect of a Workplace Wellness Program on Employee Health and Economic Outcomes: A Randomized Clinical Trial," JAMA 321, no. 15 (2019): 1491–1501; Damon Jones, David Molitor, and Julian Reif, "What Do Workplace Wellness Programs Do? Evidence from the Illinois Workplace Wellness Study," Quarterly Journal of Economics 134 (2019): 1747–1791; Julian Reif, David Chan, Damon Jones, et al., "Effects of a Workplace Wellness Program on Employee Health, Health Beliefs, and Medical Use: A Randomized Clinical Trial," JAMA Internal Medicine 180, no. 7 (2020): 952–960; and Nathan A. Barleen, Mary L. Marzec, Nicholas L. Boerger, Daniel P. Moloney, Eric M. Zimmerman, and Jeff Dobro, "Outcome-Based and Participation-Based Wellness Incentives: Impacts on Program Participation and Achievement of Health Improvement," Targets Journal of Occupational and Environmental Medicine 59, no. 3 (2017): 304–312.

93. See Jeffrey Pfeffer, Dying for a Paycheck: How Modern Management Harms Employee Health and Company Performance, and What We Can Do about It (New York: Harper Business, 2019).

94. Roy Maurer, "Nearly 8 in 10 Employers Screen for Alcohol, Drugs," Society for Human Resource Management, May 31, 2023, https://www.shrm.org/ResourcesAndTools/hr-topics/risk-management/Pages/Employers-Screen-Alcohol-Drugs.aspx.

95. Bill Current, "COVID and the Future," Current Consulting Group, August 5, 2020, https://www.currentconsultinggroup.com/marijuana-covid-19-and-the-future-of-drug-testing/.

96. For examples, see Roy Maurer, "Creative Approaches to Drug-Testing Remote Workers Will Persist," Society for Human Resource Management, May 21, 2021, https://www.shrm.org/ResourcesAndTools/hr-topics/risk-management/Pages/Employers-Screen-Alcohol-Drugs.aspx.

97. See "Average Hours Actually Worked per Worker," Organisation for Economic Co-operation and Development Data, 2020, https://data.oecd.org/emp/hours-worked.htm. In terms of hours worked per year, the United States trails only Mexico and South Korea among all industrialized countries; much of that is driven by the lower levels of vacation time in the United States. South Korea has fifteen days of annual leave mandated, while the United States has none. These estimates are complicated by part-time work, which is not distributed equally across countries.

98. "Employee Benefits Survey," Bureau of Labor Statistics, https://www.bls.gov/ebs/home.htm (accessed April 2022).

99. For the fine points on how this accounting works, see Mark P. Holtzman, "Vacation and Sick Pay Accruals Resulting from the Pandemic," *Journal of Accountancy,* July 1, 2021, https://www.journalofaccountancy.com/issues/2021/jul/vacation-sick-pay-accruals-resulting-from-coronavirus-pandemic.html.

100. "Fact Sheet: Paid Time Off Trends in the US" (Washington, DC: US Travel Industry Association, 2019).

101. "How to Effectively Manage Employee Paid Time Off," Glassdoor for Employers, https://www.glassdoor.com/employers/resources/effectively-managing-employee-time-off/ (accessed January 30, 2023).

102. Kyle Schnitzer, "Experts Explain the Reason Your Boss Is Desperate for You to Take Vacation Right Now," *The Ladders,* July 9, 2020.

103. "An Assessment of Paid Time Off in the US," Oxford Economics, February 2014, available at https://time.com/wp-content/uploads/2015/02/oxford_pto_final.pdf.

Final Thoughts

1. The evidence of earnings management is ample. See, e.g., S. Das, P. K. Shroff, and H. Zhang, "Quarterly Earnings Patterns and Earnings Management," *Contemporary Accounting Research* 26 (2009): 797–831.

2. Thomas Gryta, "GE Puts Its Famed Crotonville Management Academy up for Sale," *Wall Street Journal,* October 18, 2022. For an account of its financial practices and downfall, see David Gelles, *The Man Who Broke Capitalism: How Jack Welch Gutted the Heartland, Widened the Wealth Gap, and Crushed the Soul of Corporate America—and How to Undo His Legacy* (New York: Simon and Schuster, 2022).

Index

For the benefit of digital users, indexed terms that span two pages (e.g., 52–53) may, on occasion, appear on only one of those pages.

Figures and boxes are indicated by f and b following the page number.

health maintenance organizations
    (HMOs), 100–2, 167–68
Henly, Julia, 133
Heskett, James, 119
Highhouse, Scott, 66
hiring
    as alternative to skills training, 157
    contemporary practices, 53–56, 104
    costs per hire, 4
    electronic, 57–63, 104
    expenses, 54
    from liquid workforce, 63
    funnel, 56–57
    internal, 55–56, 78
    as managers' responsibility, 5–6
    measures of success, 52–53
    platform model, 104
    referrals, 60–61
    statistics, 56–57, 60f
    through acquiring other companies, 81
Hoffman, Mitchell, 65
hoteling, 31
HP, 42–43
human capital under financial accounting,
    17–21, 26
Human Relations School, 117–18
human resources, 11, 38–39, 86
    analysis by, 6
    as administrative expense, 23
    budget for, 6
    consulting, 76, 100f
    cutting of, 23, 72, 75
    outsourcing of, 13–14, 76–77, 100f
    software, 49, 76
    as tool for CEO, 38–39
    training, 41
human resource accounting, 25–26
Human Resource Policy Association, 27
hybrid work, 31, 32–33

Iacocca, Lee, 38
IBM, 12–13, 30–31, 84, 157
immigration, 115
income inequality, 140, 142
Indeed.com, 57
independent contractors, 94–95
industrial engineers, 11–12, 118, 131
industrial-organizational psychology, 12
industrial sociology, 80
Ingleheart, Austin S., 82

inside contracting, 80
Instacart, 128–29
institutional investors, 15–16
intangible assets, 26
internal accounting, 16
internal hiring, 12–13, 55–56, 78, 159–62
Internal Revenue Code, 143
International Financial Reporting
    Standards (IFRP), 28
interviews, 7, 66–72
    behavioral, 66–67
    exit, 80
investment bankers, 36
investors, power of, 36
IRS regulations, 114
IT industry, 21, 100–2, 157

Jacoby, Sandy, 80, 82
Jassy, Andy, 138
Jensen, Michael, 15
job boards, 57–58
job-hopping, 13, 56
job insecurity, 1
Job Openings and Labor Turnover Survey
    (JOLTS), 91
Job Seeker Nation, 64
Jobs, Steve, 42
JobTestPrep, 71
Jobvite.com, 59
Johnson & Johnson, 168

Kahn, Lisa B., 65
Kantor, Jodi, 129
karat.com, 71
Keller, JR, 160
Kellogg's, 168
Kelly, Erin, 130
Kesavan, Saravanan, 23–24
Khurana, Anuj and Rajat, 121b
Kim, Walter, 13
Kochan, Thomas, 38–39
Krueger, Alan, 154
Kuhn, Peter, 23–24
Kuhnen, Camilia, 23–24
Kuncel, Nathan, 65

Lambert, Susan, 133
Lampert, Edward, 47
layoffs, 87–88, 177
    as cost-cutting tactic, 24